MW00649500

Institutions Count

The publisher gratefully acknowledges the generous support
of the General Endowment Fund of the University
of California Press Foundation.

Institutions Count

Their Role and Significance in Latin American Development

Alejandro Portes and Lori D. Smith

UNIVERSITY OF CALIFORNIA PRESS

Berkeley Los Angeles London

University of California Press, one of the most distinguished university presses in the United States, enriches lives around the world by advancing scholarship in the humanities, social sciences, and natural sciences. Its activities are supported by the UC Press Foundation and by philanthropic contributions from individuals and institutions. For more information, visit www.ucpress.edu.

University of California Press
Berkeley and Los Angeles, California

University of California Press, Ltd.
London, England

© 2012 by The Regents of the University of California

Library of Congress Cataloging-in-Publication Data

Portes, Alejandro, 1944–
Institutions count : their role and significance in Latin American development / [written and edited by] Alejandro Portes and Lori D. Smith.
p. cm.
Includes bibliographical references and index.
ISBN 978-0-520-27353-5 (cloth : alk. paper) — ISBN 978-0-520-27354-2 (pbk. : alk. paper) — ISBN 978-0-520-95406-9 (ebook)
1. Social institutions—Latin America. 2. Economic development—Social aspects—Latin America. 3. Public administration—Latin America. 4. Institutional economics. I. Smith, Lori D., 1982– II. Title.
HN110.5.A8P665 2012
303.4098—dc23 2012021915

Manufactured in the United States of America

21 20 19 18 17 16 15 14 13 12
10 9 8 7 6 5 4 3 2 1

In keeping with a commitment to support environmentally responsible and sustainable printing practices, UC Press has printed this book on Rolland Enviro100, a 100% post-consumer fiber paper that is FSC certified, deinked, processed chlorine-free, and manufactured with renewable biogas energy. It is acid-free and EcoLogo certified.

CONTENTS

List of Illustrations vii
Preface ix
Acknowledgments xiii

1. Institutions and Development: A Conceptual Reanalysis 1
Alejandro Portes

2. The Comparative Study of Institutions: The "Institutional Turn" in Development Studies 24
Alejandro Portes and Lori D. Smith

3. Institutional Change and Development in Argentina 39
Alejandro Grimson, Ana Castellani, and Alexander Roig

4. Institutional Change and Development in Chilean Market Society 60
Guillermo Wormald and Daniel Brieba

5. The Colombian Paradox: A Thick Institutionalist Analysis 85
César Rodríguez-Garavito

6. Development Opportunities: Politics, the State, and Institutions in the Dominican Republic in the Twenty-First Century 113
Wilfredo Lozano

7. The Uneven and Paradoxical Development of Mexico's Institutions 130
José Luis Velasco

8. Conclusion: The Comparative Analysis of the Role of Institutions in National Development 167
Alejandro Portes and Lori D. Smith

Appendix: Investigators 191
Contributors 193
Index 195

ILLUSTRATIONS

FIGURES

1.1 Elements of Social Life *7*
1.2 Participatory Democracy and Institutional Monocropping *11*
1.3 The Divestiture of Parastate Corporations in Mexico *13*
1.4 Levels and Forces of Change *17*
5.1 Electoral Risk for Mayors' and Governors' Elections in Colombia (2011) *102*
7.1 Per Capita GDR in Mexico and Latin America (2000 Constant Dollars) *135*
7.2 Percentage of People in Poverty in Mexico *135*
7.3 Income Inequality in Mexico: Gini Coefficient *135*
7.4 Market Capitalization of Listed Companies (% of GDP) *139*
7.5 Public Expenditure on Health (% of GDP), 2000–2008 *140*
7.6 Per Capita Total Expenditure on Health (PPP int. $), 2000–2006 *141*
7.7 Government and Private Contributions to Total Expenditure on Health, 2000–2006 *141*
7.8 SAT's Efficiency: Cents Spent for Every Peso Collected *142*
8.1 Membership in the Causal Solution "ABC (D+E)" and Institutional Adequacy *174*
8.2 Membership in the Causal Solution "ABCE" and Institutional Adequacy *175*
8.3 Membership in the Causal Solution "(AD+BD) (E+F)" and Contribution to Development *177*
8.4 Membership in the Causal Solution "D (A+C)" and Contribution to Development *178*

TABLES

2.1 Institutions Included in the Comparative Study, 2006–2008 *30–31*
2.2 Truth Table of Institutional Adequacy and Contributions to National Development *34*
2.3 Truth Table of Scores Assigned to Institutions in Hypothesized Predictors and Outcomes *35*
3.1 A Typology of Public Institutions in Argentina *57*
5.1 Evans's Institutional Typology *96*
6.1 Composition of the Income of the Central Government *115*
6.2 Participation of Tourism in the Economy *115*
7.1 Budget of the Four Government Institutions *158*
7.2 Ratings by Institution across the Eight Indicators *159*
7.3 Ratings by Indicator across the Five Institutions *159*
7.4 Truth Table Analysis: Causal Combinations Associated with Contribution to Development *160*
8.1 Necessary and Sufficient Conditions in Fuzzy-Set Algebra *173*
8.2 Fuzzy-Set Sufficient and Necessary Conditions for Institutional Adequacy *173*
8.3 Fuzzy-Set Sufficient and Necessary Conditions for Contributions to Development *176*

PREFACE

The idea for the study that gave rise to this book came from a graduate seminar in economic sociology and a series of conversations with colleagues and students at Princeton University about the rise of the "new institutionalism" in economics and sociology. Several articles by Peter Evans of the University of California, Berkeley, about the "institutional turn" in the field of development were also influential in calling attention to the need for new empirical studies concerning what this "turn" meant in reality.

While the decision of several prominent economists to abandon conventional wisdom about determinants of development in favor of privileging the role of institutions was a welcome event, a sense of incompleteness still lingered. The definition of *institutions* raised in these economic discussions was vague, to say the least, encompassing a variety of distinct elements of social life. In some analyses, institutions were defined as akin to norms; in others, they were assimilated to the concept of values; and in still others, they were synonymous with organizations. This theoretical disorder made it impossible to gain a firm grip on the actual role played by institutions in processes of national development. If they were to encompass each and all relevant elements of society, the argument that they "matter" would become a tautology.

Accordingly, the first task was to try to put some order in this conceptual scenario by arriving at a tight, limited, and measurable definition of institutions, separating it, at the same time, from other distinct elements of culture and social structure. Results of this exercise led to the theoretical framework presented in chapter 1. It draws on the classic literature in sociology and social psychology to arrive at a schematic representation of the various elements of culture and social structure and the place of institutions within it. It then seeks to put this framework into motion by showing how it helps to clarify the failure of wholesale attempts to transplant First World models and practices to less developed countries—what Evans (2004) labels "institutional monocropping"—and by showing how processes of social change actually occur.

With this conceptual spadework out of the way, the next question was how to bring institutions to bear on empirical reality and specifically on those elements relevant to national development. Conversations with Miguel Centeno and Viviana Zelizer at Princeton, as well as with Peter Evans and other colleagues elsewhere, persuaded us that the path ahead consisted of detailed studies of real institutions that could be assumed to play a significant role on the societies in which they are embedded.

With support from the Princeton Institute for International and Regional Studies, we proceeded to start moving in this direction by selecting three such institutions in three Latin American countries. These institutions—the postal system, the civil aeronautics authority, and the national stock exchange—were selected as entities amenable to study and that prima facie could be assumed to play a significant role in their respective spheres of action. A discussion of the rationale for selecting these institutions is presented in chapter 2. Chile, Colombia, and Mexico were selected for this initial phase of the study as important countries that encompass the length of the continent and that represent very different political and economic systems. Reasons justifying their selection are also discussed in chapter 2.

Initially, we had no certainty that the study could be carried out or that it would meet a receptive audience in the selected countries. To find out, the senior author traveled to each country to meet with local social scientists, explain the purpose of the study, and try to identify prospective counterparts. Happily, the presentation of the theoretical framework of the project and the next steps to move it forward met with a receptive and thoughtful response in each country. As an outcome of these conversations, teams were formed, with individual investigators assigned to specific institutions. The methodology for the study was also refined during conversations with our Colombian, Chilean, and Mexican collaborators, who made valuable contributions.

We monitored the progress of the nine institutional studies along the twelve months of fieldwork. For this purpose, the senior author traveled at least once during this period to each country to meet with national teams, review the progress of the studies, and try to find solutions to obstacles met in the course of data collection. Assembling the requisite data was not easy and required all the experience and commitment of each investigator. Frequently, top-level administrators were difficult to contact, and some delayed face-to-face interviews for months. There was no ready guide for the compilation of documents and other secondary data; they had to be slowly assembled through the exploration of multiple channels. In one case, the investigator in charge just gave up in exasperation and a replacement had to be found. This experience attested to the multiple challenges faced by each researcher in conducting his or her respective study.

Shortly after completion of the final reports, a conference was convened to discuss them and provide guidelines for their revision for publication. This event took place in Buenos Aires in August 2006. Final revised versions of each institutional study were subsequently posted on the webpage of the Center for Migration and Development (CMD) at Princeton University (http://cmd.princeton.edu/papers.shtml). Scores provided by each investigator for each hypothesized determinant of institutional quality and contribution to development formed the basis for a synthetic final analysis by the authors. Hypothesized determinants and the methodology for this analysis are explained in chapter 2. Results of this exercise were first published in English and were subsequently incorporated as the conclusion of the volume presenting results of this phase of the project.

This book, featuring chapters for each of the nine institutions written by the respective investigators, a theoretical introduction, and an analytic conclusion, was published in Spanish by Siglo XXI in Mexico.[1] The encouraging results of this initial phase led us to seek additional resources for its extension to new institutions and new countries. Such an extension would provide a means to increase the coverage of the study and test the validity of results obtained thus far. With the support of a grant from the National Science Foundation, this new phase was launched that included two additional countries—Argentina and the Dominican Republic—and two new institutions per country—the public health service and the national tax authority. The rationale for each of these additions and the methodological adjustments required for their inclusion are also described in chapter 2.

This extension led to an increase in the sample of institutions from nine to twenty-five. Eventually, the sample was reduced to twenty-three completed studies. There is no national stock exchange in the Dominican Republic, and, because of budget and time limitations, a study of the Argentine public health service was not completed. The experience accumulated in the first phase of the project led to a more careful selection of participants and a more detailed discussion of the requirements for successful fieldwork so that, this time, there were no casualties, and all planned studies were completed. A second conference took place in Santo Domingo, Dominican Republic, in August 2008. All new reports were presented and discussed with a view toward their publication. As before, final versions of all fourteen new studies were uploaded on the CMD webpage at Princeton.

Scores provided by each researcher on the six hypothesized factors defining a developmental institution furnished the basis for a new synthetic analysis with the same methodology outlined in chapter 2 but with a much-expanded sample. Partial results of this analysis have been published in English.[2] The full results are reported in the concluding chapter of this book.

The expanded sample of institutions made it unfeasible, however, to attempt to include them in a single volume. Instead, we asked leaders of national teams to draft summary essays synthesizing results from their respective country studies and to reflect on how they bear on their nation's past and future development prospects. These summary reports were completed in March 2010 and discussed at a final seminar at Princeton University the following month. Senior economists, sociologists, and political scientists served as discussants of each national report and provided valuable suggestions for revision. Based on these, each report was revised one last time, translated into English, and reedited. These are the texts presented in this book. Leaders of each national team either wrote them alone or with the collaboration of other investigators. In either case, the names of all participants and brief professional biographies are provided at the end of this study. The participants are also recognized in each of the following chapters.

As this narrative makes clear, this book is not a standard edited volume but the final product of a collaborative research effort conducted with a common theoretical framework and the same methodology. It would be unfeasible to recognize all investigators as coauthors, but this was, in every sense, a joint endeavor involving twenty-two investigators across the Americas. We are hopeful that this final product justifies their efforts.

NOTES

1. *Las instituciones en el desarrollo latinoamericano: Un estudio comparado* (Mexico City: Siglo XXI, 2009). A summary version in English is found in Alejandro Portes and Lori D. Smith, "Institutions and Development in Latin America: A Comparative Analysis," *Studies in Comparative International Development* 43 (2008): 101–28.

2. Alejandro Portes and Lori D. Smith, "Institutions and National Development in Latin America: A Comparative Study," *Socio-Economic Review* (September 2010): 1–37.

ACKNOWLEDGMENTS

We acknowledge the support of the Princeton Institute for International and Regional Studies (PIIRS) and the National Science Foundation (grant #SES–0647030). In addition to financial support, the PIIRS director at the time, Professor Miguel Centeno, provided strong encouragement for the initial launching of this study. We are indebted to him for his insights and faith in what was then an unproven research plan.

The real heroes of this comparative project are the authors of the institutional studies in each country without whose talent, dedication, and enthusiasm the study could not have been implemented or have reached a successful conclusion. Their names are acknowledged in the appendixes to the respective country chapters. From beginning to end, the study was based at the Center for Migration and Development at Princeton, whose associate director, Nancy Doolan, provided invaluable administrative and logistical support for every phase of the project and for the three successive seminars that anchored it.

Portes's two assistants at Princeton, first Barbara Lynch and then Christine Nanfra Coil, patiently typed and edited successive versions of all chapters and assembled the final manuscript. Without their dedication, skills, and upbeat attitude at all times, the successive complex tasks leading to this final volume could not have been completed. Our editor of many years at the University of California Press, Naomi Schneider, deserves credit for her faith in the project and the recognition that this was not an edited volume but the product of a joint cooperative effort. The senior author acknowledges the support and insights of his spouse,

Patricia Fernandez-Kelly, who also contributed mightily to bringing this project to a successful conclusion. The second author owes a special debt to Javier Rivera Frias, whose love and support was critical during the years this project was under way.

A. P. and L. D. S.
Princeton
November 2011

1

Institutions and Development

A Conceptual Reanalysis

Alejandro Portes

Recent years have brought a significant change in the evolution of economics and sociology, including an unexpected convergence in their approach to issues like firms and economic development. This convergence has pivoted around the concept of "institutions," a familiar term in sociology and social anthropology but something of a revolution in economics, dominated so far by the neoclassical paradigm. This development has been accompanied by confusion about what the new master term means and, importantly, by a failure to mine prior theoretical work that sought to order, classify, and relate the multiple aspects of social life that are now brought under the same umbrella concept.

This chapter seeks to reverse these trends by recalling key concepts and distinctions in sociological theory and illustrating their analytic utility with examples from the recent literature on economic development. The argument is that recourse to these concepts and distinctions enhance our ability to analyze economic and "economically relevant" phenomena (Weber [1904] 1949).

THE NEW INSTITUTIONALISM

As Peter Evans (2004b) has pointed out, the long-held consensus in economics that equated increasing capital stocks with national development has given way to an emerging view that the central role belongs to "institutions." He approvingly quotes Hoff and Stiglitz (2001: 389) to the effect that "development is no longer seen

Revised version of Alejandro Portes, "Institutions and Development: A Conceptual Re-analysis," *Population and Development Review* 32 (June): 233–62.

as a process of capital accumulation, but as a process of organizational change." Sociologists of development, including Evans himself and several nonorthodox economists, have been saying the same thing for decades without their arguments succeeding in swaying the economic mainstream (Evans 1979, 1995; Hamilton and Biggart 1988; Portes 1997; Hirschman 1958, 1963). Not until two Nobel laureates in economics, Joseph Stiglitz and Douglass North, elaborated the same arguments were some of those in the mainstream convinced. When North declared that "institutions matter," other analysts started to take them into account.

By 2004 the development economist Gerald Roland (2004: 110) declared that "we are all institutionalists now." Sociologists have generally welcomed this "institutional turn" (Evans 2004a; Nee 2005) as a vindication of their own ideas, albeit with a critical omission. Swayed perhaps by the promise of interdisciplinary collaboration in the wake of the new ideas, they have overlooked a fundamental fact: economists do not routinely deal with the multiple elements of social life or their interaction, and, in their attempts to do so, they often confuse them, producing impoverished or simply erroneous perceptions of reality.

Other observers have noted the same problem and put it in still more critical terms. Geoffrey Hodgson (2002: 148) states, "The blindness may be partial, but the impairment is nevertheless serious and disabling. What is meant by this allegation of blindness is that, despite their intentions, many mainstream economists lack the conceptual apparatus to discern anything but the haziest institutional outlines. . . . [They] have not got adequate vision tools to distinguish between different types of institutions, nor to appraise properly what is going on in them."

This judgment may be too harsh because, after all, institutional economists have taken the first steps toward incorporating key elements of social reality into their analyses. However, the level of interdisciplinary collaboration needed to do this optimally is still lacking. The first question is what institutions actually are. The answer that emerges from economics is a disparate set of factors that range from social norms to values and all the way to "property rights" and complex organizations such as corporations and agencies of the state (Haggard 2004; Williamson 1975, 1985). North (1990: 3) defined institutions as "any form of constraint that human beings devise to shape human interaction," a vague definition that encompasses everything from norms introjected in the process of socialization to physical coercion.

From this thin definition, all that can be said is that institutions exist when something exerts external influence on the behavior of social actors: the same notion that Durkheim identified as "norms" more than a century ago and not sufficient to capture the dynamics of communities and societies.

Neoinstitutionalism has also traveled to the realm of politics, where it has been used, as in economics, to denote the constraints that the social context puts on the actions of "rational man," thus leading to "bounded rationality" (Dolsak and

Ostrom 2003; Elster, Offe, and Preuss 1998). While itself unimpeachable, this assertion leaves open the question of what are the features of social context that actually "bound" rational action. Saying simply that everything depends on time and place leads us nowhere theoretically, as this statement is nonfalsifiable.

Moving things further, Elinor Ostrom has proposed a neoinstitutional analysis of the "Commons," seeking to solve the dilemma between self-interest and the collective good among users of the same readily available, but exhaustible common property resources. Ostrom (1990; Ostrom et al. 2002) argues that neither the state nor the market does a very good job in these situations, since they seek to impose external rules on the relevant actors. Rather, actors can devise their own enforceable institutional arrangements (i.e., norms) to escape the tyranny of atomized self-interest. These norms again vary with time and place. As we will see shortly, Ostrom's analysis is compatible with a sociologically informed analysis of institutional development, but the latter has the advantage of going beyond the simple assertion that such arrangements vary with the local context.

In sum, development economists and neoinstitutionalists seek to flesh out North's insight that social constraints matter. But in the absence of a solid theoretical framework, the practical results of this institutional turn have been what might be expected. In the hands of development practitioners, the new consensus has led to the attempted export of legal codes and organizational blueprints to the global South. The dismal results of such attempts have already been recognized (Evans 2004b; Hoff and Stiglitz 2001). However, we can do more than point out that such efforts are doomed from the start. Economists and other social scientists can draw on established theoretical traditions to sharpen their conceptual tools and devise a more sophisticated and useful mapping of social life. Sociologists can contribute to this enterprise by refining their own conceptual legacy. The resulting "thick institutionalism" seems preferable, in most instances, to the "thin" version now making the rounds in several disciplines.

The basis for interdisciplinary collaboration is already at hand and consists of a body of knowledge containing key elements for the analysis of what actually takes place in society and for the proper placement of the concept "institution." These elements include (1) a distinction between the symbolic realm and the material reality; (2) an understanding of the hierarchical character of both realms; (3) an identification of the linchpin concepts linking both; and (4) a theory of social change that goes beyond current institutionalist understandings of this process.

CULTURE AND SOCIAL STRUCTURE

From its classical beginnings, modern sociology developed a central distinction, consolidated by the mid-twentieth century, between culture and social structure. There are good reasons for this distinction. Culture embodies the symbolic elements crucial for human interaction, mutual understanding, and order. Social structure is composed of actual persons enacting roles organized in a status hierarchy of some kind. The distinction is analytic because only human beings exist in reality, but it is fundamental to understand both the motives for their actions and the consequences. Culture is the realm of values, cognitive frameworks, and accumulated knowledge. Social structure is the realm of interests, individual and collective, backed by different amounts of power. The symbolic distinction provides the basis for analyzing the difference between what "ought to be" or "is expected to be" and what actually "is" in multiple social contexts (Merton 1936, 1968a).

The diverse elements that compose culture and social structure can be arranged in a hierarchy of causative influences from "deep" factors, often concealed below everyday social life but fundamental for its organization, to "surface" phenomena, more mutable and more readily evident. Language and values are the deep elements of culture, the first as the fundamental instrument of human communication and the second as the motivating force behind "principled" action, individual or collective. The importance of values can range, in turn, from fundamental moral imperatives of a society to traditions prized mostly out of custom. In every instance, values point toward a clear continuum between the good and desirable and the bad and abhorrent. "Neutrality" is the exact opposite of this basic element of culture (Durkheim [1897] 1965; Weber [1904] 1949). Values are deep culture because they are seldom invoked in the course of everyday life. Values come to the fore only in exceptional circumstances (Weber [1904] 1949; Merton 1989). Yet they underlie, and are inferred from, aspects of everyday behavior that are the opposite of unrestrained self-interest, the "constraints" that North, Ostrom, and others refer to.

Norms are such constraints. Values are not norms. The distinction is important: values represent general moral principles, and norms embody concrete directives for action (Newcomb, Turner, and Converse 1965; MacIver and Page [1949] 1961). Values underlie norms, which are rules that prescribe the do's and don'ts of individual everyday conduct. These rules can be formal and codified into constitutions and laws, or they can be implicit and informally enforced. The concept of norms has been used, at least since Durkheim ([1901] 1982), to refer to this restraining element of culture. Neglect of these classical analyses has led to lumping norms with the term *institution*, which has another, and important, connotation, as seen below. The significance of the values embodied within norms is reflected in practice in the level of sanctions attached to the latter. Thus life in prison or the death penalty awaits those found guilty of deliberate murder, while loud protest and insulting remarks may be the lot of those seeking to sneak ahead of a queue (Cooley 1902, 1912; Simmel [1908] 1964; Goffman 1959).

Norms are not free floating but come together in organized bundles known as *roles*. This sociological concept has been neglected in the institutionalist literature, which thus deprives itself of a key analytic tool. For it is as role occupants that individuals enter into the social world and are subject to the constraints and incentives of norms. Roles are generally defined as the set of behaviors prescribed for occupants of particular social positions (Linton 1945; Newcomb 1950: chap. 3). Well-socialized persons shift from role to role effortlessly and often unconsciously as part of their daily routines. The normative blueprints that constitute a role generally leave considerable latitude for their individual enactment. An extensive literature in both sociology and social psychology has analyzed roles as the building blocks of social life and as one of the linchpin concepts linking the symbolic world of culture to real social structures. The same literature has examined such dynamics as the "role set" enacted by given social actors and the "role conflict" or "role strain" created when normative expectations in an actor's role sets contradict each other (Cottrell 1933; Linton 1945; Merton 1957; Goffman 1959, 1961; Goode 1960). None of these concepts has made its appearance in the sociology being created in economics. Roles are an integral part of institutions, but they are *not* institutions, and confusing the two terms weakens the heuristic power of both concepts.

Along with normative expectations, roles embody an instrumental repertoire of skills necessary for their proper enactment. Language is the fundamental component of this repertoire for, without it, no other skills can be enacted. These cultural "tool kits" also contain many other elements—from scientific and professional know-how to demeanor, forms of expressions, manners, and general savoir faire suitable for specific social occasions. In the modern sociological literature, these elements are referred to by the concepts "cultural capital" and "skills repertoires" (Bourdieu 1979, 1984; Swidler 1986; Zelizer 2005).

POWER, CLASS, AND STATUS

Parallel to the component elements of culture run those of social structure. These are not made up of moral values or generalized do's and don'ts but involve the specific and differentiated ability of social actors to compel others to do their bidding. This is the realm of power, which, like that of values, is situated at the "deep" level of social life influencing a wide variety of outcomes. Weber's classic definition of power as the ability of an actor to impose his or her will despite resistance is still appropriate, for it highlights the compulsory and coercive nature of this basic element of social structure. It does not depend on the voluntary consent of subordinates, and for some actors and groups to have power others must be excluded from access to it (Weber [1922] 1947; Veblen [1899] 1998; Mills 1959). While values motivate or constrain, power enables. Naturally, elites in control of power-conferring resources seek to stabilize and perpetuate their position by molding values so that the mass of the population is persuaded of the "fairness" of the existing order. Power thus legitimized becomes *authority*, in which subordinates acquiesce to their position (Weber [1922] 1947; Bendix 1962: chaps. 9, 10).

In Marx's classic definition, power depends on control of the means of production, but in the modern postindustrial world this definition is too restrictive (Marx [1939] 1970; [1867] 1967: pt. 7). Power is conferred as well by control of the means of producing and appropriating knowledge, by control of the means of diffusing information, and by the more traditional control of the means of violence (Weber [1922] 1947; Wright 1980, 1985; Poulantzas 1975). In the Marxist tradition, a hegemonic class is one that has succeeded in legitimizing its control of the raw means of power, thus transforming it into authority (Gramsci [1927–33] 1971; Poulantzas 1975). Power is not absent from contemporary institutional economics, but the emphasis is on authority relations—what Williamson (1975, 1985) calls "hierarchies." Although these analyses are important, they neglect more basic forms of power. This omission supports Hodgson's argument on the lack of tools in modern economics to understand what institutions really are. For, as we shall see shortly, actual institutions are molded, to a large extent, by power differentials.

Just as values are embodied in norms, so power differentials give rise to social classes—large aggregates whose possession of or exclusion from resources leads to varying life chances and capacities to influence the course of events. Classes need not be subjectively perceived by their occupants in order to be operative, for they underlie the obvious fact that people in society are ranked according to how far they are able to implement their goals when confronted with resistance (Wright 1985; Wright and Perrone 1976; Poulantzas 1975). Class position is commonly associated with wealth, but it is also linked to other power-conferring resources such as expertise or the "right" connections (Hout, Brooks, and Manza 1993; Bourdieu 1984, 1990; Portes 2000a). As emphasized by Bourdieu (1985), dominant classes generally command a mix of resources that include not only wealth but also ties to influential others (social capital) and the knowledge and style to occupy high-status positions (cultural capital).

The deep character of power seldom comes to the surface of society, for its holders aim to legitimize it in the value system in order to obtain the voluntary consent of the governed. For the same reason, class position is not readily transparent, and it is a fact, repeatedly verified by empirical research, that individuals with very different resources and life chances frequently identify themselves as members of the same "class" (Hout, Brooks, and Manza 1993; Grusky and Sorensen 1998). Legitimized power (authority) produces, in turn, status hierarchies. Most social actors actually perceive the underlying structure of power on the basis of such hierarchies and classify themselves accordingly. In turn, status hierarchies are commonly linked to the performance of occupational roles (MacIver and Page [1949] 1961; Newcomb, Turner, and Converse 1965: 336–41; Linton 1945).

The various elements of culture and social structure, placed at different levels of importance and visibility, occur simultaneously and appear, at first glance,

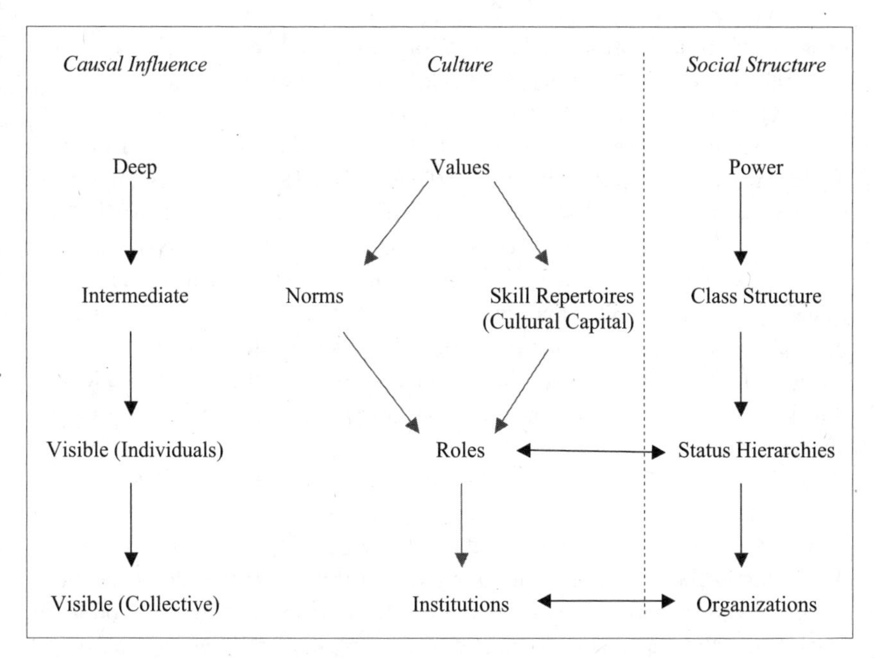

FIGURE 1.1. Elements of Social Life

as an undifferentiated mass. Their analytic separation is required, however, for the proper understanding of social phenomena, including economic phenomena. Not everything is "constraints on behavior"; some elements constrain, others motivate, and still others enable. Economists have not done the conceptual spadework required to understand these differences. The framework outlined thus far is summarized in figure 1.1. As the citations accompanying the text suggest, this framework is neither new nor improvised but forms part of a classical intellectual legacy neglected in the current enthusiasm for the institutionalist turn.

INSTITUTIONS IN PERSPECTIVE

As indicated in figure 1.1, status hierarchies with attached roles do not generally exist in isolation but as part of social organizations. Organizations, economic and otherwise, are what social actors inhabit, and they embody the most readily visible manifestations of the underlying structures of power (Powell 1990; DiMaggio 1990; Granovetter 2001). Institutions represent the symbolic blueprint for organizations; they are the set of rules, written or informal, governing relationships among role occupants in social organizations like the family, schools, and other major institutionally structured areas of organizational life: the polity, the economy, religion, communications and information, and leisure (MacIver and Page [1949] 1961; Merton 1968b; North 1990; Hollingsworth 2002).

This definition of institutions is in close agreement with everyday uses of the term, as when one speaks of "institutional blueprints." Its validity does not depend, however, on this overlap but on its analytic utility. The position advanced here is nominalist: Concepts are mental constructs whose usefulness is given by their collective capacity to guide our understanding of social phenomena, including the economy. If North and his followers denominate norms "institutions," then they must cope with the conceptual problem of the relationship between such "institutions" and the roles in which they are embedded, as well as the symbolic blueprints specifying relationships among such roles and, hence, the actual structure of organizations.

A "thick" institutionalism that limits the scope of this concept, while systematically relating it to other elements of social life, gives us the necessary analytic leverage to understand phenomena that otherwise would be obscured. For example, the distinction between organizations and the institutions that underlie them provides a basis for analyzing how events actually occur in social and economic life. For it is not the case that once institutional rules are established, role occupants blindly follow. Instead, they constantly modify the rules, transform them, and bypass them in the course of their daily interaction.

No doubt, "institutions matter," but they are themselves subject to what Granovetter (1985, 1992) referred to as "the problem of embeddedness": The fact that the human exchanges that institutions seek to guide in turn affect these institutions. That is why formal goals and prescribed organizational hierarchies come to differ from how organizations operate in reality (Dalton 1959; Morrill 1991; Powell 1990). Absent this analytic separation, as well as the understanding that institutions and organizations flow from deeper levels of social life, everything becomes an undifferentiated mass where the recognition that "contexts matter" produces, at best, descriptive case studies and, at worst, circular reasoning. The following sections seek to put this conceptual framework into motion on the basis of two recent examples from the development literature.

The Failure of Institutional Monocropping

The most tangible practical result of the advent of institutionalism in the field of economic development has been the attempt to transplant the institutional forms of the West, especially the United States, into the less developed world. The definition of *institutions* employed in such attempts is in close agreement with that advanced here: blueprints specifying the functions and prerogatives of roles and the relationships among their occupants. Institutions and the resulting organizations may be created from scratch—as a central bank, a stock exchange, or an ombudsman office—or they may be remolded—as in attempts to strengthen the independence of the judiciary or streamline the local legislature (Haggard 2004).

Many authors have noted that these attempts to put the ideas of North and other institutionalists into practice have not yielded the expected results and have frequently backfired. Evans (2004b), in particular, calls these exercises in transplantation institutional monocropping, whereby the set of rules constructed by trial and error over centuries in the advanced countries is grafted into different societies and expected to have comparable results. Roland (2004) diagnoses the cause of the failures of such efforts as lying in the gap between "slow-moving" and "fast-moving" institutions, but the actual forces at play are much more complex.

Institutional grafting takes place at the surface level of society and, as such, faces the potential opposition of a dual set of forces grounded in the deep structure of the receiving countries: those based on values and those based on power. Within the realm of culture, consider the different bundles of norms and cultural tool kits that go into formally similar roles. That of "policeman" may entail, in less developed societies, the expectation to compensate paltry wages with bribe taking, a legitimate preference for kin and friends over strangers in the discharge of duties, and skills that extend no further than using firearms and readily clubbing civilians at the first sign of trouble. The role of "government minister" may similarly entail the expectation of particularistic preferences in the allocation of jobs and government patronage, appointments by party loyalty rather than expertise, and the practice of using the power of the office to ensure the long-term economic well-being of the occupant.

Such role expectations are grounded in deeply held values that privilege particularistic obligations and ascriptive ties and that encourage suspicion of bureaucracies and seemingly universalistic rules. When imported institutional blueprints are superimposed on such realities, the results are not hard to imagine. Blueprints do not necessarily backfire, but they can have a series of unexpected consequences following from the fact that those in charge of their implementation and the presumed beneficiaries view reality through very different cultural lenses (O'Donnell 1994; Portes 1997, 2000b).

Several authors, including economists who have analyzed these dynamics, recognize the importance of power. Karla Hoff and Joeseph Stiglitz (2001: 418–20) note, for example, that imposing new sets of formal rules without simultaneously reshaping the distribution of power is a dubious strategy. Similarly, Roland (2004: 115) recognizes that "whatever group holds power will use that power in its own best interest." Less well understood are two other key features of social structures. The first is that "power" is not free floating but depends on control of certain strategic resources—capital, means of production, organized violence—that vary from country to country. Second, and more important, the existing class structure may be legitimized by the value system in such a way that change is resisted not only by those in positions of privilege, but by the mass of the population. As Weber and Gramsci recognized, legitimized power is particularly hard to dislodge because the masses not only acquiesce to their own subordination, but stand ready to defend the existing order. The experiences of "modernizing" regimes seeking to dislodge entrenched theocracies in the Middle East and elsewhere illustrate the decisive role of this kind of power (Lerner 1958; Levy 1966; Bellah 1958).

Following the argument of another Nobel Prize winner, Amartya Sen, Evans (2004b) offers an alternative to institutional monocropping, which he labels "deliberative development." Sen's argument for participatory democracy starts with the notion that "thickly democratic" initiatives, built on public discussion and free exchange of ideas, offer the only way to reach viable developmental goals. For Sen (1999), thickly democratic participation is not only a means to an end, but a developmental goal in itself. Evans agrees and cites the "participatory budgeting" process in Brazilian cities dominated by parties of the left as examples of the viability of deliberative development (Baiocchi 2003).

The conceptual framework discussed previously is useful for envisioning the contrast between institutional grafting and deliberative development. As shown in figure 1.2, the idea of importing institutions begins at the surface level and tries to push its way "upward" into the normative structure and value system of society. For reasons already seen, such efforts are likely to meet resistance and frequent failure. The participatory strategy begins at the other end, by engaging the population in a broad discussion of developmental goals (values) and the rules (norms) and technical means (skill repertoires) necessary to attain them. Although the process is messy and complicated, the institutional blueprints that eventually emerge from these discussions are likely to be successful because they correspond to the causal directionality of culture itself.

A key problem with deliberative development proposals is that they ignore the right-side elements of society, as outlined in figure 1.1, namely, those grounded in power and crystallized in the class structure. Unless the dominant classes are somehow persuaded or compelled to go along with such experiments, the latter are not likely to succeed. If implemented against elite resistance, they are bound to be derailed into just talk—deliberation as an end in itself. When the population mobilized to take part in such meetings sees that they lead to nothing or produce outcomes predetermined by the authorities, participation drops rapidly and generalized discontent sets in (Roberts and Portes 2005; Roberts 2002).

As Sen (1999) himself recognizes, technocrats (i.e., technically trained elites) prefer to impose institutional blueprints that enhance their power and external image rather than subordinate themselves to the messy deliberations of ordinary people. Evans (2004b: 40) acknowledges as well that the dynamics of power are likely to be the biggest impediment to the "institutionalization of deliberative institutions." Not surprisingly, only when parties of the left have gained solid

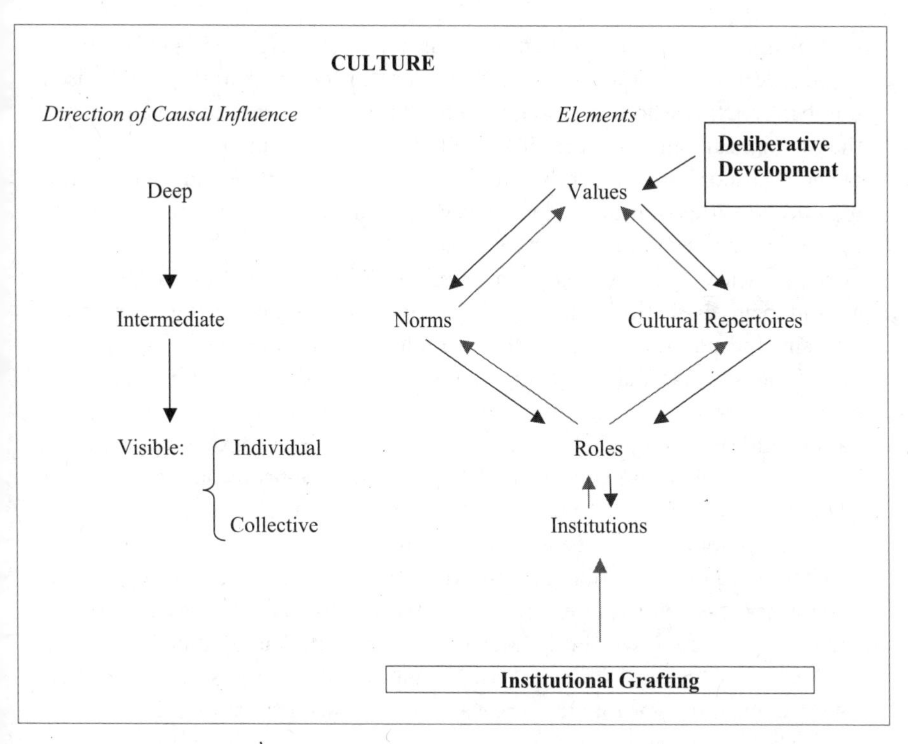

FIGURE 1.2. Participatory Democracy and Institutional Monocropping

control of governments have experiments in participatory democracy been given a reasonable chance of success. This occurs because authorities can mobilize the resources of government to neutralize resources possessed by local elites, persuading them that it is in their interest to join the deliberative process (Biaocchi 2003; Agarwala 2004).

The Privatization of the Mexican Economy

Starting in 1982, the Mexican government began a massive program of divestiture of the many companies that it had created. This program amounted to a radical departure from the previous state-centric model of development and touched the interests and life chances of almost everyone in Mexican society (Centeno 1994; Ariza and Ramirez 2005). The shift came in the aftermath of the Mexican default of 1982 and the conditions imposed by the International Monetary Fund (IMF) and the U.S. Treasury to bail out the country. Over the next three *sexenios* (presidential terms), the Mexican state divested itself of almost everything—from the telecommunications company to the two national airlines (Mexicana and Aeromexico).

This massive economic realignment was not accomplished without resistance. A great deal of money was to be made from privatizations, but there were also a number of actors who lost power, wealth, or their jobs. Mexico's privatization of the economy amounted to drastic institutional change—a profound modification of the legal/normative blueprints under which firms operate and their internal organization. This transformation, however, could not have been accomplished at the level of the institutions themselves.

State-owned firms operated with a logic of their own, creating constituencies around themselves. Although frequently inefficient, they gave secure employment to many and political capital to the line ministers and managers that operated them (Lomnitz 1982; Eckstein 1977). Thus Aeromexico operated with a staff of 200 employees per airplane at a time when the inefficient and about-to-be-bankrupt Eastern Airlines had 146. Yet the minute that plans for Aeromexico's restructuring were announced, its employees struck, arguing that the firm would be profitable "if only" management were more efficient (MacLeod 2004: 123, 133).

The battle for divestment and market opening pitted the unions, the managers of state-owned industries, and the ministries that supervised them against a group of reformers imbued with the new neoliberal doctrines at the Treasury Ministry and other strategic places in the Mexican bureaucracy. Large capitalists, foreign multinationals, and the IMF supported divestiture and opening; small firm owners who had much to lose from the removal of state protection opposed it (MacLeod 2004: 96).

During President Miguel de la Madrid's *sexenio,* only smaller and relatively marginal firms were privatized. Defenders of the status quo could keep faith that the strong corporatist traditions of the ruling party, the PRI, would in the end prevail. Despite sustained external pressure, institutions (i.e., state-owned corporations) would not reform themselves, and attempts at reform were effectively resisted: "From their positions on the executive committees and boards of directors of parastate firms, line ministers could keep a watchful eye on the efforts of would-be reformers... line ministers withheld data or presented contradictory or incorrect data, making it virtually impossible to evaluate the company" (MacLeod 2004: 75–76, see also 71).

True reform, as the IMF and the multinational corporations envisioned it, could only come from the top of the power structure. This actually happened during the next *sexenio* under President Carlos Salinas de Gortari. A convinced free marketeer, Salinas appointed economists of the same persuasion to key positions in the Central Bank and the Treasury Ministry. Once there, they created new, compact, and powerful agencies to ensure that privatization would move forward. Not willing to believe that things would take such a turn for the worse, union leaders and firm managers bypassed the new bureaucratic structures to take their case directly to the president. To no avail: "When the UDEP (Unit for the Divestiture of

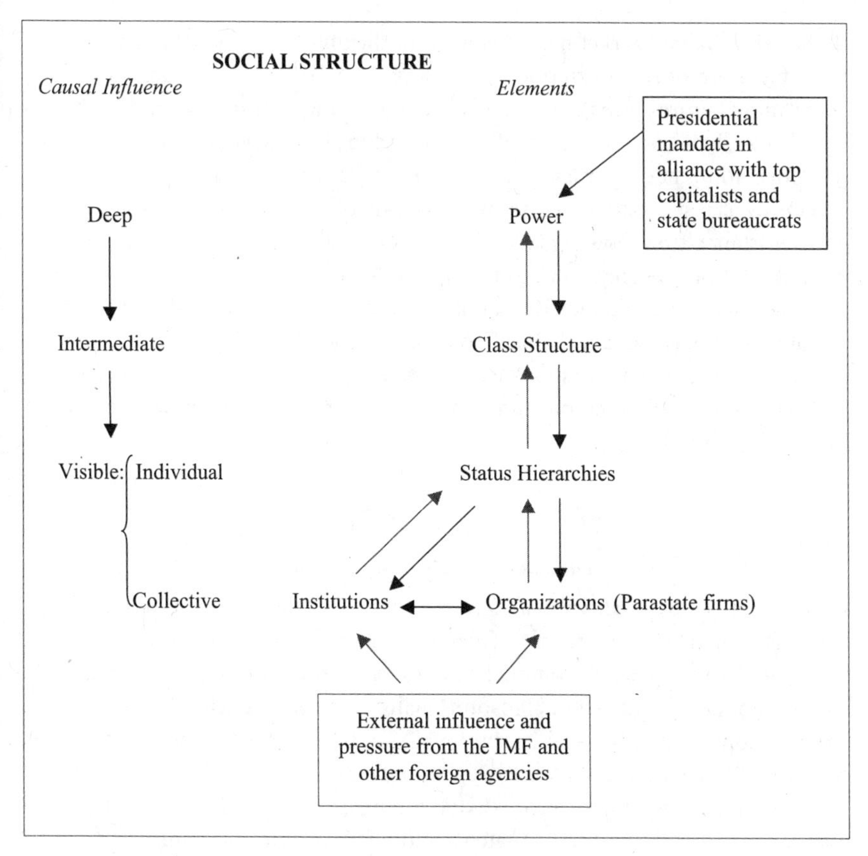

FIGURE 1.3. The Divestiture of Parastate Corporations in Mexico

Parastate Entities) began the process of privatizing parastate firms, labor leaders, line ministers, and executives of parastate firms often sought to circumvent the authority of UDEP by appealing directly to the President. President Salinas regularly sent these supplicants back to the director of UDEP. . . . [T]his process quickly consolidated UDEP's authority within the Mexican bureaucracy" (MacLeod 2004: 81–82).

The "sale of the state" engineered by UDEP in subsequent years amounted to a major case of institutional transformation; it also represents a clear example of the dynamics of power. As shown in figure 1.3, reforms initiated from the outside barely made a dent in the Mexican corporatist structure. It was necessary for the country's top political and economic leadership to get involved in order to overcome strong and organized resistance from various classes. Unionized workers and national entrepreneurs became the losers in this giant power struggle that saw the Mexican labor market become far more "flexible" and the Mexican corporations far more open to external competition and takeover (Shaiken 1990, 1994; Ariza and Ramirez 2005). As elsewhere, significant institutional and organizational change did not originate with organizations themselves but required major transformations at deeper levels of the social structure.

However, just as attempted transformations of existing institutions can meet with resistance from power holders in the social structure, power plays that impose institutional change can produce generalized opposition when the underlying values remain unaltered. The Salinas reforms took place against a background of public skepticism about the need to denationalize the economy and strong opposition from many sectors of Mexican society (MacLeod 2004). Salinas ended his term in disgrace, becoming an unpopular figure and eventually being forced to leave the country.

THE PROBLEM OF CHANGE

Diffusion and Path Dependence

In his recent book, *Institutional Change and Globalization* (2004), John Campbell systematically describes the different schools of institutional analysis that exist today. These he labels "rational choice institutionalism," associated primarily with economics; "organizational institutionalism," associated with the sociology of organizations; and "historical institutionalism," based on political economy and certain strands of political science. Depending on the school, social change is seen primarily as an evolutionary process, developing gradually over time, or as a combination of evolution and "punctuated evolution" when drastic shifts occur.

Despite these differences, Campbell characterizes all three schools as favoring two major determinants of change. These are "path dependence," meaning the tendency of events to follow a set course where what existed yesterday determines what happens today and what is likely to occur tomorrow (Thelen 2004; North 1990); and "diffusion," meaning the tendency of established institutional patterns to migrate, influencing the course of events. Diffusion is identified by the school led by John Meyer as a master process in the contemporary global system in which the institutions of the advanced countries are commonly reproduced in weaker societies, either under the aegis of international agencies or out of the desire of local rulers to imitate the modern world (Meyer and Hannan 1979; Meyer et al. 1997).

Campbell argues that "the problem of change" has been a thorny one for institutional analysis. This is not difficult to understand. First, with a vague and contested definition of *institution,* the analysis of change confronts an elusive target. When institution can be anything—from the incest taboo to the Central Bank—we do not have a sufficiently delimited object to examine how it changes over time. The definition advanced here—sets of rules that govern the regular relationships among role occupants—is sufficiently specific to allow consideration of how processes of change take place in this sector of social life. Thus defined, institutional change is *not* the same as change in the class structure or in the value system, processes that ultimately affect institutions but that occur at other levels.

Second, with concepts such as path dependence and diffusion as its main tools for the analysis of change, it is not difficult to understand how the predicted course of events for institutional analysis would be either evolution or punctuated evolution. It is a fact that, at the surface level of social life, change tends to be gradual, with patterned ways of doing things largely determining the future course of events.

Intersocietal diffusion of cultural elements operates at a deeper level, affecting the normative and skill contents of specific roles. Diffusion of new technologies and patterns of consumption from the advanced world to the less developed countries is indeed one of the most common and most important sources of change in these countries (Sassen 1988; Meyer et al. 1997).

But dynamics of change are not limited to diffusion and path dependence; they can also exist at deeper levels of the culture and social structure, producing drastic and nonevolutionary outcomes. To be sure, as argued by some institutionalists, radical change tends to have long periods of gestation, but this does not negate the fact that once such change occurs, consequences can be abrupt and often traumatic. Technological changes, to take one example, can be endogenous rather than brought about by diffusion. Once they occur, technological breakthroughs can affect, in a very short time, the skills repertoires and, hence, the roles of large numbers of social actors. One such example is the advent of the Internet, an innovation that has altered the content of occupational roles and the rules linking them in most institutions of modern society (Castells 1998, 2001).

Religion and religious prophecies can affect the culture in still more radical ways because they impinge directly on the value system (Wuthnow 1987, 1998). Weber's theory of social change focuses on the history of religion and specifically on the role of charisma and charismatic prophecy as forces capable of breaking through the limits of reality, as hitherto known, and providing the impetus necessary to dismantle the existing social order and rebuild it on a new basis. The influence of the Protestant Reformation, especially Calvinism, in revolutionizing economic life in Western Europe is perhaps the best-known illustration of the effects that charismatic prophecy can have on society (Weber [1922] 1964, [1915] 1958).

The advent of charismatic prophecy capable of revolutionizing the value system and, hence, an entire civilization occurs after a long period of historical gestation, but this does not prevent it from having immediate and profound consequences once it bursts onto the scene. After Calvinism had transformed the social order of much of Western Europe, historians had little difficulty tracing the concatenation of events that led to it. But they would not have bothered to engage in such an exercise had Luther not nailed his theses at Wittenberg and had Calvin not risen to power in Geneva. Post hoc reconstruction of revolutionary social change can always be "evolutionary."

For those who dismiss the role of religious charisma as a thing of the past, one need only point to the decisive influence that Evangelical Christianity continues to have in transforming large portions of American society (Wuthnow 1998; Roof 1999) and to the emergence of a fundamentalist brand of Islam set on ultimate confrontation with the West. The "war on terrorism" that is today the overriding concern of states in North America and Europe is interpretable as a direct consequence of a reenergized, charismatic religious prophecy seeking to remake the world in its own image (Kastoryano 2004; Kepel 1987).

Revolutionary change can also occur in the realm of social structure, as when power is wrested from its current possessors and vested in a new elite. The question of power and of class struggles has been addressed by a long line of historians and social scientists, classic and contemporary. Vilfredo Pareto's ([1902] 1966) theory of the circulation of elites and his remark that "history is but a graveyard of aristocracies" focus on the fact that dominant groups have never been able to maintain power indefinitely and on the analysis of the mechanisms leading to their demise. From very different theoretical quarters, Marx privileged the class struggle and, at a deeper level, the conflict between new modes of production and entrenched "social relationships of production" as the master mechanism leading to revolutionary change. For Marx and his numerous followers, the internal contradictions of feudalism that brought about its end were being re-created anew under capitalism, as rising social classes clashed with the dominant class structure (Marx and Engels [1847] 1959: 20).

Much of contemporary historical sociology—including the writings of Barrington Moore (1966), Theda Skocpol (1979), Charles Tilly (1984), Immanuel Wallerstein (1974, 1991), and Giovanni Arrighi (1994)—is concerned with the same question of revolutionary change and elite replacement. To take one example, Skocpol's (1979) theory of social revolutions highlights interelite conflict, external military pressure, and an oppressed peasantry as factors that, when coming together, can drastically transform the class structure and bring about a new social order. While structural change of this magnitude occurs after a lengthy concatenation of events, this is made evident only by the moment of social explosion itself and the ensuing events.

From the perspective of the profound consequences wrought by transformations in a society's value system or class structure, a theory of change based on path dependence and cultural diffusion looks limited indeed. Change—whether revolutionary or not—at deeper levels of the culture and social structure filters upward to the more visible levels, including institutions and organizations. Thus

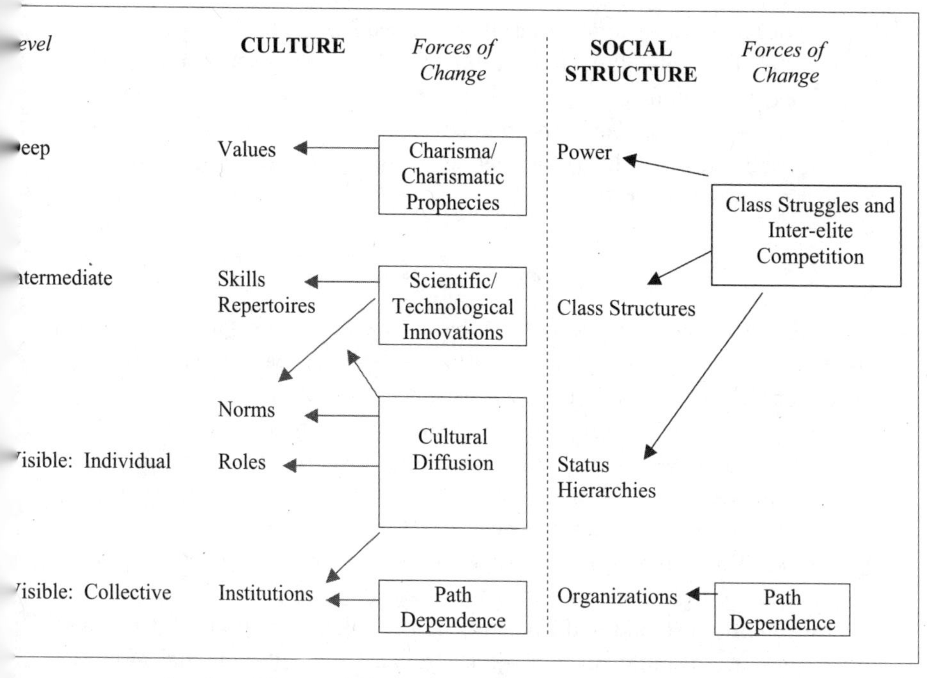

FIGURE 1.4. Levels and Forces of Change

it is possible to distinguish at least five forces impinging on institutions and leading to their transformation: path dependence, producing evolutionary change at the more visible institutional level; diffusion, also leading to evolutionary and sometimes "punctuated" change at the intermediate levels of culture; scientific/technological breakthroughs affecting the cultural skills repertoires and normative order; at a deeper level, charismatic prophecy—religious or secular—capable of transforming the value system and, hence, the rest of the culture; and interelite and class struggles with the potential for transforming the distribution of power. The last three sources hold the potential for profound institutional change, of the type seen in the aftermath of social revolutions and epoch-making inventions.

Figure 1.4 summarizes this discussion. Campbell (2004) concludes his review of institutional change by recommending that we consider such a process only within well-limited time frames and "in its multiple dimensions." These recommendations are unobjectionable, but they do not go far enough. While limited time frames prevent infinite regress into history, they do not distinguish between evolutionary change over a given period and abrupt, revolutionary transformations. Similarly, the "multiple dimensions" to be considered in the analysis of change are left unspecified.

A conceptual framework such as that outlined here helps distinguish between different elements of culture and social structure and the relative impact of processes of change taking place at different levels. An institutional analysis of change limited to institutions themselves produces an impoverished account of these processes, relative to what the social sciences in general and sociology in particular have already accomplished.

CONCLUSION

Disciplinary amnesia is perhaps inevitable as new generations of scholars seek to make their mark in the world. The unfortunate consequence, however, is the rediscovery or reelaboration of what had already been found.

Advocates of the "institutions are everything" approach may reply that the conceptual framework proposed in this chapter is dated since it is based on the work of nineteenth- and early-twentieth-century precursors. They may add that there has been progress since then, and that "thin institutionalism"—a loose definition of the concept—is more flexible and, for that reason, preferable in many circumstances. To this, we answer that progress is indeed desirable but that, with the exception of debunking the patently implausible assumptions of neoclassical economics, neoinstitutionalism is still far from achieving its potential. We would attribute this failure, first, to the neglect of a rich theoretical heritage and, second, to careless definitions. It is impossible to cumulate scientific knowledge when master concepts can mean practically anything. No better conceptual framework has been devised to replace that which is our legacy from earlier generations of thinkers and researchers. For that reason alone, thick institutionalism—a precise definition of the concept placed within a systematic framework—is preferable as the basis for cumulative progress.

The theoretical synthesis presented here is tentative and subject to modification. No intrinsic truth is claimed for it, save its utility for delimiting the scope of the concept of institutions and moving us away from an impoverished understanding of social change. The comparative study described next puts this agenda into motion by analyzing really existing institutions and their bearing on national development.

REFERENCES

Agarwala, Rina. 2004. "From Work to Welfare: The State and Informal Workers' Organizations in India." Working Paper #04-07. Center for Migration and Development, Princeton University.

Ariza, Marina, and Juan Manuel Ramírez. 2005. "Urbanización, mercados de trabajo y escenarios sociales en el México finisecular." In *Las ciudades latinoamericanas a comienzos del siglo,* edited by A. Portes, B.R. Roberts, and A. Grimson, 299–361. Buenos Aires: Prometeo Editores.

Arrighi, Giovanni. 1994. *The Long Twentieth Century: Money, Power, and the Origins of Our Times.* London: Verso.

Baiocchi, Gianpaolo. 2003. *Radicals in Power: The Workers Party and Experiments in Urban Democracy in Brazil.* London: Zed.

Bellah, Robert N. 1958. "Religious Aspects of Modernization in Turkey and Japan." *American Journal of Sociology* 64 (July): 1–5.

Bendix, Reinhard. 1962. *Max Weber: An Intellectual Portrait.* Garden City, NY: Anchor Books.

Bourdieu, Pierre. 1979. "Les trois états du capital culturel." *Actes de la Recherche en Sciences Sociales* 30: 3–6.

———. 1984. *Distinction: A Social Critique of the Judgment of Taste.* Cambridge, MA: Harvard University Press.

———. 1985. "The Forms of Capital." In *Handbook of Theory and Research for the Sociology of Education,* edited by J.G. Richardson, 241–58. Westport, CT: Greenwood Press.

———. 1990. *The Logic of Practice.* Stanford: Stanford University Press.

Campbell, John L. 2004. *Institutional Change and Globalization.* Princeton, NJ: Princeton University Press.

Castells, Manuel. 1998. *End of Millennium: The Information Age.* Oxford: Blackwell Publishers.

———. 2001. *The Internet Galaxy.* New York: Oxford University Press.

Centeno, Miguel A. 1994. *Democracy within Reason: Technocratic Revolution in Mexico.* University Park: Pennsylvania State University Press.

Cooley, Charles H. 1902. *Human Nature and the Social Order.* New York: Charles Scribners and Sons.

———. 1912. *Social Organization.* New York: Charles Scribners and Sons.

Cottrell, Leonard S. 1933. "Roles and Marital Adjustment." *Publications of the American Sociological Society* 28.

Dalton, Melville. 1959. *Men Who Manage: Fusions of Feeling and Theory in Administration.* New York: Wiley.

DiMaggio, Paul. 1990. "Cultural Aspects of Economic Action and Organization." In *Beyond the Marketplace,* edited by R. Friedlander and A.F. Robertson, 113–36. New York: Aldine de Gruyter.

Dolsak, Nines, and Elinor Ostrom. 2003. *The Commons in the New Millennium: Challenges and Adaptation.* Cambridge, MA: MIT Press.

Durkheim, Emile. [1897] 1965. *Suicide, a Study in Sociology.* Translated by J.A. Spaulding and G. Simpson. New York: Free Press.

———. [1901] 1982. *The Rules of the Sociological Method.* Translated by W.D. Halls. New York: Free Press.

Eckstein, Susan. 1977. *The Poverty of Revolution: The State and the Urban Poor in Mexico.* Princeton, NJ: Princeton University Press.

Elster, Jon, Claus Offe, and Ulrick K. Preuss. 1998. *Institutional Design in Post-Communist Societies: Rebuilding the Ship at Sea.* Cambridge: Cambridge University Press.

Evans, Peter. 1979. *Dependent Development: The Alliance of Multinational, State, and Local Capital in Brazil.* Princeton: Princeton University Press.

———. 1989. "Predatory, Developmental, and Other Apparatuses: A Comparative Political Economy Perspective on the Third World State." *Sociological Forum* 4: 561–87.

———. 1995. *Embedded Autonomy: States and Industrial Transformation.* Princeton: Princeton University Press.

———. 2004a. "The Challenges of the 'Institutional Turn': Interdisciplinary Opportunities in Development Theory." In *The Economic Sociology of Capitalism,* edited by V. Nee and R. Swedberg, 90–116. Princeton: Princeton University Press.

———. 2004b. "Development as Institutional Change: The Pitfalls of Monocropping and the Potentials of Deliberation." *Studies in Comparative International Development* 38 (Winter): 30–52.

Giddens, Anthony. 1987. *Las nuevas reglas del método sociológico.* Buenos Aires: Amorrortu.

Goffman, Erving. 1959. *The Presentation of Self in Everyday Life.* Garden City, NY: Doubleday.

———. 1961. *Encounters: Two Studies in the Sociology of Interaction.* Indianapolis, IN: Bobbs-Merrill.

Goode, William J. 1960. "A Theory of Role Strain." *American Sociological Review* 25 (August): 483–96.

Gramsci, Antonio. [1927–33] 1971. "State and Civil Society." In *Prison Notebooks,* translated and edited by Q. Hoare and G. N. Smith, 206–76. New York: International Publishers.

Granovetter, Mark. 1985. "Economic Action and Social Structure: The Problem of Embeddedness." *American Journal of Sociology* 91: 481–510.

———. 1992. "The Sociological and Economic Approaches to Labor Market Analysis: A Social Structural View." In *The Sociology of Economic Life,* edited by M. Granovetter and R. Swedberg, 233–63. Boulder, CO: Westview Press.

———. 2001. "Coase Revisited: Business Groups in the Modern Economy." In *The Sociology of Economic Life,* 2nd ed., edited by M. Granovetter and R. Swedberg, 327–56. Boulder, CO: Westview Press.

Grusky, David B., and Jesper B. Sorensen. 1998. "Can Class Analysis Be Salvaged?" *American Journal of Sociology* 103 (March):1187–1234.

Haggard, Stephan. 2004. "Institutions and Growth in East Asia." *Studies in Comparative International Development* 38 (Winter): 53–81.

Hamilton, Gary, and Nicole W. Biggart. 1988. "Market, Culture, and Authority: A Comparative Analysis of Management and Organization." *American Journal of Sociology* 94 (Supplement): 552–94.

Hirschman, Albert O. 1958. *The Strategy of Economic Development.* New Haven, CT: Yale University Press.

———. 1963. *Journeys toward Progress.* New York: Twentieth Century Fund.

Hodgson, Geoffrey M. 2002. "Institutional Blindness in Modern Economics." In *Advancing Socio-Economics: An Institutionalist Perspective,* edited by J. R. Hollingsworth, K. H. Muller, and E. J. Hollingsworth, 147–70. Landham, MD: Rowman and Littlefield.

Hoff, Karla, and Joseph Stiglitz. 2001. "Modern Economic Theory and Development." In *Frontiers of Development Economics,* edited by G. Meier and J. Stiglitz, 389–460. New York: Oxford University Press.

Hollingsworth, J. Rogers. 2002. "On Institutional Embeddedness." In *Advancing Socio-Economics: An Institutionalist Perspective*, edited by J. R. Hollingsworth, K. H. Muller, and E. J. Hollingsworth, 87–107. Landham, MD: Rowman and Littlefield.

Hout, Michael, Clem Brooks, and Jeff Manza. 1993. "The Persistence of Classes in Post-industrial Societies." *International Sociology* 8 (September): 259–77.

Kastoryano, Riva. 2004. "Religion and Incorporation: Islam in France and Germany." *International Migration Review* 38 (Fall): 1234–55.

Kepel, G. 1987. *Les Banlieues de l'Islam*. Paris: Ed. du Seine.

Lerner, David. 1958. *The Passing of Traditional Society: Modernizing the Middle East*. New York: Free Press.

Levy, Marion. 1966. *Modernization and the Structure of Societies*. Princeton: Princeton University Press.

Linton, Ralph. 1945. *The Cultural Background of Personality*. New York: Appleton, Century, Crofts.

Lomnitz, Larissa. 1982. "Horizontal and Vertical Relations and the Social Structure of Urban Mexico." *Latin American Research Review* 17: 51–74.

MacIver, R. H., and Charles H. Page. [1949] 1961. *Sociologia*. Translated from English by J. Cazorla Perez. Madrid: Tecnos Editores.

MacLeod, Dag. 2004. *Downsizing the State: Privatization and the Limits of Neoliberal Reform in Mexico*. University Park: Pennsylvania State University Press.

Marx, Karl. [1939] 1970. *The Grundrisse*. Edited and translated by D. McLellan. New York: Harper and Row.

Marx, Karl, and Friedrich Engels. [1847] 1959. "Manifesto of the Communist Party." In *Marx and Engels: Basic Writings on Politics and Philosophy*, edited by L. S. Feuer, 1–41. Garden City, NY: Doubleday.

Merton, Robert K. 1936. "The Unanticipated Consequences of Purposive Social Action." *American Sociological Review* 1: 894–904.

———. 1957. "The Role-Set: Problems in Sociological Theory." *British Journal of Sociology* 8 (June): 106–20.

———. 1968a. "Manifest and Latent Functions." In *Social Theory and Social Structure*, edited by R. K. Merton, 73–138. New York: Free Press.

———. 1968b. "Social Structure and Anomie." In *Social Theory and Social Structure*, edited by R. K. Merton, 175–214. New York: Free Press.

———. 1989. "Unanticipated Consequences and Kindred Sociological Ideas: A Personal Gloss." In *L'Opera di R. K. Merton e la sociologia contemporanea*, edited by C. Mongardini and S. Tabboni, 307–29. Genova: Edisioni Culturali Internazionali.

Meyer, John, John Boli, George M. Thomas, and Francisco Ramirez. 1997. "World Society and the Nation State." *American Journal of Sociology* 103 (July): 144–81.

Meyer, John, and Michael T. Hannan. 1979. *National Development and the World System: Educational, Economic, and Political Change, 1950–1970*. Chicago: University of Chicago Press.

Mills, C. Wright. 1959. *The Power Elite*. London: Oxford University Press.

Moore, Barrington. 1966. *Social Origins of Dictatorship and Democracy*. Boston: Beacon Press.

Morrill, Calvin. 1991. "Conflict Management, Honor, and Organizational Change." *American Journal of Sociology* 97: 585–621.

Nee, Victor. 2005. "The New Institutionalisms in Economics and Sociology." In *The Handbook of Economic Sociology*, 2nd ed., edited by N. J. Smelser and R. Swedberg, 49–74. Princeton: Princeton University Press and Russell Sage Foundation.

Newcomb, Theodore M. 1950. *Social Psychology.* New York: Holt, Rinehart, Winston.

Newcomb, Theodore M., Ralph H. Turner, and Philip E. Converse. 1965. *Social Psychology: The Study of Human Interaction.* New York: Holt, Rinehart, and Winston.

North, Douglass C. 1990. *Institutions, Institutional Change, and Economic Performance.* Cambridge: Cambridge University Press.

O'Donnell, Guillermo. 1994. "The State, Democratization, and Some Conceptual Problems." In *Latin American Political Economy in the Age of Neoliberal Reform*, edited by W. C. Smith, C. H. Acuña, and E. A. Gamarra, 157–79. New Brunswick, NJ: Transaction.

Ostrom, Elinor. 1990. *Governing the Commons: The Evolution of Institutions for Collective Action.* Cambridge: Cambridge University Press.

Ostrom, Elinor, Thomas Dietz, Nives Dolsak, Paul C. Stern, Susan Stonich, and Elke Weber. 2002. *The Drama of the Commons.* Washington, DC: National Academy Press.

Pareto, Vilfredo. [1902] 1966. "Les systèmes socialistes." In *Vilfredo Pareto: Sociological Writings*, edited by S. E. Finer, 123–42. New York: Praeger.

Portes, Alejandro. 1997. "Neoliberalism and the Sociology of Development: Emerging Trends and Unanticipated Facts." *Population and Development Review* 23 (June): 229–59.

———. 2000a. "The Resilient Significance of Class: A Nominalist Interpretation." *Political Power and Social Theory* 14: 249–84.

———. 2000b. "The Hidden Abode: Sociology as Analysis of the Unexpected." *American Sociological Review* 65: 1–18.

Poulantzas, Nicos. 1975. *Classes in Contemporary Capitalism.* London: New Left Books.

Powell, Walter W. 1990. "The Transformation of Organizational Forms: How Useful Is Organization Theory in Accounting for Social Change?" In *Beyond the Marketplace: Rethinking Economy and Society*, edited by R. Friedland and A. F. Robertson, 301–29. New York: Aldine de Gruyter.

Roberts, Bryan R., and Alejandro Portes. 2005. "Coping with the Free Market City: Collective Action in Six Latin American Cities at the End of the Twentieth Century." *Latin American Research Review* 41 (June): 233–62.

Roberts, Kenneth. 2002. "Social Inequalities without Class Cleavages in Latin America's Neoliberal Era." *Studies in Comparative International Development* 36 (Winter): 3–33.

Roland, Gerard. 2004. "Understanding Institutional Change: Fast-Moving and Slow-Moving Institutions." *Studies in Comparative International Development* 38 (Winter): 109–31.

Roof, Wade Clark. 1999. *Spiritual Marketplace: Baby Boomers and the Remaking of American Religion.* Princeton, NJ: Princeton University Press.

Sassen, Saskia. 1988. *The Mobility of Labor and Capital: A Study in International Investment and Labor Flow.* New York: Cambridge University Press.

Sen, Amartya. 1999. *Development as Freedom.* New York: Knopf.

Shaiken, Harley. 1990. *Mexico in the Global Economy: High Technology and Work Organization in Export Industries.* Monograph Series 33. San Diego: Center for U.S.-Mexican Studies, University of California.

———. 1994. "Advanced Manufacturing and Mexico: A New International Division of Labor?" *Latin American Research Review* 29: 39–72.

Simmel, Georg. [1908] 1964. "The Stranger." In *The Sociology of Georg Simmel,* edited and translated by K. H. Wolff, 402–8. New York: Free Press.

Skocpol, Theda. 1979. *States and Social Revolutions, A Comparative Analysis of France, Russia, and China.* Cambridge: Cambridge University Press.

Swidler, Ann. 1986. "Culture in Action: Symbols and Strategies." *American Sociological Review* 51: 273–86.

Thelen, Kathleen. 2004. *How Institutions Evolve: The Political Economy of Skills in Germany, Britain, the United States, and Japan.* New York: Cambridge University Press.

Tilly, Charles. 1984. *The Contentious French: Four Centuries of Popular Struggle.* Cambridge, MA: Harvard University Press.

Veblen, Thorstein. [1899] 1998. *The Theory of the Leisure Class.* Amherst, NY: Prometheus Books.

Wallerstein, Immanuel. 1974. *The Modern World-System: Capitalist Agriculture and the Origins of the European World-Economy in the Sixteenth Century.* New York: Academic Press.

———. 1991. *Geopolitics and Geoculture: Essays on the Changing World-System.* Cambridge: Cambridge University Press.

Weber, Max. [1904] 1949. *The Methodology of the Social Sciences.* Translated by E. A. Shils and H. A. Finch. New York: Free Press.

———. [1915] 1958. "Religious Rejections of the World and Their Directions." In *From Max Weber: Essays in Sociology,* edited by H. H. Gerth and C. Wright Mills, 323–59. New York: Oxford University Press.

———. [1922] 1947. "Social Stratification and Class Structure." In *The Theory of Social and Economic Organization,* edited by T. Parsons, 424–29. New York: Free Press.

———. [1922] 1964. *The Sociology of Religion.* Translated by E. Fischoff. Boston: Beacon Press.

Williamson, Oliver. 1975. *Markets and Hierarchies.* New York: Free Press.

———. 1985. *The Economic Institutions of Capitalism.* New York: Free Press.

Wright, Erik O. 1980. "Varieties of Marxist Conceptions of Class Structure." *Politics and Society* 9: 299–322.

———. 1985. *Classes.* London: Verso.

Wright, Erik O., and Luca Perrone. 1976. "Marxist Class Categories and Income Inequality." *American Sociological Review* 42: 32–55.

Wuthnow, Robert. 1987. *Meaning and Moral Order: Explorations in Cultural Analysis.* Berkeley: University of California Press.

———. 1998. *After Heaven: Spirituality in America since the 1950s.* Berkeley: University of California Press.

Zelizer, Viviana. 2005. "Culture and Consumption." In *The Handbook of Economic Sociology,* 2nd ed., edited by N. J. Smelser and R. Swedberg, 331–54. Princeton: Princeton University Press and Russell Sage Foundation.

2

The Comparative Study of Institutions

The "Institutional Turn" in Development Studies: A Review

Alejandro Portes and Lori D. Smith

North's pronouncements concerning the role of institutions on development were followed by a series of studies, historical and contemporary, on the role of various social forces, collectively lumped under the rubric "institutions." Among the most influential was the study by Acemoglu, Johnson, and Robinson (2003) that focused on the path dependence of institutions created by Europeans in their areas of concentration. Colonies where Europeans created permanent settlements developed solid institutional frameworks copied from the mother countries, which, in turn, created the basis for sustained economic development. Aware of the perennial endogeneity problem between institutions and development, Acemoglu and colleagues instrumented their main determinant—European settler concentration—on prior reported death rates among early colonists, soldiers, and even bishops. They reasoned that areas where high death rates were reported among early settlers because of malaria and yellow fever were confined to an extractive role and that only healthier ones were conducive to concentrated settlement by Europeans.

Like almost all studies in this field, Acemoglu and colleagues depended for their measure of institutional quality on reputational indices that assign a single score per country. In their case, they draw on Political Risk Services Inc. for a measure of "average protection against expropriation," supplemented by a measure of "constraints on the executive" taken from the Polity III data by Gurr (1997). The industry standard in this field appears to have become the International Country Risk Guide (ICRG) compiled by Knack and Keefer (1995). Another important

Revised and abridged version of A. Portes and L. D. Smith, "Institutions and National Development in Latin America: A Comparative Study," *Socio-Economic Review* (September 2010): 1–37.

measure is the Rule of Law index employed, among others, in Dollar and Kraay's (2002) influential study. As Jutting (2003:19) notes in his review of this literature, "Nearly all the studies use as a proxy for 'institutions' variables that measure the quality and performance of institutions rather than the institution itself." These reputational measures risk tautology, because the assembled opinions on "institutional quality" can be influenced by the level of economic development achieved by different countries.

Finally, a debate has been raging between researchers grouped around Dani Rodrik (Rodrik, Subramanian, and Trebbi 2002) that stress the role of institutions as "trumping everything else" (Jutting 2003: 19) and another group around Jeffrey Sachs (2003) that emphasizes the role of geography, especially distance from the equator. None of these approaches makes allowance for subnational differences in institutional performance, or for the dynamics of real-life organizations. The image that emerges from most of this literature is that of a static world with countries frozen in a hierarchy of "good governance," indexed by a single number.

A more nuanced, sociological account of the role of institutions in development is provided by Nee and Opper (2009). After carefully building a Weberian ideal type of bureaucracy, they go on to argue that it is the quality of this apparatus, not legal formal protections of shareholders, that foster long-term capitalist development: "The lower the bureaucratic quality, the higher the level of uncertainty faced by economic actors and the less the calculability in both short and long-term planning" (299).

To buttress the argument, these authors also rely on an index of "government effectiveness" compiled by the World Bank (Kaufmann, Kraay, and Mastruzzi 2005) that, because of its numerous indicators and inclusion of objective measures, is believed to provide "the least noisy signal of the underlying notion of bureaucratic quality" (Nee and Opper 2009: 301). Not surprisingly, African countries, such as Nigeria, rank at the very bottom of this scale, while the Netherlands and the Scandinavian countries rank at the very top. Predictably, the index has a strong positive "effect" on capitalistic development.

Reviewing this literature, a strong sense emerges that studies at closer range are needed to develop nuance and bar tautology. It is possible that not all governmental agencies and quasi-governmental institutions in Nigeria are hopeless; nor are all Dutch and Scandinavian ones paragons of excellence. Moreover, as sociologists of organization have repeatedly noted, these are dynamic entities that change over time and can adapt rather rapidly to shocks and transformations in their environment. Seeking to move beyond the present research literature, we make use of the theoretical scheme presented in chapter 1 to identify a sample of institutions sufficiently important and diverse to tell us something about subnational diversity and to clarify the extent to which organizations correspond or not to institutional blueprints.

RESEARCH DESIGN

For this purpose, the study recruited teams of experienced researchers in five countries to conduct yearlong studies of target institutions on the basis of a common research design. Latin American countries were selected because of their common historical origins and culture and their comparable levels of development. The intent was to see if differences existed between a sample of countries that commonly receive comparable scores in cross-national indices of "institutional quality." Specifically, the study sought answers to the following questions:

1. Whether systematic differences could be uncovered in the developmental contribution of a sample of institutions within the same country and a sample of the same institution across different countries.
2. If such differences could be identified, whether they are due to idiosyncratic characteristics of each country's history and culture or whether common external forces influence them.
3. Whether a common profile of characteristics making up "developmental" institutions could be identified in the data.
4. Whether a rank order could be established among countries, based on the relative presence of such institutions.

The countries included in the study are Argentina, Chile, Colombia, Mexico, and the Dominican Republic. Brazil was excluded because of its size and its somewhat different historical origins as a Portuguese colony. The five countries selected cover the geographic length of Latin America, from south to north, and represent a fair sample of the relative levels of development found in the region. There were, in addition, specific theoretical reasons to include each individual country. They are omitted here but will be raised in the intercountry comparison in the final chapter.

The study selected institutions of national scope that differed, in their respective functions, along an axis ranging from "primarily economic" to "mostly technical" to "primarily social." Most of these were state agencies, although they included an important private entity—the national stock exchange. While the universe of institutions amenable for study is quite large, those selected are emblematic of economic, technical, and social functions deemed fundamental for the proper organization and advancement of most nations. They are as follows:

Stock exchanges have been studied in the past as the ideal-type of unfettered capitalism, evolving in time from closed clubs to regulated entities open to public investment (Weber [1904] 1949; Abolafia 1996). Even small nations currently possess a stock exchange, though they vary greatly in scope and modes of operation. Although private entities, stock exchanges play a potentially strategic role in economic development as vehicles to capitalize a wide range of enterprises, both public and private. The extent to which they do so depends, nevertheless, on the transparency of their operations and on the trust that companies and investors have in the inviolability of their rules (Sabel 1994; Hollingsworth 2002).

Tax authorities underwrite the capacity of states to foster economic development and social equity. Traditionally, Latin American states have financed themselves through taxes on commodity exports and manufactured imports, external indebtedness, and inflation (Wormald and Cárdenas 2008; Velasco 2008). The imperatives of global trade and finance have progressively reduced each of these avenues, forcing states to turn inward toward value-added and income taxes. This has raised the profile of tax authorities and added urgency to reforming them. The extent to which such efforts have been successful in the face of generalized resistance to fiscal demands remains uncertain and was one of the specific questions posed by the study.

Public health services are redistributive institutions that seek to compensate for economic disparities by making a basic good available to all the citizenry. In this pursuit, these services must balance scarcity of resources with a rising demand. The long-term mission of this institution entails a notable dilemma: past successes in reducing infant mortality and preventing epidemics translate into increasing pressure on scarce resources by a larger and longer-living population (Cereceda, Hoffmeister, and Escobar 2008). The field studies focused on how managers and health providers seek to cope with these tensions and fulfill (or not) the redistributive goals for which the institution was created.

Postal systems are a traditional public service, much maligned in many countries for their inefficiency and slowness but still vital for communication and the conduct of trade. The unreliability of the mails in many Latin countries has led governments to partially privatize the service, allowing private operators to compete head-on with the public agency (Díaz 2006; Luján Ponce 2008). This decision has challenged the very existence of the institution. Our study targeted the postal system as a strategic site in order to examine how past operational practices have led to its present crisis and the various ways in which the system is seeking ways to reinvent itself in order to cope with challenges threatening its survival.

Civil aviation authorities were selected because of their vital role in enabling international communication and trade. Airports, especially in capital cities, are the face of the nation and, as such, are objects of great attention by governments and economic elites alike. Airport construction and operation and the regulation of civil aviation are "modern" pursuits that require

> considerable technical expertise. This led us to the initial expectation that civil aviation authorities would represent what Evans (1989) has called "islands of excellence" within the government apparatus since otherwise the country would be decertified by international agencies and vital communications with the outside world would be disrupted.

Of the five institutions targeted for study, the stock exchange and the tax authority can be categorized as mostly economic agencies, although tax collection can also have an important redistributive function. Public health services and the postal system are mostly socially oriented agencies, the first because of its intrinsic welfare mission and the second because of its mandate to link all regions of the country and make its services available to everyone. Civil aeronautics falls in between as a mostly technical organization entrusted with a strategic mission.

DATA COLLECTION AND ANALYSIS

The units of analysis are complex organizations, each governed by its respective institutional blueprints. Their study required an intensive effort of data collection. This task was entrusted to teams of investigators in each country, with individual members charged with a particular institution. Data collection included the following: (a) compilation of the legal rules defining the mission and governing the activities of the organization; (b) compilation of internal reports and evaluations; (c) compilation of external academic and journalistic reports; (d) interviews with institutional personnel at the levels of top management, midlevel management and technical personnel; (e) interviews with expert informants; (f) interviews with strategic users of institutional services (i.e., commercial airlines, pension funds investing in the stock market, mass mail marketers, etc.) For each institution and each country, fifteen to thirty detailed interviews were conducted, divided about equally between internal personnel at different levels and external informants.

By combining these different forms of data collection, investigators were able to arrive at an authoritative assessment of all the dimensions of interest. These took the form of both discursive reports and a scoring of the organization on a list of characteristics, to be described next. The final sample comprises twenty-three institutional studies. (There is no stock exchange in the Dominican Republic, and, due to time limitations, the Argentine public health service was not included.) Table 2.1 presents a list of the sampled institutions, their titles, electronic addresses, dates of formal establishment, and historical antecedents.

Analyzing this large sample to answer the questions listed above requires more than simple intuition. For this purpose, we arranged scores for each institution in truth tables, as proposed by Ragin (1987, 2000). This method allows the identification of basic patterns and differences that may be obscured in discursive reports. Once such patterns are identified, it is possible to return to the reports for illustrative and supportive evidence. In addition, organizational scores can be subjected to systematic analysis employing Qualitative Comparative Analysis (QCA). QCA uses Boolean algebra to identify causal determinants that are sufficient, necessary, or neither for a particular outcome to exist. The method does justice to the combinatorial logic of social causation by identifying interaction effects among determinants, so that factors that may not produce by themselves the outcome do so in combination with others (Ragin 1987; Vaisey 2009).

QCA methodology requires reliable indicators of both potential causal factors and effects. For this, we relied on the experience and investigative effort of each research team. While the institutional scores do contain a "reputational" element, its validity is checked against the evaluations of a plurality of informants and by months of observation of the actual performance of each organization. In addition, institutional scores were assigned independently by each investigator.

HYPOTHESES

From the research literature, we drew six factors that have been associated with bureaucratic quality and developmental performance in the past. The work of Rodrik, Subramanian, and Trebbi (2002) and Nee and Opper (2009) proved particularly useful in this regard. The identified factors are not long-term historical forces, such as those examined by Acemoglu, Johnson, and Robinson (2003), but proximate characteristics of institutional quality. For purposes of the study, *development* was defined as a composite of economic growth, greater social equity, and democratic rights (Sen 1999; Portes 1997). More broadly, the concept was equated with sustained improvements in the well-being of a nation's population.

Investigators were asked to evaluate the extent to which the organization studied contributed to this goal *in its respective institutional sphere.* One cannot expect the postal system to improve university education or the civil aeronautics agency to increase agricultural productivity. Each agency was evaluated as "developmental" to the extent that it fulfilled its mission and, in addition, sought to improve the quality of its services and extend them to all sectors of the nation. Factors hypothesized to lead to this outcome can be categorized as those internal to the organization and those affecting it from the outside. The theoretical work of Evans (1979, 1995, 2004) identifies two internal conditions necessary for developmental institutions:

I) Meritocratic recruitment and promotion
II) Immunity from bribe taking and "capture" by special interests

TABLE 2.1 Institutions Included in the Comparative Study, 2006–2008

Country Institution	Name	Website	Year of Establishment	Historical Antecedent[a]	Historical Establishment
Argentina					
Postal Service	Correo Oficial de la República Argentina (CORASA)	www.correoargentino.com.ar	2004	Dirección General de Correos, Postas y Caminos	1810
Civil Aviation	Comando de Regiones Aéreas (disbanded)/ Administración Nacional de Aviación Civil (ANAC)	www.anac.gov.ar	1966/2007	Dirección Nacional de Aviación Civil	1954
Stock Exchange	Bolsa de Comercio de Buenos Aires (BCBA)	www.bcba.sba.com.ar	1854	—	
Tax Agency	Dirección General Impositiva (DGI)	www.afip.gob.ar	1947/1997[b]	Administración General de Impuestos Internos & Dirección General del Impuesto sobre los Réditos	1891; 1932
Chile					
Postal Service	Empresa de Correos de Chile (CorreosChile)	www.correoschile.cl	1981	Dirección General de Correos	1794
Civil Aviation	Dirección General de Aeronáutica Civil (DGAC)	www.dgac.cl	1968	Dirección de Aeronáutica	1930
Stock Exchange	Bolsa de Comercio de Santiago de Chile (BCSC)	www.bolsadesantiago.com	1893	—	
Health Care System	Complejo Asistencial–Barros Luco/Ministerio de Salud	redsalud.gov.cl	2003	Sistema Nacional de Salud (SNS)	1952
Tax Agency	Servicio de Impuestos Internos (SII)	www.sii.cl	1980	Dirección General de Impuestos Internos	1916
Colombia					
Postal Service	La Administración Postal Nacional (Adpostal)	www.adpostal.gov.co (disbanded)	1992	Ministerio de Correos y Telégrafos	1923

Civil Aviation	Unidad Administrativa Especial de la Aeronáutica Civil (Aerocivil)	www.aerocivil.gov.co	1992	Departamento Administrativo de Aeronautica Civil	1960
Stock Exchange	Bolsa de Valores de Colombia (BVC)	www.bvc.com.co	2001	Regional Exchanges (in Bogotá, Medellín, and Cali)	1928;1961; 1983
Health Care System	Clínica San Pedro Claver/ Empresas Promotoras de Salud (EPS)	(disbanded)	1962/2003	Caja Nacional de Previsión	1945
Tax Agency	Dirección de Impuestos y Aduanas Nacionales (DIAN)	www.dian.gov.co	1993	Dirección de Impuestos Nacionales and Dirección de Aduanas Nacionales	1991
Dominican Republic					
Postal Service	Instituto Postal Dominicano (INPOSDOM)	www.inposdom.gob.do	1985	Dirección General de Correos	1963
Civil Aviation	Instituto Dominicano de Aviación Civil (IDAC)	www.idac.gov.do	2006	Dirección General de Aviación	1955
Health Care System	Sistema Público de Salud	www.sespas.gov.do	2001	Secretaría de Estado de Salud Pública y Asistencia Social	1956
Tax Agency	Dirección General de Impuestos Internos (DGII)	www.dgii.gov.do	2006	Departamento de Rentas Internas	1935
Mexico					
Postal Service	Servicio Postal Mexicano (Sepomex)	www.sepomex.gob.mx	1986	Dirección General de Correos	1901
Civil Aviation	Dirección General de Aeronáutica Civil (DGAC)	dgac.sct.gob.mx	1956	Departamento de Aeronáutica Civil	1928
Stock Exchange	Bolsa Mexicana de Valores (BMV)	www.bmv.com.mx	1975	Bolsa Privada de México; Bolsa de Valores de México S.A.	1907/1932
Health Care System	Hospital General Manuel Gea González (HGMGG)	www.hospitalgea.salud.gob.mx	1972	Sanatorio Hospital "Dr. Manuel Gea González"	1946
Tax Agency	Servicio de Administración Tributaria (SAT)	sat.gob.mx	1995	Subsecretaría de Ingresos	1977

[a] Institutions typically have more than one historical antecedent; this table focuses on antecedent entities that encompassed similar functions and activities but were quite differently organized.

[b] The DGI was founded in 1947 but was fundamentally reorganized in 1997 following the establishment of a superordinate entity (AFIP).

The recent research literature on actual organizational experiences in Asia and Latin America (Kochanowicz 1994; Gereffi 1989; Nee 2000; MacLeod 2004) identifies a third key internal determinant:

III) Absence of entrenched "islands of power" capable of subverting institutional rules to their own ends.

Recruitment and promotion based on family connections or other personalistic ties is the opposite of condition I. A poorly paid or otherwise demoralized bureaucracy "for sale" to outside bidders is the alternative to condition II. Powerful managerial cliques and self-seeking union bureaucracies negate condition III. All three internal conditions are related, but they are not the same: initial meritocratic recruitment and promotion may be subsequently corrupted by special interests; entrenched "islands of power" may be immune to outside corruption to the extent that they can channel significant internal resources to their own ends, thus subverting the original institutional goals (MacLeod 2004).

Evans's work can again be drawn upon as the source of the first external determinant:

IV) Proactivity or the ability of the organization to involve itself with clients, users, and other relevant actors in its institutional environment.

Evans (1995) labels this condition "embeddedness." Here, we will use "proactivity" given the prior association of "embeddedness" with the theoretical work of Granovetter (1985), which has an important but different meaning, as seen in chapter 1. The final external conditions are derived from the work of John Meyer and his associates (Meyer and Boli 1997; Meyer and Hannan 1979) on global diffusion of institutional forms and those of Cardoso and Faletto (1979), O'Donnell (1994), Zeitlin (1984), and Portes and Hoffman (2003) on Latin American class structures and their role in perpetuating socioeconomic inequality:

V) Technological flexibility and openness to external innovation
VI) Countervailing power, either by the organization itself or its external allies, to prevent control by particularistic interests.

Condition IV is negated by inward-looking institutions that seek to protect their own interests and internal cohesiveness, turning a deaf ear to clients, users, and potential outside opportunities. The opposite of condition V is institutional rigidity with entrenched traditions—"the way things have always been done"—prevailing over external opportunities for innovation.

Reflecting the hierarchies of power portrayed in the study's theoretical framework (chapter 1), an institution, no matter how well designed, that lacks backers and sponsors among top officialdom or among influential elites is likely to fall prey to dominant class interests or to find a "class wall" frustrating its mission. The experiences of numerous failed agrarian reform programs in Latin America and the well-studied demise of the early Mexican privatization program confronted with unified class resistance (MacLeod 2004) provide object lessons of the role of power in subverting the best laid out institutional plans.

Research teams used these hypotheses as guides to organize their respective studies and, in addition, were asked to rank each individual organization on each predictor in each of the scales described above. These evaluations and the accompanying narratives form the database for the analysis presented in the following chapters.

GENERAL TRENDS

Table 2.2 presents a truth table drawn from the dichotomous scores produced by the twenty-three institutional studies. Prior to subjecting these data to detailed analysis, it is possible to identify several preliminary trends. These have to do both with differences among institutions and with differences among countries. The table breaks down outcomes into two components: first, an initial assessment of whether the organization meets the institutional goals for which it was created, as reflected in the relevant enabling law or formal regulation; and second, a summary assessment of whether it is "developmental" in its institutional sphere, as defined previously. A perusal of scores in the table indicates a marked divide between organizations and agencies whose prime mission is economic and those that focus on services to the general population. Consistently, stock exchanges and, especially, tax authorities rank high, while zeros in the binary scale tend to cluster in the post office, the national health service, and, to a lesser extent, civil aeronautics.

The crisp binary logic of Boolean algebra commends itself for clarity but imposes strict limits on reality and on researchers' evaluations. To address this problem, Ragin (2001, 2008) introduced an alternative methodology based on "fuzzy-set" algebra that allows the analysis of cases coded along a conceptual continuum. Accordingly, each organization studied received a second code for each hypothesized determinant and each outcome in a 1-to-5 scale. Table 2.3 presents results of this exercise. The conceptual meaning of each score in the scale is specified at the bottom of this table. The trend of scores in table 2.3 is essentially the same as that observed in the binary rankings. Again, economic institutions score consistently higher than others, especially those dedicated to social services. A second trend in the data is the marked differences in institutional rankings among the five countries included in the study.

These differences are central to one of the key research questions posed above. Their historical origins are discussed in detail in the following chapters. The plan for the rest of the book consists of detailed summary chapters for each country written by the investigators themselves, followed by an analysis of the tables

TABLE 2.2 Truth Table of Institutional Adequacy and Contributions to National Development (*1 = Presence; 0 = Absence*)

Country / Institution	Determinants						Results	
	A. MERITOCRACY	B. IMMUNITY TO CORRUPTION	C. NO "ISLANDS OF POWER"	D. PROACTIVITY	E. TECHNOLOGICAL FLEXIBILITY	F. EXTERNAL ALLIES	I. INSTITUTIONAL ADEQUACY	II. CONTRIBUTION TO DEVELOPMENT
Chile								
Postal Service	1	1	1	1	0	0	1	1
Civil Aviation	1	1	1	1	1	0	1	1
Stock Exchange	1	1	1	1	1	1	1	1
Health Care System	1	1	1	1	1	0	1	1
Tax Agency	1	1	0	1	1	1	1	1
Colombia								
Postal Service	0	0	0	0	0	0	0	0
Civil Aviation	1	1	1	0	1	0	1	0
Stock Exchange	1	1	1	0	1	1	1	0
Health Care System	0	0	0	0	1	0	0	0
Tax Agency	0	0	0	1	1	0	0	0
Mexico								
Postal Service	0	0	0	1	0	1	0	1
Civil Aviation	1	1	1	0	1	0	1	0
Stock Exchange	1	1	1	1	1	1	1	1
Health Care System	1	1	1	1	1	1	1	1
Tax Agency	0	1	1	1	1	1	1	1
Argentina								
Postal Service	0	0	0	1	1	1	1	0
Civil Aviation	0	0	0	0	0	0	0	0
Stock Exchange	0	1	0	1	1	1	1	0
Tax Agency	1	0	0	1	1	1	1	1
Dominican Republic								
Postal Service	0	0	0	0	0	0	0	0
Civil Aviation	1	1	1	1	1	1	1	1
Health Care System	0	0	0	0	0	0	0	0
Tax Agency	0	0	1	1	1	1	1	1

TABLE 2.3 Truth Table of Scores Assigned to Institutions in Hypothesized Predictors and Outcomes (1 = *"Entirely outside the conceptual set defined by the variable"*; 2 = *"More outside than inside"*; 3 = *"Neither"*; 4 = *"More inside than outside"*; 5 = *"Entirely inside"*)

Country Institution	Determinants						Results	
	A. MERITOCRACY	B. IMMUNITY TO CORRUPTION	C. NO "ISLANDS OF POWER"	D. PROACTIVITY	E. TECHNOLOGICAL FLEXIBILITY	F. EXTERNAL ALLIES	0_1 INSTITUTIONAL ADEQUACY	0_2 CONTRIBUTION TO DEVELOPMENT
Chile								
Postal Service	4	3	4	5	3	2	4	5
Civil Aviation	3.5	4	3	4	5	3	5	4
Stock Exchange	4	4	3.5	5	4	5	4	4
Health Care System	3.5	3.5	2.5	3.5	2	1	4	3.5
Tax Agency	4	4	2.5	4	5	4	3.5	4
Colombia								
Postal Service	2	2	3	2	2.5	1	1	1
Civil Aviation	4	3	3.5	2	5	2.5	4	3
Stock Exchange	4	3.5	3.5	2	3.5	4	4	2
Health Care System	2	2	3	2	4	3	1	1
Tax Agency	2	1	2	4	4	2	2	2
Mexico								
Postal Service	1	2	1	3.5	1	3.5	1	3.5
Civil Aviation	4	3.5	4	1.5	3.5	1.5	4	2.5
Stock Exchange	4	3.5	3.5	3.5	5	3.5	4	4
Health Care System	4	3	4	4	4	3	4	4
Tax Agency	2	4	5	4	5	3	4	4
Argentina								
Postal Service	2	1	2	3	4	4	3	2
Civil Aviation	2	2	2	1	2	1	2	1
Stock Exchange	3	3	2	4	3	3	4	2
Tax Agency	4	1	3	4	5	5	4	4
Dominican Republic								
Postal Service	1	1	2	2	2	2	2	2
Civil Aviation	3.5	3.5	3.5	5	3.5	4	4	4
Health Care System	1	2	1	2	2	1	1	2.5
Tax Agency	3	3	4	4	5	4	4	4

presented in this chapter on the basis of both Boolean and fuzzy-set algebra. A final discussion of the interinstitutional and intercountry differences uncovered by the study wraps up its answers to the original questions posed above and then its implications for theory and practice.

REFERENCES

Abolafia, Mitchell. 1996. *Making Markets: Opportunities and Restraint on Wall Street.* Cambridge, MA: Harvard University Press.

Acemoglu, Damon, Simon Johnson, and James A. Robinson. 2001. "The Colonial Origins of Comparative Development: An Empirical Investigation." *American Economic Review* 91(5): 1369–1401.

Cardoso, Fernando H., and Enzo Faletto. 1979. *Dependency and Development in Latin America.* Translated by M. M. Urquidi. Berkeley: University of California Press.

Cereceda, Luz Eugenia, Lorena Hoffmeister, and Constancia Escobar. 2008. "Institucionalidad, organización y reforma de la salud en Chile." Final report to the project *Latin American Institutions and Development: A Comparative Analysis.*

Díaz, Luz Marina. 2009. "Vida, pasión y muerte de la Administración Postal Nacional Colombiana." In *Las instituciones en el desarrollo latinoamericano: Un estudio comparado,* edited by A. Portes, 292–316. Mexico City: Siglo XXI.

DiMaggio, Paul. 1990. "Cultural Aspects of Economic Action and Organization." In *Beyond the Marketplace,* edited by R. Friedlander and A. F. Robertson, 113–36. New York: Aldine de Gruyter.

Dollar, David, and Aart Kraay. 2002. "Institutions, Trade, and Growth." Paper prepared for the Carnegie-Rochester Series on Public Policy.

Evans, Peter. 1979. *Dependent Development: The Alliance of Multinational, State, and Local Capital in Brazil.* Princeton: Princeton University Press.

———. 1989. "Predatory, Developmental, and Other Apparatuses: A Comparative Political Economy Perspective on the Third World State." *Sociological Forum* 4: 561–87.

———. 1995. *Embedded Autonomy: States and Industrial Transformation.* Princeton: Princeton University Press.

———. 2004. "The Challenges of the 'Institutional Turn': Interdisciplinary Opportunities in Development Theory." In *The Economic Sociology of Capitalism,* edited by V. Nee and R. Swedberg, 90–116. Princeton: Princeton University Press.

Gereffi, Gary. 1989. "Rethinking Development Theory: Insights from East Asia and Latin America." *Sociological Forum* 4: 505–33.

Granovetter, Mark. 1985. "Economic Action and Social Structure: The Problem of Embeddedness." *American Journal of Sociology* 91: 481–510.

Gurr, Robert Ted. 1997. "Polity II: Political Structures and Regime Change, 1800–1986." Manuscript. Department of Political Science, University of Colorado.

Hollingsworth, J. Rogers. 2002. "On Institutional Embeddedness." In *Advancing Socioeconomics: An Institutionalist Perspective,* edited by J. R. Hollingsworth, K. H. Muller, and E. J. Hollingsworth, 87–107. Lanham, MD: Rowman and Littlefield.

Jutting, Johannes. 2003. "Institutions and Development: A Critical Review." Working Paper 210. OECD Development Centre.

Kaufmann, Daniel, Aart Kraay, and Massimo Mastruzzi. 2005. "Governance Matters IV: Governance Indicators for 1996–2004." Working Paper S3630. Washington, DC: World Bank.

Knack, Steve, and Philip Keefer. 1995. "Institutions and Economic Performance: Cross-Country Tests Using Alternative Institutional Measures." *Economics and Politics* 7: 207–27.

Kochanowicz, J. 1994. "Reforming Weak States and Deficient Bureaucracies." In *Intricate Links: Democratization and Market Reforms in Latin America and Eastern Europe*, edited by J. M. Nelson, J. Kochanowicz, K. Mizsei, and O. Muñoz, 195–227. New Brunswick, NJ: Transaction.

Luján Ponce, Noemí. 2008. "El tiempo se acabó: El servicio postal mexicano en la encrucijada de su modernización." Final report to the project *Latin American Institutions and Development: A Comparative Analysis.*

MacLeod, Dag. 2004. *Downsizing the State: Privatization and the Limits of Neoliberal Reform in Mexico.* University Park: Pennsylvania State University Press.

Meyer, John, and John Boli. 1997. "World Society and the Nation State." *American Journal of Sociology* 103 (July): 144–81.

Meyer, John, and Michael T. Hannan. 1979. *National Development and the World System: Educational, Economic, and Political Change, 1950–1970.* Chicago: University of Chicago Press.

Nee, Victor. 2000. "The Role of the State in Making a Market Economy." *Journal of Institutional and Theoretical Economics* 156: 64–88.

Nee, Victor, and Sonja Opper. 2009. "Bureaucracy and Financial Markets." *Kyklos* 62: 293–315.

O'Donnell, Guillermo. 1994. "The State, Democratization, and Some Conceptual Problems." In *Latin American Political Economy in the Age of Neoliberal Reform,* edited by W. C. Smith, C. H. Acuña, and E. A. Gamarra, 157–79. New Brunswick, NJ: Transaction.

Portes, Alejandro. 1997. "Neoliberalism and the Sociology of Development: Emerging Trends and Unanticipated Facts." *Population and Development Review* 23 (June): 229–59.

Portes, Alejandro, and Kelly Hoffman. 2003. "Latin American Class Structures: Their Composition and Change during the Neoliberal Era." *Latin American Research Review* 38 (February): 41–82.

Ragin, Charles. 1987. *The Comparative Method: Moving beyond Quantitative and Qualitative Strategies.* Berkeley: University of California Press.

———. 2000. *Fuzzy-Set Social Science.* Chicago: University of Chicago Press.

———. 2008. *Redesigning Social Inquiry: Fuzzy Sets and Beyond.* Chicago: University of Chicago Press.

Rodrik, Dani, Arvind Subramanian, and Francesco Trebbi. 2002. "Institutions Rule: The Primacy of Institutions over Integration and Geography in Economic Development." IMF Working Paper WP/02/189. Washington, DC: International Monetary Fund.

Sabel, Charles. 1994. "Learning by Monitoring: The Institutions of Economic Development." In *The Handbook of Economic Sociology,* edited by N. J. Smelser and R. Swedberg, 137–65. Princeton: Princeton University Press and Russell Sage Foundation.

Sachs, Jeffrey. 2003. "Institutions Don't Rule: Direct Effects of Geography on Per Capita Income." National Bureau of Economic Research Working Paper W9490, February.

Sen, Amartya. 1999. *Development as Freedom.* New York: Knopf.

Vaisey, Stephen. 2009. "The 'Ragin' Revolution Continues." *Contemporary Sociology* 38 (4): 308–12.

Velasco, José Luis. 2008. "Servicio de Administración Tributaria de México." Final report to the project *Latin American Institutions and Development: A Comparative Analysis.*

Weber, Max [1904] 1949. *The Methodology of the Social Sciences.* Translated by E. A. Shils and H. A. Finch. New York: Free Press.

Wormald, Guillermo, and Ana Cárdenas. 2008. "Formación y desarrollo del Servicio de Impuestos Internos (SII) en Chile: Un análisis institucional." Final report to the project *Latin American Institutions and Development: A Comparative Analysis.*

Zeitlin, Maurice. 1984. *The Civil Wars in Chile.* Princeton: Princeton University Press.

3

Institutional Change and Development in Argentina

Alejandro Grimson, Ana Castellani, and Alexandre Roig

For a number of authors, Argentina is an example of a peculiar failure in development. Using diverse indicators, its ranking among Latin American nations in the early twentieth century is frequently compared with its position in the early twenty-first century in order to illustrate a process of relative decline. The disparity between the country's potential (not only its natural resources but also the educational level of its population) and present-day reality has given rise to an abundant bibliography that delves into Argentine history and the country's development process, singling out diverse factors to account for this relative decline. The economic devastation perpetrated by the last military dictatorship, the "lost decade" in the 1980s, and neoliberalism in the 1990s are the latest additions to a list that includes intersectoral conflict, the absence of a hegemonic socioeconomic group after the 1930 crisis, and the ups and downs of the Peronist/anti-Peronist dichotomy, among others.

All things considered, when compared with the parallel history of Brazil, it is clear that going back as far as the nineteenth century the historical process shaping the Argentine national state has been characterized by discontinuity. In regional terms, Brazil has experienced remarkable political, institutional, and territorial continuity, without this constituting an obstacle to change. In contrast, following the war of independence, Argentina suffered a long period of civil war and cyclical institutional instability, together with a confrontation between the provinces and Buenos Aires whose effects were still being felt in the late twentieth century. An eloquent example of this difference between the two countries is the fact that in 1979

Titles and authors of individual reports on which this chapter is based are found in Appendix 3.1.

the military dictatorship that took power in Brazil in 1964 itself initiated and administered the transition to civilian government; furthermore, to date, there have been no investigations of human rights violations. During the same period, Argentina had four constitutional presidents and other de facto governments; the last military dictatorship collapsed after losing the Malvinas (Falklands) war against Britain, and its members are still standing trial for crimes much more serious in quantity and quality than their counterparts in Brazil. "Discontinuity" is not necessarily a bad thing: maintaining slavery or maintaining in power authorities that violate human rights can hardly be construed as positive. But when discontinuity is a general feature of the state and of economic development, as has been the case in Argentina, institutional quality irremediably suffers.

There is an ample bibliography that approaches, from different theoretical standpoints, the reasons that explain the unique Argentine experience. From this body of work, there emerges a set of different explanations for this experience: political instability, social conflicts, excessive intervention of the state in the economy, external dependency, characteristics of the political system, and the quality of institutions (Castellani 2009a; Guillén 2001). Our purpose in this chapter is not to present an exhaustive review of this literature but to synthesize the principal lines of research that inform the debate about Argentine (under)development.

Economic and social research on development has a long tradition in Argentina. A series of authors have dedicated their efforts to explaining why Argentina has been unable to construct a path to sustained development. From an orthodox economic perspective, Llach (1996) and De Pablo (1984) focused on the high degree of state intervention in economic activity, beginning in the 1940s; the inefficiency and disintegration characterizing domestic industry; the prevalence of government subsidies (and their inflationary implications); and the excessive pressure exerted by workers for higher wages. In contrast, scholars with a more heterodox approach (Ferrer 1973, 1977; Nochteff 1994; Diamand 1973; Díaz-Alejandro 1975; Basualdo 2006; Schvarzer 1999) point to deficits in private investment and technological innovation, a chronic lack of economic equilibrium and foreign exchange, and the type of landownership and exploitation as critical factors for understanding the pitfalls that have hindered national development. All these factors were seriously aggravated during the last military dictatorship.

In their analysis of the limitations on Argentine development from a sociological perspective, Lewis (1993), Nun (1989), O'Donnell (1977), Portantiero (1978), Pucciarelli (1997), and Sidicaro (2001) emphasize the relationship between the state and the most relevant socioeconomic actors; the practices, multiple conflicts, and crosscurrents affecting diverse intraclass sectors; and the quasi-rentier nature of the local bourgeoisie. And finally, from a more politically oriented point of view, other researchers (Camou 1997; Guillén 2001; O'Donnell 1982; Orlansky 2001; Oszlak 1980, 1984, 1990; Rofman 1998) analyze institutional quality, public policy making, and the role of the latter in economic development. In general, these studies take into account both intra- and interinstitutional conflicts unleashed at different stages of state intervention, together with the progressive deterioration of certain powers of the state considered crucial for the effective application of policy.

In this regard, the relationship between institutions and development is a longstanding concern. For Portes (2009), the institutional quality of a country is an essential element in its potential for development. What is meant by "institutional quality"? Is it a question of the quality of a country's human resources and the way in which formally established blueprints are carried out? This is a subject of urgent debate in Argentina, given the large number of voices citing the need for improvement. From certain political viewpoints, "institutional quality" is taken to mean respect for the separation of powers and functionality of institutional rules. Yet comparative studies affirm that, although necessary for development, these conditions alone are not sufficient to bring it about. Indeed, any strictly formalist or reglementary view of institutional quality loses sight of crucial issues.

As seen in chapter 2, to evaluate the quality of an institution, whether in the public or private sector, three internal factors must be taken into account: the presence of meritocratic practices, immunity from corruption, and the absence of "islands of power" within the organization. And to establish, in turn, the current or potential influence of the above on development, three external factors must be evaluated: proactivity, technological flexibility, and openness to innovation, along with the capacity to construct external alliances.

In this chapter, the way these six factors function in four Argentine institutions are analyzed as part of the comparative study outlined in chapter 2. Our sample comprises a public institution responsible for linking Argentines domestically and with the world at large by means of highly specialized technology, the civil aviation service; a private institution with the potential to influence economic development, the Buenos Aires Stock Exchange; a public institution with a long history of involvement in territorial integration, the postal service; and finally, an institution that is crucial to the functioning of the state as it manages its tax revenue, the National Tax Board. During 2008 we conducted interviews, carried out direct field observations, and analyzed data from diverse sources on each of the above institutions (see Appendix 3.1). Our aim here is to broaden the scope of individual studies on the relationship between institutional quality and development by means of a systematic interinstitutional comparison.

INSTITUTIONAL TRAJECTORIES

Each of the four institutions is the product of complex historical and organizational processes within which determinants of its institutional quality must be sought.

Civil Aviation

The most recently created institution is precisely the one that disappeared in the course of the study: the Regional Air Command (Spanish acronym, CRA) which was responsible for managing civil aviation, was dissolved by a decree issued by President Nestor Kirchner in November 2007 and its functions transferred to the National Administration of Civil Aviation (ANAC), run by civilians. The chain of command of the original institution extended from the executive branch of government to the Ministry of Defense, and then to the General Staff of the Argentine Air Force. In addition to the weather forecasting service and a training center, the Command also ran a number of departments that included the Department of Air Transport, the Department of Aeronautical Licensing, and the National Department of Aerial Navigation.

CRA's primary responsibility was to administer the aeronautics sector in the name of the federal government while preserving the public patrimony and exercising planning and police functions. As the aeronautical authority, it also licensed installations, certified personnel, established rules and regulations, enforced accident prevention measures, certified airworthiness, and kept relevant records. Finally, it handled requests for the use of Argentine airspace, gathered and published information, offered search and rescue services, and supplied infrastructure for communication and self-help networks (Grimson 2009).

Stock Exchange

The Buenos Aires Stock Exchange (BCBA) was founded in 1854. Despite being one of the oldest stock exchanges in Latin America, its development has been checked by structural limitations in attracting private savings. The organizational structure of the BCBA revolves around a group of financial institutions, the most important members of which are the BCBA itself, the Security and Exchange Commission, and the Open Electronic Market (MAE) set up by the large banks. They handle the greater part of operations involving government paper in Argentina. Sharp tension exists between more traditional agents and the new actors dealing in stocks and bonds, the majority of whom have ties to the large banks. Old-fashioned practices carried over from the era when stock exchanges were essentially gentlemen's clubs are still in effect in the BCBA. This dual nature of the Argentine stock exchange persists to this day: the values, the types of organizations and actors linked to financial globalization, and the great technological leap forward in recent years have been grafted onto an institution with deep-rooted traditional values, types of organizations, and chains of command (Heredia 2009).

Postal Service

Founded before the viceroyalty of the River Plate came into existence in July 1769, the postal service filled the demand for a domestic system of communication created by the growing volume of commercial activity associated with the port of Buenos Aires. The first Postal Service Law (No. 816), passed in 1876 at the height of the nation-building period in Argentina, significantly modernized the system and merged mail and telegraph service into a single organization that operated under the direction of the Ministry of the Interior. Institutional stability was maintained in the official post office until the mid-twentieth century. But with the growing instability brought about by the alternation of civilian and military governments, administrative and normative changes became increasingly frequent.

In the early 1970s, a new postal service law (No. 20.216/73) was passed, and at almost the same time the first state enterprise to hold a monopoly on mail delivery, the national Mail and Telegraph Service, or ENCOTEL, was established. This organization operated within the orbit of the Secretariat of Communications, which answered to different ministries in the course of the next three decades. Currently part of the Ministry of Federal Planning, Public Funding and Services (MPFIPS), the Secretariat of Communications is still in charge of supervising and regulating postal services.

The official Post Office of the Argentine Republic (CORASA) is a state-owned firm created in 2004, following the rescinding by the state of a private concessionaire's permission due to serious breaches of contract. The new enterprise, whose managing style has mirrored that of a large private firm, has increased market share and sales, raised productivity, and generated a profit, while at the same time guaranteeing the universal basic postal service (SPBU), without receiving government subsidies or special privileges. Thanks to this auspicious performance, the post office once again has a positive image in the eyes of both individual and corporate users, leading CORASA to be ranked among the most prestigious institutions in the country in 2006.

Tax Authority

Notwithstanding its long institutional trajectory, the agency currently in charge of collecting taxes has been in existence for a relatively short time. In October 1996, the two main agencies handling tax revenue, the National Customs Administrations and the General Tax Department (DGI), merged. The General Direction of Social Security Resources (DGRSS) then joined these organizations, and the umbrella Federal Administration of Public Revenue (AFIP) was born in July 1997. The new institution is, hence, a product of the merging of old agencies, each with its own peculiarities in terms of human resources and policy making. In addition, federal tax-collecting bodies in Argentina are charged with fulfilling the terms of the Law of Co-participation with the provinces. The enabling law of AFIP can thus be understood as the regulatory framework within which the political tug-of-war between the provinces and the federal government over the capture and distribution of tax revenue takes place.[1]

There is no unified tax code in Argentina; instead, each individual tax has its own norms. While opening the way for frequent modifications, this modus operandi also rules out any attempt at harmonizing the tax system.[2] The aim of the government during the 1990s was to limit public spending, and any state intervention regarding taxes was considered inimical to the market. Yet, at the same time, the tax-collecting apparatus was being modernized and diverse mechanisms were being put in place to increase revenue by collecting taxes on formerly undeclared income. Tax revenue became increasingly essential for servicing Argentina's growing sovereign debt. Today tax collection takes precedence over reductions in spending, and the economic literature does not necessarily see tax collection in a negative light. Rather, taxes are part of a new discourse on the "need to reassess the state." Thus, from different political viewpoints and with different objectives, successive administrations have found it necessary to modernize tax collection mechanisms in order to service the increased financial needs of the government.

Although quite heterogeneous, the institutional trajectories described above are relevant when thinking about the variables that determine institutional quality because they provide context for the analysis of the actual organizations and a perspective to examine the institutional objectives they pursue.

ANALYSIS OF INSTITUTIONAL DIMENSIONS

According to the hypothesized determinants described in chapter 2, the following internal dimensions of each agency were evaluated: (a) the existence of a competent, strongly cohesive bureaucracy recruited in accordance with meritocratic criteria and that sets high value on the positions held; (b) transparent and predictable norms for filling positions and making promotions; and (c) a clear, stable regulatory framework governing how the organization functions. When present, these attributes indicate not only operational efficiency; they also discourage the formation of so-called islands of power within the agency.

Similarly, the external indicators examined are (d) the capacity of the organization to interact with its environment and to fulfill its assigned functions (Proactivity); (e) a high degree flexibility in adapting to changes in context that makes possible the incorporation of technological advances in inputs and processes (Technological Flexibility); (f) the capacity to construct an articulated network with other social and/or governmental actors, without sacrificing autonomy in decision making (External Allies).

Meritocracy

Whether a meritocratic system for hiring and promoting personnel exists in the organizations studied, the panorama is alarming. With the exception of the Dirección General Impositiva (DGI; Department of Revenue) where meritocratic practices and staff cohesion are very high, the other three cases employ authoritarian, informal, or traditional methods for managing personnel.

For example, informal/discretionary criteria prevail in the post office. Persons holding executive positions are named by the board of directors (whose members, in turn, are politically appointed); at present, most high-ranking executives hold the same positions they previously occupied under a private concessionaire. Administrative positions are not career appointments, and promotions in the firm are limited to those jobs covered by Convenios Colectivos de Trabajo (CCT), or collective work agreements, between labor unions and the firm. However, from 1993 to 2006, even the mechanisms for promotion established by collective labor accords were suspended, freezing employees in positions usually inferior to their capacity. This lack of incentives has generated apathy among the permanent workforce.

The situation in the former Comando de Regiones Aéreas (CRA) was much more complex, the result of superimposing a militarized system onto an organization manned by civilian personnel. Although it is assumed that modern armies function meritocratically, no provisions were made for comparing the relative merits of civilian and military staff in the CRA. The result was that the entire civilian staff was put under the orders of the armed forces. Subordinates reporting technical errors made by superiors were penalized. Thus "following orders" was often done at the expense of professionalism. For this reason, the military chain of command eroded meritocratic criteria, reproducing instead an authoritarian structure. In addition, civilian staff salaries were low, and the agency did not provide training upgrades for its personnel.[3] Hence, of all the organizations studied, the CRA had the lowest level of staff cohesion.

Finally, the case of the Buenos Aires Stock Exchange is contradictory, illustrating the pros and cons of traditional staff management: on the one hand, the organization's traditional orientation encourages job training, staff cohesion, job stability, and seniority-linked promotion; on the other, it discourages autonomy, does not attract applicants with high academic credentials, nor do productivity and training upgrades merit promotion. Despite the BCBA's traditional management style, experts with firsthand knowledge of how the organization is run still view staff members as well suited to their jobs and able to carry out their assigned tasks (Heredia 2009).

Immunity to Corruption

Although none of the organizations studied scored high on this dimension, the organization responsible for civil aviation was by far the worst. Ideally, international standards would be applied to airplanes, pilots, working conditions, and airport security, with airline profitability calculated after the cost of applying them had been factored in. However, this basic principle was apparently not always applied (Grimson 2009). Although definite proof is lacking, there are indications of corruption in diverse departments, running from reports of drug trafficking to noncompliance with the most elemental rules of safety.[4]

In none of the other organizations studied were reports of corruption as persistent as in the CRA. Enough reports circulate, however to suggest that this dimension is still low in several other agencies. For example, DGI authorities themselves recognize the existence of cases of corruption, very few of which come to light owing to the high level of intrabureaucratic cohesiveness. This is a product of job security, constant upgrading of skills, and frequent meetings to discuss internal information, all of which strengthen cohesion. Although there are no secrets within the organization, cases of corruption are used to settle internal power struggles, becoming public only as a last resort.

There have been no proven instances of corruption in the postal system since it was taken over by the state. Suspicion of corruption in CORASA is linked to the dealings of current department heads (who formerly worked for a private concessionaire) with the service's main suppliers and subcontractors. Several factors suggest that the precariousness of the institution's regulatory framework allows the spread of these practices, and collusion in general. For example, because CORASA is juridically a private corporation (although 100 percent of the stock is held by the state), it is exempt from the obligation of state firms to publicly solicit bids before making purchases and/or outsourcing services, thus opening the way for connivance between department heads, suppliers, and subcontractors.

The BCBA constitutes a partial exception among the institutions studied. Although its monitoring capacity was questioned not long ago, at present this situation has been resolved thanks to an active cross-checking policy, together with improvements in the software guaranteeing the transparency of transactions. All of our respondents expressed absolute confidence in the honesty of the different stock exchange actors (agents, firms, employees, partners, members of the regulatory commissions), and there were no reports of "malpractice." Apparently, in-house and external checks put in place by the Securities and Exchange Commission (Comisión Nacional de Valores) are satisfactory, and personnel in both the BCBA and the Commission manifest the highest degree of immunity from corruption among the organization studied

Absence of "Islands of Power"

In all the organizations, islands of power were identified in the form of key administrative departments, labor unions, a military command structure, or traditional partnerships. In civil aviation and the post office, labor unions constituted relatively autonomous power factors that conditioned the path followed by both agencies. In each case, staff members belong to different unions, each one of which exercises considerable power that is used, at times, to improve working conditions for its members and, at others, to cover up inefficiency or corruption. In any event, no reform can be undertaken in these organizations without the consent of, at a minimum, the most powerful unions in the sector.

Certain key administrative departments can also become islands of power: the Subdepartment of Systems and Telecommunication in the DGI and the Commercial and Operative sectors in CORASA are cases in point. In both cases, power arises from the handling of vital information. In CORASA, executives are, by definition, powerful because they are the only ones with experience in running a postal service and are in close touch with its main clients and suppliers (Castellani 2009b). In the DGI, the automation of data has created a spatially and symbolically dominant space within the umbrella agency, AFIP. Access to this information is wholly mediated by this department, which gives it great autonomy and negotiating power (Roig 2009).

In the remaining organizations, islands of power are linked to institutional rules and tradition. In the case of civil aviation, they are linked to diverse factors, including institutional ground rules and regulations and the political context. The Civil Air Command was responsible for security, while the Secretariat of Transportation and other organizations carrying out control functions worked on their own, with no coordination among them. Given its minimal civilian input, the Command's very structure lent itself to the persistence of islands of power.[5] Traditional partnerships constitute an island of power within the BCBA. The persistence of traditional actors and practices, which distinguishes the Argentine stock exchange from its Latin American counterparts, has prevented structural reform in both the late 1980s and the early 2000s, protecting recalcitrant directors that oppose the initiatives of modernizing agents from the banking and financial sectors.[6]

Proactivity

Despite these internal deficiencies, proactivity is high in three of the four cases studied. Indeed, with the exception of civil aviation, proactivity has been successfully incorporated into the operational domain of the remaining organizations. The tax service offers perhaps the best example. The DGI has increased its presence in the mass media over the years. Publicity campaigns promoting a "new culture of tax collection" for a "country in good shape" and a "new citizenry" have increased in number.[7] Communicational style oscillates, according to our respondents in the agency, between "selling fear or selling citizenship" (Roig 2009: 22). In fact, campaigns alternate the stigmatizing of tax evasion with opportunities for rescheduling unpaid taxes.

Furthermore, the communication activities of the organization are closely attuned to the government, constituting one of its main propaganda efforts: monthly figures on tax collection are presented by the government as "good news," since a "new record" is almost always established (Roig 2009: 22). Almost all tax transactions can be carried out on-line, allowing taxpayers to have access to the organization's databases free of charge. For this reason, the DGI is viewed as an open agency and an integral part of society. At present, approximately 500,000 transactions are carried out every day, compared to less than 500 per day in 2002.[8]

The post office has also shown a respectable degree of proactivity. Taking advantage of a broad retail network (approximately five thousand sales outlets), CORASA has adopted the marketing strategy of broadening the scope of the services and products it provides. This has allowed the agency to increase its share of the wholesale market (where it competes with large private firms) and finance the unsubsidized universal basic postal service (SPBU). This advance over private service providers has been accomplished without recourse to large-scale publicity campaigns. According to evaluations from external sources, from 2006 to the present, the quality of the services provided by CORASA has been relatively satisfactory and on par with those offered by its private competitors. The long waiting periods experienced by customers are a by-product of the increase in services offered, on the one hand, and a hiring freeze, on the other. Productivity has been raised but sometimes at the expense of longer queues.

When evaluating the degree of openness to external demands of the BCBA, certain contradictions appear that erode the organization's proactivity: it is very receptive to opportunities for offering new services and to suggestions from customers and external evaluating organizations, but its doors are often closed to other actors. Once again the case of the BCBA is contradictory. On the one hand, as an enterprise aspiring to capture new investors (and acting accordingly), results are encouraging. To this end, campaigns are launched in the provinces, conferences are organized by specialists, reports on stock market activity are telecast daily, and programs simulating trading are available online. Yet, despite this display of activity, the stock exchange does not satisfactorily fulfill its primary function: to serve as a channel for domestic savings to be invested in firms. This is largely due to the marked preference of Argentine savers for fixed-rate sources of income, a result of the aversion to risk-taking instilled in them by recurrent economic crises.

Data gathered up to the time of the demise of the CRA in 2008 indicated that a development in the field of civil aviation in Argentina was negative in a number of ways: the frequency of domestic flights decreased, as did the number of international flights, along with airport quality and operational safety. Positive action in these areas lay, nonetheless, outside the scope of responsibility of the CRA. Thus implanting proactive measures was prevented by a system in which functions were split up among different agencies, requiring complex coordination among them.

As in the case of the post office, organizational openness of the CRA to external demands was restricted. Denunciations and problems detected by others were minimized or denied by the agency without any evidence of attempts to investigate them, much less any indication of steps taken to anticipate future problems. Sectors depending and interacting with the Command were helpless, since the nature of their activity did not give them the option of choosing another interlocutor. The general opinion was that the CRA showed some openness to the requirements of the commercial sector, especially airlines and airport concessionaires, but without balancing this attitude with a serious concern for infrastructure needs.

Technological Flexibility

Evaluations of technological flexibility are quite similar to those described above. In general, with the exception of the CRA, technological flexibility is high. Once again, the tax service is at the forefront. Major technological innovation has taken place in recent years, the result of a progressive, long-range strategy carried out with resources available to the organization. The Subdepartment of Systems and Telecommunications centralized all databases in the country and put them under its control. Automation affected not only data availability but also decision making. This strategic plan was elaborated by middle-ranking personnel, that is, those functionaries who guarantee continuity over time. The plan was drawn up on the basis of five principles repeatedly mentioned by our respondent in the agency: (1) no outside consultants were called in, meaning it was an in-house plan; (2) norms are treated as data, meaning they cannot be changed; (3) the quantity and quality of authorities are also treated as data, and are thus invariable; (4) as a technical organization, the AFIP (and its components, including the DGI) cannot engage in political activities; and (5) with the exception of the above principles, everything else is subject to change.

Based on these ideas, a five-year plan was put into effect and the architecture of the system overhauled. Decisions were made to unify databases, put them on the Internet, and offer free access to them. Free software requiring no expenditure of public funds was used; the new system has received international recognition in the form of external awards for high quality (see Roig 2009).

The post office has also earned international accreditation for the mail and telegram services that it provides. In the city of Buenos Aires and Buenos Aires province, the system encompasses the following activities: (1) processing of postal products in the Buenos Aires Postal Treatment Center; (2) collection and distribution of postal and telegraphic products; and (3) client and call center services. Without being on the technological cutting edge, CORASA has shown a level of flexibility that is acceptable by international standards.

The BCBA is on a par with its Latin American counterparts in the use of advanced technology for handling stock market transactions. According to its annual reports, the organization has made a sustained effort to acquire the latest equipment and programs for facilitating operations. Unlike what had been the case at other times, there appears to be no difficulty acquiring quality infrastructure. Even when daily transactions have reached record levels, it has never been necessary to suspend trading or check transactions before closing operations. Nonetheless, this assessment is contradicted by the opinion expressed by our respondents, all of whom felt that the stock exchange is a conservative institution that resists change. According to the assistant director of human resources, "[The institution] is not proactive regarding innovative practices. It always takes four or five years before innovations are accepted and integrated. I'm referring to accounting, administrative and operational systems" (Heredia 2009: 48.)

And herein lies the ambiguity that makes it possible to speak, in the same breath, of a high level of technological flexibility for facilitating daily operations with the outside world and resistance to technological change that would modify the organization's internal structure. There has been an overwhelming lack of technological upgrading in civil aviation and its entire operational system in Argentina. The radar shutdown and subsequent crisis at the Buenos Aires international airport in 2007 was an alarming confirmation of this trend. Other evidence showing the lack of training and upgrading of personnel also point to institutional inflexibility. For example, when questioned about the poor command of English of many air traffic controllers, air force officials said that this was an individual matter and that operators were hesitant to use their free time for language study. The difficulty of solving this problem is evidence of the inflexibility of both management and staff. The absence of meritocratic incentives clearly has played a part in making this faulty upgrading tolerable (see Grimson 2009).

External Allies

With the exception of the CRA, all the organizations studied counted on significant state support. In the DGI and CORASA, top positions are filled by political appointment, and both organizations receive support from high-ranking departments in the public sector. For example, the current board of directors of the post office is made up of men with close links to the executive branch and is strongly supported by the Ministry of Planning. Up to the present, CORASA has been able to finance itself from operating revenues, and our respondents indicated that as long as this was the case the firm would remain in state hands.

Indeed, CORASA currently enjoys the full support of officials at the highest level of the executive branch, the backing of significant union leaders, and the respect of its main clients, suppliers, and private competitors. It has shown that an efficient enterprise can be run within the state apparatus. While the support of high government officials is important for guaranteeing the survival of the agency, it also signifies an important degree of dependency on these same authorities. In order for CORASA to continue functioning, the governmental decree that created it must be renewed every 180 days. This situation leads to an erosion of internal autonomy that impedes long-term planning and weakens the organization's capacity to fulfill its institutional goals.

While enjoying an equally high level of state support, the DGI does not have to contend with the juridical precariousness of the post office. The position of federal administrator (head of the umbrella agency, AFIP) is of prime importance to the government, and, hence, the person holding it must combine political loyalty with technical know-how. The political significance of the position is self-evident, not only because its holder is responsible for tax revenue, but also because the type of intelligence-sensitive information handled is crucial for maintaining Argentina's link with international credit organizations and the United States. In addition, the relationship between the federal government and the provinces is largely managed through the DGI, not only with respect to tax redistribution, but also concerning how tax data are handled. In recent years the high quality of the organization has been recognized by different social actors, and it is considered an exceptional outpost of efficiency in a state-run latticework characterized by overall low institutional quality.

Although the BCBA is not questioned by the main actors in the banking and finance sector, the government has yet to establish consistent policies for strengthening the capital market and, by extension, the role of this organization in promoting national development. For example, one unfulfilled long-term demand is to offer fiscal benefits to firms that acquire capital by issuing common stock. Current policy making is focused on promoting the national bank and creating a new development bank, initiatives that do not augur well for a greater role of the capital markets and, hence, the BCBA in financing productive activity.

The CRA was the organization mobilizing the least state or social support, despite intense public debates surrounding its 2006–7 crises. Although the progressive degradation of the service, technical difficulties, accidents, and the reduced number of domestic flights were top stories in the mass media, the middle and upper classes (the sectors of society that fly most frequently) were not moved to protest. Nor did the crisis appear to worry those economic interests based in the Buenos Aires metropolitan area and closely linked to the global economy. This situation mirrors long-standing patterns deeply rooted in the history of the country.

On their part, provincial economic sectors apparently lacked the necessary power to reverse the critical situation caused by their inadequate air links with the nation's capital. In response to the crisis in civil aviation, the government finally decreed the transfer of control from the CRA to the new National Administration for Civil Aviation, within the Secretariat of Transport within the Ministry of Planning. It is still too early to ascertain whether this change in management of a service so critical to economic development and national integration will succeed in raising its present very low standards.

In synthesis, the institutional quality of the organizations studied is quite heterogeneous: there is one extreme case (CRA) and three intermediate ones (AFIP/DGI, CORASA, and BCBA). And it is precisely these latter three that place in doubt any supposition regarding a possible correlation between internal and external dimensions of institutional development: to a greater or lesser degree, they present low levels of internal quality (meritocracy, etc.) without this significantly hindering their external dimensions or their basic capacity to fulfill their preordained institutional goals. Scores assigned to each of these agencies and presented in tables 2.2 and 2.3 in the preceding chapter tell the same story. Based on these studies, the Argentine institutional situation cannot be said to be ideal, but, by fits and starts, several agencies manage to function relatively well and make a developmental contribution. This situation is explored further next.

INSTITUTIONS, ORGANIZATIONS, AND DEVELOPMENT

A certain tension can be identified between "real" and "ideal" processes for making institutions more dynamic and generating the potential, whether activated or not, to bring about the kind of social transformations that contribute to national development. In the relationships we have been able to establish between institutions and organizations, two broad patterns emerge. The first pattern is coherence between the values of the institution and its organizational structure. This would be the case for the BCBA and the DGI. It is worth noting that both institutions bear on the financial sector of the economy and are situated at the heart of Argentine capitalism. The second pattern is divergence between institution and organization. This pattern did not prevent CORASA from carrying out its main functions; in the case of the CRA, however, the real organization placed its institutional values at risk, at least during the period covered by the study.

In the case of the DGI, there are two overriding institutional values. The first is efficiency in tax collection—either by methods characterized as "fiscal terrorism" or through educational campaigns that aim at creating a civic culture. The second is the gathering of fiscal intelligence, which requires, above all, specialized know-how in data acquisition. It can be said that the organization revolves around the production, control, and accessing of information. The link between power and information is not only found in the DGI, but it does take on special significance in an enterprise in which information itself is the bargaining chip.

In organizational terms, this relationship is expressed in the central role played by the Subdepartment of Systems and Telecommunications, the emphasis placed on technological updating, and the competition with other revenue-collecting agencies. In this sense, information is not only a means for collecting taxes; it is also an end in itself and, as such, serves as one of the symbols of the institution. The quality of the information managed by the organization guarantees its legitimacy in the eyes of the society: it is generally assumed that records on the resources of the citizenry are free from error and that no injustices have been committed.

Confidence in the institution is also associated with the information it is thought to handle, above and beyond whether the preceding supposition is true. Hence, the organization is viewed not in light of what it actually does but rather what it has the capacity to do. Fulfilling its objective in a more or less efficient way is only part of its raison d'etre; the production of an image of a potentially unlimited role in the economy also comes into play. In the economic sphere, the DGI serves a purpose not unlike that of the police in the society at large. If minimum consistency between organizational structures and institutional blueprints did not exist or if the agency were unable to generate an image of great power, an entire dimension of state sovereignty would be at risk (Roig 2009).

It might be assumed that the BCBA would correspond to the kind of institution that links the private sector to economic development. Yet what we actually observed is a private organization that is conservative, paternalistic, and traditional in nature. All things considered, the data gathered on this organization reveal a paradox: notwithstanding the strong coherence between the real organization and its institutional objectives, the small volume of transactions handled by the BCBA is conspicuous, along with the absolute predominance of trading in government paper. Consequently, it would appear that the BCBA's efforts are more oriented to financing public debt than to empowering the private sector. This situation is undoubtedly due to structural problems in the Argentine macroeconomy—an extremely low level of private savings, coupled with an extremely high public debt diverts institutions like the BCBA from their original objective (Heredia 2009).

Regarding CORASA, the long-standing deterioration in the institutional quality of the official post office accelerated in the late 1990s. Whether under private or public management, it did not meet minimum standards of institutional quality. At present, relative improvement can be observed, especially regarding proactivity and technological flexibility. Yet serious deficiencies persist that hinder further improvement and, consequently, do not allow the postal system to make a stronger contribution to development. Most difficulties fall within the confines of the internal criteria reviewed above. Any measure of these—meritocracy, the absence of islands of power, and immunity from corruption—would necessarily yield low scores. While this is not a novel phenomenon in this organization, it is nonetheless striking that a new administration that gave primacy to efficiency when it took charge has shown itself unable to improve these dimensions. One possible explanation is that the marked dependency of the postal board of directors on the executive branch of government and the precariousness of the regulatory and juridical framework under which CORASA operates conspire against putting in place additional and significant reform measures.

It should be noted, however, that, compared to its predecessor, the current administration has markedly improved the image of the postal system, and the organization now fulfills its basic institutional goal of ensuring domestic and international communications. This makes CORASA an odd case in which the combination of low administrative and operative quality still permits fulfillment of basic institutional objectives while at the same time posing questions regarding its capacity to contribute to development in the long term (Castellani 2009b).

Our evaluation of the development of civil aviation in Argentina up to 2008 is highly negative. As already noted, the number of domestic flights dropped and the increase in the number of international flights declined, as did operational security. According to Rubén Miguel Cafaro, aeronautic consultant and forensic expert on the subject of civil aviation, the ongoing transition from the CRA to the new civilian agency (ANAC) will take from five to eight years, since 70 percent of the air traffic controllers are military personnel that have the option of retiring from the armed forces in order to become civilian employees. More optimistic estimates speak of a two-year transition period. In any event, the 180 days stipulated in the official decree are obviously insufficient. If there is going to be a new era for civil aviation in Argentina, a number of pending challenges must be met. One is how personnel will be incorporated and meritocratic practices installed. Another is the need to better integrate the different agencies interacting in airports and to find ways for reaching consensus. Last but not least, one of the most daunting future challenges is how to change the work culture of the different agencies in this sector, establishing rules and regulations that standardize procedures for public safety (Grimson 2009).

Taken as a whole, certain final conclusions can be drawn from these studies. First, the state plays a critical role in determining characteristics of all institutions, including those in the private sector. Second, a diagnosis of total failure or terminal crisis is unrealistic. More to the point is our assessment highlighting how discontinuity is a key factor in the structural weakness of certain organizations and how inconsistent policy making affects institutional quality in crucial areas.

Third, the internal dimensions of institutional quality have been more negatively affected than the external ones. This obliges us to reflect on the absence of a causal relationship among these variables. In Argentina, more institutions can be found that fulfill the roles for which they were originally created than there are those that have incorporated meritocratic standards for hiring and promoting personnel and guaranteeing immunity from corruption. Could a group of agencies be imagined that meet these internal standards but do not achieve proactivity, technological innovation, or external alliances? With the information at hand, it is impossible to know, but we will offer indications below that the opposite may be the case.

CONCLUSION: THREE TYPES OF INSTITUTIONS

The four institutions analyzed are a significant but not representative sample of the relationship between institutions and development in Argentina. Only one of them, the Buenos Aires Stock Exchange, is a private organization. And of course, in order to determine the characteristics of this last type of institution, more research on a larger sample of cases would be required. However, in accordance with the institutional typology of Evans (1995), as modified by Portes (2009), it is possible on the basis of our sample to construct three ideal types that express the relationship between public institutions and development.

First, there are *developmental institutions* that serve as the basis for policy making on the part of the state. Thanks to this relationship, these institutions approximate a model featuring meritocratic organization and are staffed by a qualified, proactive bureaucracy. This is clearly the case for the DGI in Argentina, since different governments with markedly different economic policies have all felt the need to amplify and strengthen tax collecting procedures. We are by no means suggesting that the DGI is "perfect"; no real agency is, as was verified in the preceding analysis. It is also pertinent to note that in recent decades the improvement of tax collecting institutions is common to a number of Latin American countries, indicating a regional trend.

Conversely, the CRA exemplifies the opposite ideal type in which the failure to fulfill any internal criteria leads to nonfulfillment of external ones. This would make it an example of what Rodríguez-Garavito (see chapter 5) terms *predatory institutions*. The empirical fact is that the CRA has ceased to exist, but institutions of this type could continue to emerge, thereby creating serious obstacles to future national development.

The two preceding types can be combined into a third, exemplified by the postal system: failing to meet internal criteria, the institution is functioning well and showing significant levels of proactivity. In this particular case, discontinuity was caused by privatization, but in other Argentine institutions discontinuity might be the product of contradictory policies applied by successive governments. It is common in Argentina for high-ranking authorities in public service to set up direct hiring networks instead of holding meritocratic contests to fill jobs. By placing a premium on personal loyalty, islands of power tend to be constructed, and such practices are sure to make any institution less immune to the risk of corruption.

One could assume that this situation would inevitably weaken the proactivity of the real organization. Yet the Argentine case shows that this is not necessarily so. The agency can be in the hands of a nonpredatory political group seeking to accumulate power and prestige by running it well. But accumulating power in this manner makes any long-term planning impossible, and also requires the use of direct networks for hiring personnel. The result is a proactive organization built on a nonmeritocratic foundation of patronage and populist practices. This patronage-oriented type, which can be labeled an *intermediate* institution, is widespread in Argentina. Its viability, in the short term, is exemplified by CORASA. But the organization has no immunity or solidity in the face of abrupt political change: it is as likely to remain in existence as to collapse. This means that its contribution to development is highly contingent.

In the Argentine sample, one ideal type is missing: an institution with strong internal standards and weak proactivity. In other countries, such as Colombia, institutions of this type do exist and are termed *reactive* by Rodríguez-Garavito. These are cases in which a quality institution, forged during a favorable period in the past, has now lost its way. It is possible that such institutions also exist in the fields of public health and education in Argentina. Table 3.1 presents our typology.

There is no doubt that a critical factor for development in any society is to count on bureaucratically rational and proactive institutions. In other historical moments in Argentina, public institutions grew up that were situated midway between the meritocratic proactive ideal type, on the one hand, and the patronage-oriented one, on the other. Solid institutions were created not only in the fields of education and public health but also among public enterprises in areas ranging from oil exploration to mining. The problems created by patronage practices in these institutions are common knowledge, as is the fact that eminently meritocratic and proactive organizations like the Argentine flagship airline Aerolineas Argentinas were destroyed by military dictatorships and by neoliberalism.

As a result, the new millennium has found the country with a dearth of solid, proactive institutions. It is plausible that in a larger and representative sample public institutions of the type exemplified by the postal system would predominate. As mentioned above, the problem is that while, in the short term they may make a contribution to development, there is no way of knowing if this will be the case over the long term. In this sense, the Argentine dilemma is whether to continue along the road of the institutional ups and downs that adversely affect the internal

TABLE 3.1 A Typology of Public Institutions in Argentina

Type	Example
Predatory	Civil Aviation (DRA—dissolved in 2008)
Reactive	Absent
Intermediate	Postal System (CORASA—operating under 180 days renewable decree)
Developmental	Tax Authority (DGI—part of a broader agency under the president of the republic)

quality of its public agencies or whether a political consensus can be forged to protect at least the more developmentally central agencies from this cyclical discontinuity. It is highly unlikely that individual institutions can resolve this dilemma on their own.

APPENDIX 3.1: INSTITUTIONAL STUDIES IN ARGENTINA

The reports on which this chapter is based are listed below with English translation of the original Spanish titles. The individual studies can be downloaded from the webpage of the Center for Migration and Development, Princeton University: http://cmd.princeton.edu.

Castellani, Ana. "The Case of the Official Postal System of the Argentine Republic."
Grimson, Alejandro. "Civil Aviation in Argentina."
Heredia, Mariana. "The Stock Exchange of Buenos Aires."
Roig, Alexandre. "The General Tax Office of the Federal Tax Agency of Argentina."

NOTES

1. The Argentine Constitution grants the exclusive faculty to tax imports and exports to the national Congress. Responsibility for collecting the remaining taxes is shared by Congress, provincial legislatures, and the municipal legislature of the autonomous city of Buenos Aires.

2. The federal government is responsible for collecting taxes on income and personal possessions, the value-added tax, and all indirect taxes. The resulting revenue is then "co-participated" to each province in accordance with a prior agreement.

3. An eloquent example of this lack of training is that a number of air traffic controllers did not have adequate command of English.

4. In 2004, for example, a scandal erupted when sixty kilograms of cocaine that had passed through the control systems in Buenos Aires and were loaded in Argentine planes were captured in Spain. In consequence of this and similar scandals, responsibility for airport security was transferred to the Ministry of the Interior and the Airport Security Police Force was created.

5. Among the norms favoring this institution, the most surprising was that accidents were investigated by the Board for Accident Investigation in the very air force that was one of the subjects under investigation. See Grimson 2009.

6. For a detailed description of this conflict between traditional and modernizing agents within the BCBA, see Heredia 2009.

7. These ad campaigns are available at www.afip.gov.ar/institucional/publicidadPrensa/multimedia/.

8. However, automation has come at the tax paying process. Handling transactions online requires, first of all, access to a computer (which is problematic for marginal sectors of the society and remote areas of the country). But above and beyond the question of material inequality, the technological demands made on clients are often complex. In the course of field observations made in various DGI offices, many older people were seen seeking technical help to carry out their transactions, and consultations were so frequent that employees have photocopied a set of step-by-step instructions available to the public.

REFERENCES

Basualdo, Eduardo. 2006. *Estudios de historia económica argentina desde mediados del siglo XX a la actualidad.* Buenos Aires: FLACSO–Siglo XXI.

Camou, Antonio. 1997. "Los consejeros del príncipe: Saber técnico y política en los procesos de reforma económica en América Latina." *Nueva Sociedad* 152: 54–67.

Castellani, Ana G. 2009a. *Estado empresas y empresarios: La construcción de ambitos pivilegiados de acumulación entre 1966 y 1989.* Buenos Aires: Prometeo Libros.

———. 2009b. "Instituciones y desarrollo en América Latina: El caso del Correo Oficial de la República Argentina." Final report to the project *Latin American Institutions and Development: A Comparative Analysis.*

De Pablo, Juan Carlos. 1984. *Política económica argentina.* Buenos Aires: Macchi.

Diamand, Marcelo. 1973. *Doctrinas económicas, desarrollo e independencia.* Buenos Aires: Paidós.

Díaz-Alejandro, Carlos. 1975. *Ensayos sobre la historia económica argentina.* Buenos Aires: Amorrortu.

Evans, Peter. 1995. *Embedded Autonomy: States and Industrial Transformation.* Princeton: Princeton University Press.

Ferrer, Aldo. 1973. *La economía argentina.* 2nd ed. Buenos Aires: Fondo de Cultura Económica.

———. 1977. *Crisis y alternativas de la política económica argentina.* Buenos Aires: Fondo de Cultura Económica.

Grimson, Alejandro. 2009. "La aviación civil en la Argentina." Final report to the project *Latin American Institutions and Development: A Comparative Analysis.*

Guillén, Mauro F. 2001. *The Limits of Convergence: Globalization and Organizational Change in Argentina, South Korea, and Spain.* Princeton: Princeton University Press.

Heredia, Mariana. 2009. "La Bolsa de Comercio de Buenos Aires." Final report to the project *Latin American Institutions and Development: A Comparative Analysis.*

Lewis, Meter. 1993. *La crisis del capitalismo argentino.* Buenos Aires: Fondo de Cultura Económica.

Llach, Juan. 1996. *Otro siglo, otra Argentina.* Buenos Aires: Editorial Ariel.

Notcheff, Hugo. 1994. "Los Senderos perdidos del desarrollo: Elite económica y restricciones al desarrollo en la Argentina." In *El desarrollo ausente: Restricciones al desarrollo, neoconservadurismo y elite económica en la Argentina. Ensayos de economía política,* edited by D. Azpiazu and H. Notcheff. Buenos Aires: FLACSO.

Nun, José. 1989. *La rebelión del coro.* Buenos Aires: Nueva Visión.

O'Donnell, Guillermo. 1977. "Estado y alianza de clases en la Argentina." *Desarrollo Económico* 64: 523–64.

———. 1982. *El estado burocrático autoritario.* Buenos Aires: Editorial de Belgrano.

Orlansky, Dora. 2001. "Política y burocracia: Argentina 1989–1999." Working Paper 26. Instituto de Investigaciones Gino Germani (November).

Oszlak, Oscar. 1980. *Políticas públicas y regímenes políticos: Reflexiones a partir de algunas experiencias latinoamericanas.* Buenos Aires: CEDES.

———. 1984. *Teorías de la burocracia estatal: Enfoques críticos.* Buenos Aires: Paidós.

———. 1990. "La reforma del estado en Argentina." Working Paper CEDES 36. Buenos Aires.

Portantiero, Juan Carlos. 1978. "Economía y política en la crisis argentina." *Revista Mexicana de Sociología* 2: 431–36.

Portes, Alejandro. 2009. "Prefacio." In *Las instituciones en el desarrollo latinoamericano: Un estudio comparado,* edited by A. Portes, 7–17. Mexico City: Siglo XXI.

Pucciarelli, Alfredo. 1997. "Los dilemas irresueltos en la historia reciente de la Argentina." *El Taller: Revista de Sociedad, Cultura y Política* 5: 82–121.

Rofman, Alejandro. 1998. "¿Reforma o nuevo rol para el estado?" *Aportes para el Estado y la Administración Gubernamental* 11: 1–18.

Roig, Alexandre. 2009. "La Dirección General Impositiva de la Agencia Federal de Ingresos Públicos (AFIP) de la Argentina." Final report to the project *Latin American Institutions and Development: A Comparative Analysis.*

Schvarzer, Jorge. 1999. *Implantación de un modelo económico: La experiencia argentina entre 1975 y el 2000.* Buenos Aires: AZ Editora.

Sidicaro, Ricardo. 2001. *La crisis del estado y los actores políticos y socio-económicos en la Argentina (1989–2001).* Buenos Aires: Libros del Rojas.

4

Institutional Change and Development in Chilean Market Society

Guillermo Wormald and Daniel Brieba

This chapter's main thesis is that Chile's developmental performance of recent decades was underpinned by significant and systematic institutional change and that this change is closely related to its transformation from a state-centered society to a market-centered one. The analysis focuses on the changing process in a set of institutions highly relevant for economic growth and social redistribution. In this regard, our interest is to specify the mechanisms that account for continuity and discontinuity in institutional structure, which according to some relevant authors is an important target of economic sociology (Nee and Swedberg 2005). In addition, we discuss the impact of these changes on socioeconomic development.

The analytic importance of the Chilean case is the significant transformation in the development model and institutional framework that took place in the country after the military coup of 1973. During this period, as in many other Latin American countries but probably more radically, Chile faced the economic globalization of its economy and its growing transformation into a market economy and a market society (Slater and Tonkiss 2001). Although this analysis shows the existence of forces contributing to institutional isomorphism, it also emphasizes the importance of considering some historical and sociocultural specificities when looking at institutional realities and their impact on development. These specificities reinforce the idea that the copy is never equal to the original and also the sociological idea that institutions are not simply a set of formal rules and/or economic incentives but a complex arrangement of historical and cultural values, power relations, and political and economic interests of different actors. All these

Titles and authors of individual reports on which this chapter is based are found in Appendix 4.1.

features need to be taken into account when evaluating their institutional presence and organizational performance as well as their efficacy in promoting economic growth and development. Therefore, we agree with the idea that "institutions are not disembodied rules that specify the incentive structure of social action . . . , [but] fundamentally they involve actors, whether as individuals or organizations, who pursue real interests in concrete institutional structures" (Nee and Swedberg 2005: xxxviii).

In this perspective, the concept of social institution used by Portes (2008, 2009) becomes significant and constitutes a good heuristic tool for our analytic purpose. Specifically, we want to draw attention to his idea that institutions embody and combine two central dimensions: on the one hand, those cultural values that underlie formal and informal rules and, on the other, the organizational aspects that complement these rules and specify institutional performance. When looking at these two realities—manifest and latent—in historical perspective, it is possible to better understand the forces behind stability and institutional change, as well as their contribution to development.

Our analysis focuses on the transformation path experienced by five institutions, all of them challenged by a new market-oriented development model and the consolidation of a market society since the 1990s. In this regard, the Chilean case is just another—probably more successful—example of the way in which development societies endogenized the globalization challenge departing from their sociocultural specificities.

Our empirical evidence comes from the analysis of case studies of the national tax revenue agency (Servicio de Impuestos Internos, SII), the national aviation traffic authority (DGAC), the national post office (Correos Chile), and the public health system, especially the Barros Luco hospital in Santiago. We also considered the case of the most important stock exchange in the country, Bolsa de Comercio de Santiago, which is under private control. This evidence was gathered as part of a comparative study conducted in five Latin American countries. All these cases shared a common analytic framework and the same historical horizon (1980–2005). Thus an additional aim of this chapter is to compare and summarize some of these findings.

We begin our discussion with the conceptual framework, which allows us to define and organize the empirical analysis. Here we make more explicit our concept of institution and its importance for understanding a specific development path. We also deal with the dimensions that need to be addressed when evaluating institutional performance. The next section describes the macro forces leading to transformation in the institutional arrangements and the main characteristics of the so-called Chilean development model. The third section focuses on the way in which the state and other specific private institutions internalized this changing environment through what may be defined as a modernization impact. The analysis then returns to a theoretical reflection on the causes of this process of institutional transformation and modernization and its impact on development targets. The main lessons arising from this study are summarized in the conclusion.

CONCEPTUAL FRAMEWORK

This section seeks to synthesize some of the basic concepts used in previous research on the actual operation of five Chilean institutions and their evolution from 1980 to the present. The basic definition of *institutions* that guides this research is presented in chapter 1. The crucial distinction between institutions as symbolic instruction sets and organizations as their material, actually existing correlates allows empirical research to illuminate the distance between the two in the organizations studied. Indeed, a central conclusion of the entire project has been that in organizations where institutional blueprints and actual organizational praxis differ markedly, organizational effectiveness—that is, an organization's capacity to fulfill its basic function and to contribute to development—would suffer. Correspondingly, the empirical research sought to establish the degree to which each organization fulfilled each of six organizational performance criteria hypothesized to contribute to organizational effectiveness. Since all organizations studied were chosen because of their strategic importance for national development, it is also understood that fulfillment of their institutional role would constitute their contribution to this overarching goal; and in this sense, we can speak of more or less "developmentalist" institutions.

The six performance criteria were chosen for their potential importance for an organization's fulfillment of its mission or function and were described and justified in chapter 2. Change in the degree to which a given organization fulfills these performance criteria over time is a key indicator of institutional transformation. Therefore, since our focus is not on comparison per se but rather on institutional change, we specifically look at the way each organization evolved along these lines during the time period considered. Providing such theoretically grounded descriptions of institutional transportation is, we believe, key to understand the process of social change that Chilean society underwent in the same period.

If the six performance criteria outlined in chapter 2 provide a *description* of institutional change, we also need a conceptual framework to *explain* it. To do so, we also follow the model of institutional change originally proposed by Portes (2006), which has the virtue of integrating different theories of change into a single model derived from his understanding of institutions as organizational blueprints. In that work, reproduced in part in chapter 1 of the present volume, Portes criticizes the literature on institutional change, first, for lacking a proper definition of institutions and thus shooting at "an elusive target"; and second, for relying mostly on some version of either path dependency or diffusion, which are causal forces operating at rather superficial levels of social reality. Instead, Portes proposes five different sources of institutional change, which operate at very different levels of causality and may be located either within the social structure or in the symbolic realm of culture (see figure 1.4).

The most drastic changes tend to come from deeper forces in the social structure or value system of society. At the deepest level of cultural causality, charismatic and religious prophecies can radically change society "because they impinge directly on the value system," thus "providing the impetus necessary to dismantle the existing social order and rebuild it on a new basis" (Portes 2009: 40–41). A similarly deep factor, operating this time through the social structure, is the struggle for power either between classes or through interelite competition. Revolutions are classic examples of such conflicts and provide a graphic illustration of a radical change in the distribution of power in society. Such changes, also affecting class structure and social status hierarchies, can thus imply major institutional change.

The five potential causes of institutional change, summarized in figure 1.4, provide the hypotheses needed to examine the major transformations in Chilean institutions. Not all these potential causes of change, however, are equally interesting in the context that we are examining; religious prophecies or major transformations at the deepest levels of the value system have surely been absent. And as explained above, endogenous technological change has played no important role, even as major technological modernization has occurred through processes of diffusion. In fact, we will see how the process of organizational modernization has involved a mixture of continuity and slow evolution, on the one hand, and imported technological and organization innovations, on the other.

INSTITUTIONAL CHANGE AND THE DEVELOPMENT MODEL

From 1973 on, Chilean society reorganized its socioeconomic foundations. The deep nature of this process becomes apparent in the change in the rules of the game condensed in a new constitutional arrangement and the closely related change in its historical development model. Regarding constitutional arrangements, a first crucial transformation consisted in restoring, as fundamental principles of the new social order, private property rights and individual rights. Both were embodied in the new constitutional order imposed by the military regime since 1980. In addition, the new military government canceled the model of import substitution industrialization and adopted a new model of development oriented to export diversification and integration into global markets. This meant the growing importance of the private sector as a main economic agent and the market as the mechanism to allocate economic resources, regulate economic activity, and promote social welfare.

The evolution of this new model recognizes four crucial moments: the imposition of an authoritarian political regime and a strong neoliberal economic policy orientation; a second moment when, through deep and systematic reforms, the rules of the game of the new economic model and the future (i.e., democratic) political regime were laid down; a third one when democracy was restored and policy was reoriented to the development of a market economy, with greater emphasis on social protection and redistribution; and a final, recent moment when the political-economic model has been followed by a change in the value structure of society. The new market model is thus the result of a long historical process that started with the military coup of 1973 and has continued—with some adjustments—to the present.

The initial stage (1973–90) was characterized by a drastic change of the rules of the game vertically imposed, from "top to bottom."[1] In practice this meant a partial dismantling of the previous institutional arrangements organized around the centrality of the state. In its place, the regime promoted the development of a new market economy. In accordance with this new objective, a series of measures were implemented. The first was the liberalization of most prices so as to quickly return to a market system of production and distribution of goods. The second was the privatization of many economic activities. From 1974 on, those firms previously expropriated and operated by the state were returned to private hands. In addition, the state's enterprises linked to the provision of public utilities, such as water, gas, telephone, and electricity, were privatized. Finally, in 1979, tax duties were reduced to only 10 percent, thus leaving the Chilean economy open to global competition. These measures and others of this kind, which required administrative decisions and the use of existing state infrastructures, are the ones usually associated with "the model"—or the shift in economic policy that reoriented the economy from a closed, inward-looking import substitution model to an open, globalized, export-driven one.

We argue, however, that a *second* moment came in the early 1980s when the dictatorship went far beyond the standard economic issues related to policies such as trade and financial liberalization, competition, or the privatization of state-owned enterprises. In this second moment, the military government laid the legal foundations for the political and economic order that would fully come into its own—albeit with some important modifications—with the post-1989 democratic governments. We believe this second moment has not been given enough attention, often being confused with and subsumed under the more general change in the economic model. The most fundamental legal change was the new constitution in 1980, which had far-ranging consequences for the structuring of both economic and political life. Economically, not only was private property given enhanced juridical protection and a means for swift legal redress, but major areas of the economy were given new, comprehensive, and sometimes highly innovative regulatory frameworks. Such was the case with the Labor Law (1979), which substantially reduced the power of the unions and established new procedures for wage bargaining, arbitration, and strikes that were generally favorable to business; the Mining Law (1981), which allowed private investment and granted tax protection; the Stock Exchange Law and the Public Corporations Law (both of key relevance for the Santiago Stock Exchange's subsequent growth); and, in the area of social policy, the Pension Reform Law, the Higher Education Law (1981),[2] and the ISAPRE (private health providers) law (1981).

Thus in each of these economic sectors legislation provided the enduring framework within which organizations and economic agents would make their decisions and seek to adapt to the new free market conditions. In other words, these legal reforms stabilized and deepened the initial economic model. Finally, the maintenance of the so-called macroeconomic equilibrium was reinforced by a decree that gave total autonomy to the Central Bank in regulating inflation and money flows (Muñoz 2007: 16–18). Further,, the rationalization and shrinkage of state administration took place in accordance with the new doctrine of a "subsidiary state."

Initially, all these measures implied a process of productive rationalization that brought massive bankruptcy of small- and medium-sized enterprises. They also triggered a painful adjustment process for all those who stayed in business. Undoubtedly, the authoritarian character of the new government and its power to dismantle the previous sociopolitical network were important reasons for the imposition of these new social conditions (CEP 2000; Sabatini and Wormald 2005; Muñoz 2007). All these changes could well have been short-lived if the return to democracy had meant a swift policy reversal once the new center-left governments came into power. This is why the *political* legislation of the military government must also be considered.

For our purposes, the key aspect of this legislation was its antimajoritarian bent that, in practice, ensured that no major policy decision could be made without the consent of the opposition . By introducing a "binomial" electoral system for Congress that ensured the overrepresentation of the second largest coalition (which from 1990 until 2010 was invariably the center-right), in combination with supermajority requirements for reforming many key political and policy areas, the dictatorship successfully "locked in" the new development model and its legal foundations. In turn, this provided stability in expectations regarding the continuity of the model and therefore incentives for investing in organizational modernization to adapt to its requirements.

The main product of these two authoritarian and "neoliberal" moments was thus the firm implantation of a market economy. With the return to democracy at the beginning of the 1990s, the new ruling center-left elite faced the challenge of balancing economic growth with the necessary redistribution to palliate the social costs resulting from the application of the economic model. During this third phase, the market model partly lost its neoliberal stamp and began to assume a more social democratic orientation. The new democratic governments took advantage of market potential to attract private investments and develop innovation and entrepreneurial capacity. Thus they signed an important number of free trade agreements reinforcing the economy's openness to competition.[3] They also implemented policies to sustain macroeconomic equilibria and to develop good market practices, thus leading to the recent incorporation of the country as a full member of the Organization for Cooperation and Development (OCDE). But, at the same time, they generated new regulations to improve social efficacy. The state began to take a central role in redistribution and social protection so as to guarantee "minimum" access to social welfare for low-income groups.

The center-left Concertación governments "fully assumed [the] market economy as the main organization principle," even as they "decided to develop a commitment to social targets that the previous government lacked" (Muñoz 2007: 2). Thus both the authoritarian and democratic regimes shared a common feature: the gradual and sustained consensus of the political and entrepreneurial elite to enhance economic growth through the development of a market economy open to global competition.[4] Finally, a fourth moment in this process of institutional change has been the slow but significant support that the market economy gained among the population. The causes for this are related to the model's stability and relative success over a long period. Indeed, the new economic model has done relatively well in terms of economic growth. Between 1985 and 1990 gross national product (GNP) grew at an average annual rate of 6.4 percent and between 1990 and 2009, 5.1 percent. In turn, per capita GNP tripled during the last period.[5] Reflecting this trend, the poverty rate decreased from 38.7 percent in 1987 to 13.7 percent in 2006 (Casen 2006). This sustained growth opened new life chances in terms of income, employment, and consumption, especially for those middle-class sectors that have had access to education. During these decades, Chile experienced an important increase in social mobility and became an urban middle-class society not dependent on state employment (Torche and Wormald 2004).

As regards welfare services, Chile evolved toward a mixture of private and public sources—a situation that introduced a cleavage in society, as middle-class and high-income groups have access to services through market provision that are generally better than public services and are commonly perceived to be so. This is just one indicator of a more general realignment in favor of a market society. In fact, what was for many decades a purely elite decision to sustain and develop a market-oriented model has increasingly gained not only economic but also socio-cultural legitimacy.

This subjective dimension refers to personal experiences in which identities, valuations, and expectation of material and social conditions interweave, thus contributing to system legitimacy. A recent national survey, conducted with a representative sample of individuals age eighteen and older, shows that 65 percent agreed that work, personal effort, and initiative are the main resources for improving life conditions. Sixty-eight percent said that these are the main factors in overcoming poverty. The majority (60 percent) also agreed that economic success depends on personal effort and that remuneration should be tied to productivity (68 percent). Similarly, in another recent survey, 62 percent trust that Chile will become a developed country in the next ten years (Encuesta Bicentenario 2009).[6] These data suggest that the relative success of the market economy increasingly became legitimized through the expansion of market values. That is to say, a growing segment of middle-class people think that progress in life is closely related to market opportunities, personal initiative, and hard work. Probably this social change is behind the recent electoral success of a new right-wing coalition that came into power in the presidential period 2010–14.

The development of the market model has not been free of social contradictions. Income inequality, ecological imbalances, capital centralization and concentration, social vulnerability, and the reproduction of precarious labor conditions are some of the most significant.[7] However, these are consequences that the same model has tried to correct. Current critics argue against the idea of market self-regulation more than against the market model itself (Muñoz 2007: 17), although recent student movements challenge the model's efficacy in providing equal opportunities. In sum, the institutional changes that have taken place for more than three decades have produced a new market model with the following features:

- A coherent and strategic economic orientation of the ruling (political and economic) elite has been sustained for more than thirty-five years.
- Initially imposed from the top down using military power, this orientation has become legitimated by its own relative economic success
- This orientation came from outside the traditional institutional order in Chile, with globalization playing a central role.
- The impact of the new model has been broad ranging, affecting multiple other dimensions of culture and society.

STATE MODERNIZATION: THE INSTITUTIONAL RESPONSE

State Modernization as Strategic Aim

The change toward a market economy had a strong impact on the previous state's institutional reality. During the first neoliberal phase, the state reduced its size, redefined some of its functions, and started a process of modernization of the public administration mainly oriented to introducing technical improvements and management innovation in some services. Since 1990, however, the new democratic governments enhanced different modernization policies to improve state performance. Actually, this turned out to be a strategic aim of most of the new administrations as a result of the growing demand for state efficiency and efficacy imposed by global competition. The state needed to improve its performance as a way to promote economic growth and legitimated its role vis-à-vis private capital on a global scale. In addition, it needed to respond more effectively to social demands.

A final motivation related to guidelines provided by significant global institutions such as the World Bank, which, by the mid-1990s abandoned the idea of a "minimum state" and replaced it with what it defined as an "effective state" (World Bank 1997). Thus it no longer recommended state reduction but state effectiveness. This agenda incorporated various initiatives aimed at state transparency, introducing administrative processes and organizational controls to reinforce the honesty of the public administration (Waissbluth 2005: 56). This modernization agenda has continued, with some ups and downs, to the present.

State institutions have had to confront two related issues: on the one hand, their adaptation to the new development model, and, on the other, the governmental decision to include the modernization of public performance as a strategic aim.

The Internal Response: Institutional Change and the Modernization Path

A good empirical approach to evaluating the nature of the modernization process is to look at the way in which each of the five institutions studied performed. We do this following the theoretical framework described in the initial section. Below we analyze to what extent the six hypothesized institutional/organizational characteristics—defined in chapter 2—evolved during the time period considered, describe the forces leading to each specific process of institutional change and, finally, evaluate the way in which they fulfill their institutional functions.

Public Health Service. From 1981 on, the health system has been structured around the mixed provision of health care: private; and public, run by the state. In practice this mixed supply has meant a social segmentation based on users' socioeconomic status. The public system provides health care for a growing number of low and middle income groups who are not able to pay private security programs. In this regard, the Chilean health system's modernization responds to the political necessity faced by the new democratic governments to provide wider and better health coverage to beneficiaries of the public sector who represented over 75 percent of the total Chilean population by 2006. Although material resources for public health provision have increased substantially since 1990, it became increasingly evident that further improvements depended on better administration of these resources.

In this context, the modernization path of this sector concentrated on two basic aims: autonomous management of hospitals and the so-called Plan AUGE.[8] The first of these initiatives responds to an effort to rationalize the use of human and material resources within the public system.[9] The second was a top-to-bottom policy promoted by the Lagos government (2000–2006) as a way to provide at least a minimum level of social protection, especially to the most vulnerable sectors. The result of these two initiatives has been mixed: on the one hand, beneficiaries of the Plan AUGE are satisfied with the state provision of minimum health protection; on the other, hospitals administrators are increasingly concerned with tensions arising from excessive demand and medical resistance to the new economic-oriented administrative criteria, including some rationalization measures.[10]

According to Cereceda, Hoffmeister, and Escobar (2008), the modernization path was characterized by a new impulse toward meritocratic recruitment and promotion, especially in the higher managerial positions. However, they also noted that clientelistic and political criteria are still being used at different organizational levels. In addition, they pointed out that the new managerial criteria have been resisted by medical and nonmedical personnel. The former resented the loss of autonomy in the performance of their work, as well as the imposition of a new economic rationality that does not necessarily consider medical criteria. The latter resisted the new labor conditions which are seen as a menace to the traditional power of trade unions.

The reform has been relatively successful, however, in stamping out corruption. The new administrative controls increased transparency in the acquisition of medical supplies and also allowed greater control over the use of resources. Here a tension arose between the state's and physicians' interests, which sometimes induced the latter to guide patients to take medical exams in their private clinics.

Modernization in the health system entailed an important turn toward technical innovation, especially investment in new medical equipment. This works in favor of improved medical practice, as well as an incentive to recruit qualified medical personnel. Similarly, the reform entailed significant innovations in organizational processes, data gathering, and human development resources. In spite of these improvements, deficiencies in material infrastructure, personnel recruitment, and management practices persist. Paradoxically, although health reform was supported by a wide political consensus, institutional actors claim a lack of support. The explanation has to do in part with the endemic resource shortage of any health system threatened by excessive demand. It also has to do with the specific nature of this institutional reform, which emphasized patient rights to health care as a strategic aim to which other considerations were subordinated. After three years of the Plan AUGE, the figures show an important increase in access to hospital services; they also show that about 75 percent of the beneficiaries of this program are low income, especially children and the aged (Cereceda, Hoffmeister, and Escobar 2008: 33).

Thus health reform is a good example of the difficulties associated with a process of institutional change aimed at redefining power relations, norms, and values within a complex organization. In this case, the strengthening of institutional efficacy necessarily involved a long-term process of diffusion, legitimated by wide public support and open to continuous bargaining among key players.

The Post Office. The salient features affecting the national post office were the expansion of communications and competition within the new market economy, the revolution in communication technologies, and internal competition from myriad small private firms and more efficient international ones. This was possible because from 1981 on, the law removed the national post office monopoly on internal postal services. All these factors represented a serious threat to the continuation of the "old" organization and thus turned out to be a powerful stimulus for change. In this regard, the changing path within the post office is a clear example of cultural diffusion and technological innovation as vehicles for change.

Traditionally, the post office has performed a significant social integration role. By delivering correspondence and other communications it connects the country. It provided universal postal service at a reasonable price. This is probably the main reason for its maintenance and development as a state institution today.[11] However, under the new competitive conditions, modernization became an imperative for survival. This was the basic aim of the new strategic plan elaborated from 2000 on. This plan was actually the organizational response to a long history of unsuccessful initiatives. After the last of these failures, the central government promoted a complete change of management. This time, directors were selected by a central government agency (SEP) according to meritocratic criteria and with the deliberate aim of allowing the post office to compete under the new circumstances. Increasingly, the new organizational policies, based on more transparency and dialogue with trade union leaders, were able to gain the trade unions' engagement with and support of the service.[12] This new long-term plan reinforced organizational change toward a more competitive position by consolidating the use of technological innovation, both in production processes and in management.

It also increased meritocracy in terms of recruitment and promotion, drastically reducing the old clientelistic practices.

Market and flexible salary incentives were negotiated against productivity gains and better client satisfaction. New external and internal controls were introduced to avoid corruption. Finally, a systematic effort was made to change organizational values. In this regard, the basic idea was to transform the previous organizational culture by introducing new priorities in day-to-day performance, such as client satisfaction and personal commitment to a job well done and to the organization's success. The leitmotiv was, "If the Post Office performs well, I win; if not we all lose" (Cereceda 2009: 231; see also 231–35). This process of institutional change is a good example of adjustment where institutional survival is on the line. Modernization became an imperative to face the new competitive environment, support a crucial state role through the adequate provision of communication services, and, last but not least, maintain jobs for a significant number of state employees.

The National Revenue Agency. Change within the tax revenue service (SII) is the most impressive evidence of a deliberate attempt at institutional reform aimed at building state capacity. This is undoubtedly one of the most strategic agencies within the state, aimed at extracting the economic resources needed by the government. As Wormald and Cárdenas (2008: 20) show, the founding policy document of the military dictatorship regarded the tax system as key to preventing "excessive concentration of wealth" and looked to the tax collection agency to make a "decided effort in enforcing taxes." That these were not mere words was shown by the radical reform the SII underwent under the new director appointed by the Pinochet dictatorship:

> When I came into the tax agency, there was just one out-of-order old computer. There were also a bunch of corrupt lawyers. All processes were done by hand. . . . Then we started the modernization of the service. The first step was to rationalize goods acquisition so as to avoid waste. . . . The existing number of employees was cut to half. This allowed us to improve salaries and to professionalize management. We also introduced tax payment through the banks, and the service started to exert real control over tax revenues. Taxpayers who did not declare their income properly started to be afraid. Imagine the effect of having a service which could effectively act against tax evasion. This power of control was reinforced by political support from the Ministry of Finance and the president himself. (Wormald and Cárdenas 2008: 20)

We see that the means to achieve this change were not subtle: a staff reduced to half, rationalization of resources, investment in qualified personnel, and, above all, the will to enforce taxes so that "no one got away." Significantly, the support of the finance minister and the president himself are explicitly recognized, thus confirming not just the top-down nature of the reform itself but also the source of the political will that drove it. After the return to democracy, this modernizing drive did not lose momentum. Once again, the consistent and long-term support of two successive presidents of a technically trained and honest director bent on radical agency modernization proved effective. Under the democratic regime, technological change and organizational redesign in order to improve user-friendliness and collection rates became the goal. Increased user satisfaction with the agency and, above all, a reduction in overall tax evasion from over 30 percent in 1990 to an estimated 18 percent in 2005 are proofs of this success. "Institutional engagement, with a sustained increase in tax collection and with a better discharge of fiscal duties, has been the explicit aim assumed by the different governments during the last decades" (Wormald and Cárdenas 2008: 14).

From this followed a related improvement in meritocracy. Technical cadres became an organizational necessity, reinforced by the professionalization of top management. This last feature is probably one of the most salient characteristics in the modernization path followed by this institution. In 1991 leadership was assumed by a new team of highly qualified engineers, backed by strong political support and with the explicit aim of reinforcing institutional efficacy. The head of this team served twelve years in his post. The success of this team in reducing tax evasion, reducing collection costs, and increasing state revenues at a much faster rate than economic growth point to a "developmental agency" nested within a state whose very top personnel—from the president down—has been its key allies.

The Air Traffic Authority. The air traffic authority (Dirección General de Aeronáutica Civil, or DGAC) is also an example of successful modernization "from above," by accommodation of military interests with the culture of the organization itself. Since its inception, the DGAC has been predominantly under military control, in spite of its strategic civil and commercial functions. It remains subordinated to the commander of the air force. As Thumala (2009: 184) notes, "This link has determined not only the nature of its institutional dependency but also its ways of operation. The military tradition of the organization has determined that its structure and organizational culture are markedly hierarchical, even to this day."

The institution's modernization process must be understood in the context of an external environment that changed significantly during the 1980s and 1990s. Three major changes were the exponential growth in air traffic caused by economic growth and deregulation of the market, the privatization and concession of airport infrastructure, and the internal state modernization process undertaken by successive democratic governments. A crucial change in the external environment was the growing importance of air traffic that demanded the expansion of airport infrastructure. This demand was met through Build, Operate, and Transfer (BOT) agreements with the private sector, thus taking airport management and maintenance functions out of the DGAC's direct control. The DGAC's main function became limited to guaranteeing safe airspace and security in all flights and airports in the country. Successful provision of this service is crucial for the cargo and passenger industries and thus constitutes a strategic task of the state. The DGAC's success in providing this service is reflected in its very low rate of accidents or incidents in the country (a rate of 0 accidents per 100,000 flights in 2005) and by the fact that it has been granted "Category 1" status by the U.S. Federal Aviation Authority (FAA) since 1996. This status allows commercial airlines to pay lower insurance premiums while allowing direct commercial exchanges with the United States.

The organization's strengths lie in its relative immunity to corruption, which would jeopardize safety standards and the DGAC's critical oversight functions; its close connection to client needs (mainly the commercial airlines) for whom it is critical; and its technological openness and flexibility.[13] The agency is less strong in other criteria. The absence of meritocratic recruitment stems from limitations in the ability to fire deficient or poorly qualified personnel once they have become protected by the Civil Service Statute and the role of the DGAC as a rehirer of retired air force personnel, possibly sidelining qualified civilian candidates. As Thumala reports (2009: 184), "All departmental directors of the DGAC are former or active members of the Air Force, and at the vice-director level almost all of them are also former members."

Nonetheless, the report on this institution concludes that these limitations do not fundamentally impair the fulfillment of the agency's mission since it hires mostly highly specialized and trained personnel. Thus, whether or not hiring allegedly cheaper retired military personnel is economically efficient or if competition is truly open to all, chosen candidates do possess the required qualifications for the critical functions they perform. Yet the clear dominance of military personnel in an agency performing essentially civilian functions does raise questions regarding the presence of an island of power—a military caste—inside the organization. Thumala (2009) also finds that the DGAC does not have powerful external allies. Indeed, the DGAC is a little-known agency in spite of the importance of its functions; moreover, its military personnel and culture, and direct dependence on the commander of the air force, have made it a subordinate and less prominent agency. This has had the positive effect of preventing it from being colonized by powerful interests, as had happened in other state agencies. However, the DGAC's influence on key policy decisions in its sphere of influence is very low; it is an agency whose opinion is not much considered but must, nevertheless, obey.

The Santiago Stock Exchange. The Santiago Stock Exchange has been a remarkable case of institutional modernization in response to the market pressures unleashed by the economic development model during the military dictatorship. As the only nonstate institution in our sample, the stock exchange provides unique insights into the way the private sector reacted to these pressures and adapted to them independently. As discussed in Wormald and Brieba (2009), the stock exchange has undergone in the past thirty years a sustained process of change, from what was essentially a gentleman's club with economic, social, and even political functions to a professional exchange where maximizing profits amid increasing competition is almost the sole objective. This transformation, however, required major external shocks to eventually trigger an internal response that sent the stock exchange along a modernization path. Two changes in its environment were key: the constitutional and legal changes that fundamentally altered the economic development model and the threat from an alternative stock exchange that could take over its business.

As pointed out, changes in the Chilean legal framework, particularly in the early 1980s, were both wide and deep. The much greater security of property rights established in the 1980 Constitution was an important foundation on which to build after a protracted period of government intervention and expropriation. A crucial boost to the stock exchange came in 1982, when the new private pension law channeled workers' contributions into it and other financial instruments. This provided much-needed liquidity and "depth" to a market that had hitherto lacked both. The opportunities opened up by this expansion in financial flows were not immediately taken up by an organization that still operated as a closed elite club. For a while it resisted the entrance of corporate financial entities (mainly banks) and also technological modernization. Only when these new players set up an electronic stock exchange and provided a real threat to the traditional stock exchange did the older organization allow corporate players to become brokers and part of the organization. Coupled with the ensuing and thorough technological modernization, the Santiago Stock Exchange was able to keep and consolidate its primacy as the financial hub of the Chilean economy.

Institutional change in the stock exchange was not merely technological. Through a sustained modernization drive led by its long-term management team, plus the gradual incorporation of corporate and other more market-oriented players, the organization moved consistently in a direction that facilitated the fulfillment of its institutional mission: the channeling of savings into productive investments. The Santiago Stock Exchange scored high in most of the six institutional criteria discussed previously. Recruitment is undertaken on almost purely meritocratic criteria; this has become more necessary as competition between brokers has increased and the financial markets have gained in complexity. Nonetheless, in what remains a relatively small market operating in a business where trust is of such fundamental importance, personal connections and family background retain a fraction of their former relevance. Purely meritocratic recruitment is most observable in the "new" corporate actors that have been the backbone of the modernization process.

Regarding immunity to corruption, throughout its long history the Santiago Stock Exchange was never considered a corrupt institution; nonetheless, technological modernization has allowed a much greater degree of transparency in all transactions. More important, the stock exchange management understands trust as the key intangible asset for the market to work smoothly and, as such, has sought to lead the way in improving standards of transparency and disclosure. Nonetheless, the thorny issues relating to the regulation of conflicts of interest and access to privileged information have not been regulated at the level with which such issues are dealt with in more developed markets. On the other hand, internal islands of power are no longer a major obstacle to modernization and to fulfillment of the institutional function: Once the hold of the old families was broken by the "modern" corporate financial firms, the institution has not been subjected to the interests of any particular group of actors. This is not to say that no tensions remain between the two groups but rather that they have been contained within the stock exchange's institutional framework.

Regarding the external criteria considered in this study, the stock exchange performs reasonably well in all three. It has successfully established close relations with its most immediate clients in the corporate world, has begun to establish regional alliances with foreign stock exchanges, has diversified its business, and has inserted itself in the global financial market. Its weakest point remains its level of proactivity vis-à-vis the public at large, whose financial knowledge and education remain very limited. This is a serious concern in a business that still struggles with problems of depth and liquidity, and doubly so in a country where a great proportion of pension savings are invested by pension funds in local financial instruments. Openness to technological innovation is, conversely, the strongest feature of the institution to the point that it has now developed and exports financial software.

Finally, the capacity of the Santiago Stock Exchange to establish powerful alliances outside its immediate environment is manifest and, in fact, constitutes another strategic asset of the organization. Historically, its ties with major business and corporate actors were very strong, given the family connections between brokers and businesses. Nonetheless, because financial markets were depressed at low levels of activity in the past, the stock exchange was seldom able to influence policy making. This situation has now changed, and within the present market-oriented economy it has become a respected and important actor in all matters relating to the regulation and oversight of financial and capital markets.

Isomorphism and Particularism

All these cases are clear examples that institutional modernization made significant inroads during these decades. Tables 2.2 and 2.3, above, summarize the specific shape of the process by scoring each selected institution on the six hypothesized determinants of quality and contribution to development.

From these figures emerges a general modernization path, irrespective of institutional specificity. The descriptive analysis undertaken here shows that all institutions, without exception, have improved their performance and efficacy during the period considered. As noted earlier, this was induced by the need to adjust their traditional performance to the new environmental requirements in order to deliver more and better services. Globalization and market competition played a key role in raising quality standards and developing new organizational blueprints. The new democratic turn and the growing educational levels of the population have also played an important role by reinforcing the idea of the rights of citizens to better services.

Another isomorphic force behind this path has been the common institutional move toward blueprint copying. This has been especially strong when dealing with new technical procedures or devices. The recruitment of professional cadres and directives, usually trained in good European or North American universities, who tended to reproduce the responses and priorities learned abroad, was another push in this direction. In the specific case of state institutions, a further step toward isomorphism has been the recent successful attempt to join the OCDE. In the words of its general secretary, "During the last two decades, Chile has done a good job in terms of democratic and economic policies. The country joins an organization that works to find common solutions to global problems and establishes global standards and common policies in areas such as education, employment, public accountability to reinforce a solid and open global economy. Being an OCDE member means to be at the center of the design and promotion of those rules which define the global economy and society in the future" (Curria 2010: 1).

In spite of these common characteristics, particularism also played a role in the modernization path. Institutions reacted in different ways to similar stimuli. Reasons have to do with their different functions, relations, relevant institutional environment, and historical and cultural specificities. Thus while the national aeronautic agency (DGAC) responds to a military culture that specifies its organizational performance, the public health service is largely conditioned by a medical culture in many ways opposed to economic and administrative criteria. In addition, it is clear that there is not just one best modernization case but different roads according to institutional specificities. Again, the case of the DGAC shows that the adoption of the new values—such as transparency, flexibility, client orientation—coexist and often clash with traditional military values, which tend to reinforce loyalty, obedience, and discipline. Interestingly, this mix of "traditional" and "modern" values can sometimes lead to good outcomes, for example, in the adoption of new management rules. This seems to be the case within SII and the DGAC itself where a rather traditional "authoritarian" style was adopted by the new technocratic and modernizing elite. In other cases, however, this mixture of values may represent an obstacle to the adoption of new, modern blueprints.

Institutions also have historical specificities that tend to reinforce the traditional way in which things have been done. This is especially true within state organizations with a definite function and a relatively stable environmental context and personnel.[14] Bureaucracy is adverse to risk, and the fear of many public officials that they will be charged with some procedural mistake turns "rational" the traditional way of doing things. As DiMaggio and Powell (1983) have noted, organizational blueprints tend to sustain enduring patterns of reliability and accountability in organizational behavior. Therefore, path dependency is an important force to take into account when dealing with modernization targets in existing institutions.

DISCUSSION: INSTITUTIONAL CHANGE IN CHILE

In the preceding sections we described the macrolevel changes in Chilean society as a result of the military coup of 1973. Subsequently, we provided a description of changes in the five organizations covered by the study, both in terms of their overall performance and in terms of the six specific institutional criteria that have guided this comparative project. We saw that all five organizations underwent a process of intense change and modernization under pressures triggered by major changes in their external environments; albeit to a varying degree, all have succeeded in adapting to the new democratic and free market society.

In this section, we attempt to explain this relatively successful institutional transformation by first applying to the Chilean case Portes's theory of institutional change and then drawing further attention to the importance of legal reform for the stability and permanence of the market model. We conclude by suggesting there may be a space for integrating the "political economy" focus on "rules of the game" in a sociological explanation of institutional change. If we review the five forces of change presented in figure 1.4, over, our analysis shows that it was the use of *power* by the military dictatorship from 1973 on that was the prime mover and initial cause of the country's subsequent institutional transformation. The previously existing interelite and class conflict for control of the state was ultimately resolved by force in favor of a right-of-center neoliberal project. Yet limiting the role of power to this initial moment would be inappropriate. Both the second and third "moments" described above—the enactment of comprehensive economic and political reform and the maintenance of the economic model (with some modifications) by the democratic Concertación governments in the 1990s—were also based on the use of political power to change past realities.

Only in the most recent "moment"—the progressive transformation of Chile into a market society, in which market values are increasingly internalized—have changes initially imposed from above through the use of power begun to gain broad support in society, or, in Portes's conceptualization, have become embedded in the country's values. Nonetheless, while this change may bode well for the model's future stability, value change must be understood as a *consequence* of the permanence and success of the economic model over several decades rather than as its cause. At less deep levels of causality, we can also detect forces that had a more direct bearing on the specific ways in which institutions modernized and changed. Among them, forces of *cultural diffusion* played a crucial role in pushing all organizations studied in the direction of greater meritocracy, lower corruption, and enhanced technological innovations. The deliberate copying of institutional blueprints from the developed world and the recruitment to top positions of managerial cadres trained in elite European and North American universities were of greatest importance. Through these channels, technological innovation and internal modernization were undertaken in forms specific to each institution's needs.

We saw as well that while cultural diffusion provided the main isomorphic force behind institutional change, the main particularistic influence was each organization's past history and specific culture. Looking again at the conceptual framework in figure 1.4, these forces can be readily identified with path dependence—the most superficial, but no less real, influence on institutions. However, we also noted that the specific culture of each institution has been not only a force of resistance to change but also sometimes a force through which change itself was effected. Overall, this brief application of the model to the Chilean case shows that the conceptual framework laid out in chapter 1 is highly useful for explaining institutional change in an integrated way across forces located at different levels of causal influence.

To conclude, we wish to highlight the special importance of the "second moment" in our narrative, both because of its intrinsic importance for the Chilean case and because of its theoretical significance for refining our understanding of institutional change. While we have just seen that the original cause of such reforms was political power, the most remarkable thing was that these reforms were not reversed once the military dictatorship had left office and democratic center-left governments came to power. As argued above, the initial change in economic orientation may well have been short-lived if more fundamental steps had not been taken through comprehensive legal reform of the economic and political rules of the game. Indeed, these reforms were central for *deepening* the market model, on the one hand, and for *stabilizing* it, on the other. Deepening took place through those reforms that changed, sometimes in quite fundamental ways, the rules that had hitherto framed economic activity so as to make them more business-friendly.

In terms of stabilizing the new model, from an economic standpoint, the creation of a host of new regulatory frameworks can be seen as an investment, with significant sunk costs once enacted. This means that even a hostile incoming government would have found it difficult and time-consuming to reverse all the reforms. After 1990 there was an important degree of cross-party elite consensus regarding economic policy that made continuity possible. Nonetheless, this consensus took place after the military had politically "locked in" such reforms via the new electoral and supermajority rules laid down in the 1980 Constitution.

It is worth noting here that in the fields of political science, institutional economics, and political economy, "institutions" are usually understood in the sense discussed in the preceding paragraphs: as the rules of the game that govern interactions among organizations. While this is *not* the definition of institutions we have employed in this study, our analysis suggests that changes in these rules can be crucial for understanding institutional change at the organizational level. In this sense, a "thin" institutional focus on these rules should be explicitly integrated into an analysis of the ways in which power can affect social structure. Two related conceptual distinctions can help us do this in a simple way. The first is the distinction between *de facto* and *de jure* power, which authors such as Acemoglu and Robinson (2006) have recently used to differentiate between the power some actors or group of actors have at one point in time and the one that is embodied in the formal rules of social interaction and that thus constrain actors over long periods. If our analysis of the Chilean case is correct, a crucial step for the stability of the new economic model was the dictatorship's capacity to translate its de facto power into de jure power, by locking in, in the way described above, the fundamental rules of the game. The problem, however, is that by calling such rules of the game "institutions," political economists fall into the traps described by Portes and make potentially confusing conceptual claims about the relationship between institutions and development.[15]

For this reason, we suggest that by calling such rules of the game not institutions as such but *institutional arrangements,* we can link them more clearly to institutions. Conceptually, we think this can be done in a simple way. If institutions are "the set of rules, written or informal, governing relationships among role occupants in social organizations" (see chapter 1), then we can define institutional arrangements as *the set of rules, written or informal, governing relationships between social organizations.* Just as institutions prescribe a set of rules that really existing organizations may only partially follow, so the rules prescribed by these institutional arrangements may or may not be followed by organizations in engaging with each other. Institutional arrangements would thus refer to the rules of the game that define and structure social interaction between institutions. This role can be seen most clearly in texts such as the Constitution that specify, at the highest order, the rules of the game between institutions such as Congress, the judiciary, and the executive.

We believe that the proposed distinction between institutions as organizational blueprints and institutional arrangements as interorganizational blueprints is analytically useful for several reasons. In the first place, unlike organizations that mostly set their own internal rules, rules for interorganizational engagement are usually externally created and enforced. In this sense, most organizations are "rule takers" when it comes to dealing with their environment, and it makes sense to treat these rules as exogenous to them. Moreover, the source of most of these rules—at least the formal ones—is the political system. Key institutional relationships for a country's policy environment, for its ability to provide public goods, and for specific outcomes depend to an important degree on these ultimate sources of de jure power. Institutions and their interrelationships produce an emergent reality that is not reducible either to individual institutions or to the underlying power distribution that gave rise to them.

Thus, inasmuch as there is some degree of institutional autonomy, looking at this complex and crucial system of rules for its effects not just on political performance but also on development may require a direct focus on them instead of a mediated one through their impact on individual institutions. Last, we note that, just as Portes (2009: 29) highlights that his definition of institutions "is in close agreement with everyday uses of the term," the somewhat more unwieldy concept of institutional arrangements points to another dimension of the usage of the term *institutions*, as when one says that a certain rule or relationship has been "institutionalized," meaning that mutual expectations of behavior have been stabilized.

The importance in the Chilean case of changes in the formal rules of the game for stabilizing and deepening the initial change in the economic model suggests that there may be analytic space for explaining change at the level of concrete organizations, at least in part as due to changes in institutional arrangements. More generally, these arrangements matter because once institutionalized (i.e., as de jure power) they gain an autonomous influence that is not reducible to the original conditions of de facto power under which they were enacted (Acemoglu and Robinson 2006). On the other hand, rules of the game cannot be an "ultimate" source of change since they themselves may be affected by deeper social forces such as society's value system and its (de facto) power and class structures. This suggests that *institutional arrangements, which are the focus of most "thin" institutionalism, can best be thought of as a midlevel causal influence on institutions.*

CONCLUSION

When we are talking about development, we are dealing with a normative concept that embodies a crucial institutional dimension. In this respect, an aim of this chapter has been to reinforce North's already well known statement that "institutions matter" and that they are central to understanding economic dynamism. But then the question arises about what we are going to understand by "institution." In our view, the sociological concept of institution developed by Portes and presented in chapter 1 of this volume constitutes a good tool for empirical analysis, as does the concept of institutional arrangement that complements this analytic perspective. Both concepts are important when trying to understand the process of Chilean development during the past decades.

The important point here is that the new market-oriented economy and institutional arrangements increasingly penetrated—either in terms of values or social relations—Chilean society, thus stimulating its transformation into a new society. Institutional change was also the result of a process of cultural diffusion, reinforced by the development of some isomorphic forces. However, our case studies also noted that institutional change and modernization processes must consider historical, social, and cultural institutional specificities. It is probably at this level where the theoretical framework employed in our analysis acquires all its analytic potential by showing that the "copy is never equal to the model," precisely due to sociological considerations. Within organizations there always emerges a distance between institutional blueprints and actors' actual behavior. This distance has to do with organizational power relations, trust relations among employees, informal links and bureaucratic habits, and cultural and organizational values, which, at the end, define real institutional performance. Therefore, it is only by looking at the historical and social reality of concrete institutions and their relations with institutional arrangements in their environment that one can understand the development potentialities of a given country.

In the Chilean case, society underwent significant change leading to a consolidation of a market economy and a corresponding process of modernization of state institutions. While this institutional transformation has had a positive impact on economic growth and social citizenship, it still falls short in providing access to equal opportunities for all. In this respect, a more efficient state than the one depicted here will have to play a key role in counterbalancing market forces in the future development of the country.

APPENDIX 4.1: INSTITUTIONAL STUDIES IN CHILE

The reports on which this chapter is based are listed below with English translation of the original Spanish titles. The individual studies can be downloaded from the webpage of the Center for Migration and Development, Princeton University: http://cmd.princeton.edu.

Cereceda, Luz. "Institutionalism and Development: The Case of the Postal Service of Chile."

Cereceda, Luz, Lorena Hoffmeister, and Constanza Escobar. "Institutionalism, Organization, and Health Reform in Chile."

Thumala, Angelica M. "Military Culture and Market Demands: The Modernization of the General Aeronautics Direction of Chile."

Wormald, Guillermo, and Daniel Brieba. "The Stock Exchange of Santiago Chile: An Institutional Analysis."

Wormald, Guillermo, and Ana Cárdenas. "The Internal Tax Service of Chile: An Institutional Analysis."

NOTES

1. This new economic policy orientation was condensed in a neoliberal policy program document of the military government that criticized the excessive "statism" of the previous democratic administrations. By contrast, the authors advocated the "urgent necessity of economic power decentralization, allowing the development of a modern and efficient economic system organized through the market and competence" (*El Ladrillo*, 1992, 50; our translation).

2. This law was complemented in 1990 with the Organic Constitutional Law, which allowed private providers, subsidized by the state through an indirect voucher system, in elementary and secondary education as well.

3. Up to 1989 Chile had not signed any free trade agreements. However, by 2009 the successive democratic governments had signed twenty-four of them.

4. A good indicator of this elite consensus had been the economic policy orientation. From the military government on, the treasury minister had been an economist committed to macroeconomic equilibrium and exposure to global competition. What started in 1979 with a radical reduction in the customs tax has been reinforced by free trade agreements in the next decades and Chile's recent full membership in the OCDE.

5. GNP grew from US$ 4.542 to US$14.299 between 1990 and 2009. *EL Mercurio*, January 18, 2010.

6. This survey has been conducted annually since 2006 by the Institute of Sociology of the Catholic University of Chile and the marketing enterprise ADIMARK.

7. The new market economy actively promoted a growing differentiation in working conditions. To the traditional formal/informal cleavage, global market competition added and accelerated an important differentiation within both these sectors (Sabatini and Wormald 2005: 256–57). On the other side, the already deregulated labor code was only slightly reformulated. Therefore, trade unions and workers' organizations also fragmented and lost representation, in addition to their capacity to develop a common project.

8. The Programa de Garantías Explícitas de Salud, created in 2005, was instituted to provide universal health coverage—guaranteed by law—for a definite number of pathologies in a given time and at a given price. Between 2005 and 2010 the number of illnesses covered by this program increased from twenty-six to sixty-six.

9. This initiative started with eleven hospitals in 2006 and established that all public hospitals should have autonomous management by 2009.

10. According to figures from a recent survey, around 90 percent of the beneficiaries of the Plan AUGE agreed that the attention they received was even better than expected. Encuesta Fundación Jaime Guzman, published by *El Mercurio*, June 30, 2010).

11. In 1981 Correos de Chile replaced the old Servicio de Correos y Telégrafo de Chile. By 2007 this enterprise was organized in 1,209 offices throughout the country. It handled 80 percent of mail delivery within the country and employed 4,852 persons (Cereceda 2009: 211).

12. As a result of this modernization plan around 25 percent of the employees were dismissed through different retirement initiatives.

13. It was, for instance, a bulwark of opposition and resistance of the upper class to the Allende government in the 1970s. For more details, see Wormald and Brieba 2009.

14. In the case of the Chilean administration, a 1989 law imposed what is known as "labor immobility" (inamovilidad funcionaria), which makes it very difficult to dismiss any civil servant who occupies a permanent position.

15. See chapters 1 and 2.

REFERENCES

Acemoglu, Damon, and James A. Robinson. 2006. *Economic Origins of Dictatorship and Democracy.* New York: Cambridge University Press.

Brinton, Mary, and Victor Nee. 2001. *The New Institutionalism in Sociology.* Stanford: Stanford University Press.

CASEN. 2006. *Encuesta de caracterización socio-económica.* Módulo pobreza. Santiago: Mideplan.

Cereceda, Luz. 2009. "Institucionalidad y desarrollo: El caso de Correos de Chile." In *Las instituciones en el desarrollo latinoamericano,* edited by A. Portes, 210–37. Mexico City: Siglo XXI.

Cereceda, Luz Eugenia, Lorena Hoffmeister, and Constancia Escobar. 2008. "Institucionalidad, organización, y reforma de la salud en Chile." Final report to the project *Latin American Institutions and Development: A Comparative Analysis.*

Curria, Angel. 2010. "Página de opinión." *El Mercurio,* October 1.

Di Maggio, Paul, and Walter Powell. 1983. "The Iron Cage Revisited: Institutional Isomorphism and Collective Rationality in Organizational Fields." *American Sociological Review* 48: 147–60.

Evans, Peter, and James E. Rauch. 1999. "Bureaucracy and Growth: A Cross-National Analysis of the Effects of 'Weberian' State Structures of Economic Growth." *American Sociological Review* 64: 748–65.

Centro de Estudios Públicos (CEP). 1992. *El ladrillo, bases de la política económica del gobierno militar chileno.* Santiago: Alfabeta Impresores.

———. 2001. *La transformación económica de Chile.* Santiago: Alfabeta Impresores.

Larrain, Felipe, and Rodrigo Vergara. 2001. "Chile en pos del desarrollo: Veinticinco años de transformaciones económicas." In *La transformación económica de Chile,* edited by F. Larrain and R. Vergara. Santiago: Centros de Estudio Públicos.

Muñoz, Oscar. 2007. "El modelo económico de la Concertación, 1990–2005: ¿Reformas o cambio?" CIEPLAN/FLACSO Working Paper. Santiago.

Nee, Victor. 2005. "Organizational Dynamics of Institutional Change: Politicized Capitalism in China." In *The Economic Sociology of Capitalism,* edited by V. Nee and R. Swedberg, 53–74. Princeton: Princeton University Press.

Nee, Victor, and Richard Swedberg, eds. 2005. *The Economic Sociology of Capitalism.* Princeton: Princeton University Press.

Polanyi, Karl. 2003. *La gran transformación: Los orígenes políticos y económicos de nuestro tiempo.* Mexico City: Fondo de Cultura Económica.

Portes, Alejandro, ed. 2009. *Las instituciones en el desarrollo latinoamericano: Un estudio comparado.* Mexico City: Siglo XXI.

Portes, Alejandro, and Lori D. Smith. 2009. "Síntesis: Las causas del éxito o fracaso de las instituciones latinoamericanas." In *Las instituciones en el desarrollo latinoamericano: Un estudio comparado,* edited by A. Portes, 317–37. Mexico City: Siglo XXI.

Sabatini, Francisco, and Guillermo Wormald. 2005. "Santiago de Chile bajo la nueva economía: 1980–2000." In *Ciudades latinoamericana: En el umbral de un nuevo siglo,* edited by A. Portes, B.R. Roberts, and A. Grimson, 217–98. Buenos Aires: Prometeo Editores.

Schneider, Ben Ross, and David Soskice. 2009. "Inequality in Developed Countries and Latin America: Coordinated, Liberal, and Hierarchical Systems." *Economy and Society* 38: 17–52.

Swedberg, Richard. 2005. "The Economic Sociology of Capitalism: An introduction and Agenda." In *The Economic Sociology of Capitalism,* edited by V. Nee and R. Swedberg, 3–40. Princeton: Princeton University Press.

Thumala, M. Angélica. 2009. "Cultura militar y demandas del mercado: La modernización de la Dirección General de Aeronáutica Civil de Chile." In *Las instituciones en el desarrollo latinoamericano,* edited by A. Portes, 182–209. Mexico City: Siglo XXI.

Torche, Florencia, and Guillermo Wormald. 2004. *Estratificación y movilidad social en Chile: Entre la adscripción y el logro.* Serie Políticas Sociales, 98. Santiago: U.N. Economic Commission for Latin America (CEPAL).

Waissbluth, Mario. 2005. *La reforma del estado en Chile 1990–2005: Diagnóstico y proyectos de futuro.* Serie Gestión 76. Santiago: University of Chile.

Wormald, Guillermo, and Daniel Brieba. 2009. "La Bolsa de Comercio de Santiago de Chile: Un análisis institucional." In *Las instituciones en el desarrollo latinoamericano,* edited by A. Portes, 155–81. Mexico City: Siglo XXI.

Wormald, Guillermo, and Ana Cárdenas. 2008. "El Servicio de Impuestos Internos en Chile: Un análisis institucional." Final report to the project *Latin American Institutions and Development: A Comparative Analysis.*

5

The Colombian Paradox

A Thick Institutionalist Analysis

César Rodríguez-Garavito

Fifteen years after leaving Colombia, where he lived between 1952 and 1956, Albert O. Hirschman published a devastating review of a book on Colombian politics and institutions, written by a young American scholar, James Payne. In the review, included in *A Bias for Hope,* Hirschman lashes out against the thesis of the book (Payne 1968), which he summarizes:

> In plain language, occasionally used by the author, Colombian politicians are exceedingly demagogic—interested exclusively in increasing their own power, always ready to betray yesterday's friends and allies, and, to top it all, incapable of having friendly personal relations with anyone because they feel comfortable only with abject supplicants. On the other hand, there is the politician with a program incentive whose preferred habitat is the United States of America. *He* enjoys working on concrete policies and achieving a stated goal; hence he is principled, willing to defend unpopular causes, always ready to come to constructive agreements, hard-working, and generally lovable. (Hirschman 1971: 345; original emphasis)

In addition to calling the book biased and naive, Hirschman challenges Payne by pointing to an explanatory puzzle:

> It is easy to show that the Payne model is as wrong as it is outrageous. In the first place, it is unable to explain the very wide swings of Colombian politics; after all, during almost all of the first half of the twentieth century Colombia stood as a "stable" democracy with peaceful transfers of power from one party to another: throughout the Great Depression of the thirties when almost all other Latin American countries

Titles and authors of individual reports on which this chapter is based are found in Appendix 5.1.

> experienced violent political convulsions, constitutional government continued in spite of much social unrest.
>
> This experience is hard to explain by a theory that holds that vicious political infighting, untrammeled by any concern with programs or loyalty, holds continuous sway throughout the body politic. Moreover, such a theory ought to take a good look at—and give special weight to—the body's head: if Payne had done that he might have noticed that this stereotype . . . simply does not apply to a number of the most outstanding leaders and recent presidents of Colombia.[1] (346)

Hirschman's statement offers an ideal entry point to the content and methodology of this chapter. From the point of view of content, it offers one of the clearest and most authoritative formulations of what I call the "Colombian paradox": the coexistence of fairly stable political, economic, and social institutions on the one hand and very high levels of violence and territorial fragmentation on the other. This paradox has troubled scholars of Colombia and Latin America for decades, and it appears again, with more detailed empirical evidence, in the case studies analyzed in this chapter. Produced as part of the larger comparative project on institutions and development in Latin America on which this book is based (see also Portes 2006; Portes and Smith 2010), these studies provide institutional ethnographies of the postal service (Díaz 2009), the stock market (Rodríguez-Garavito 2009), the airport and air safety agency (Hernández 2009), the tax administration (Rodríguez-Garavito and Rodríguez Franco 2008) and the public health system (Díaz 2008).

As we shall see in detail below, the results of this regional project show that among the five countries studied,[2] Colombia receives the lowest scores on the independent variables of institutional quality and proactivity, as well as on the outcome variables of institutional adaptation and contribution to development (Portes and Smith 2010). Given these institutional uncertainties, what explains the stable Colombian economic performance in the regional context, as shown by the fact that its last episode of hyperinflation dates to 1902 (Sánchez, Hernández, and Armenta 2010)? How can we understand the fact that Colombia is one of the few Latin American countries to have escaped regional waves of economic populism (Robinson 2010; Urrutia 1991) and the only one that escaped the debt crisis cycles of the 1980s (Avella 2007)? How does institutional precariousness combine with the existence of a technocracy that, as Hirschman points out, is recognized for its professional competence? How can we explain that Colombia was and still is one of the most stable democracies in the region (indeed, one of only four that did not succumb to military coups in the 1960s and 1970s)?[3] In addition, how can we understand how all this happens in the midst of the oldest and most violent armed conflict on the continent?

The allusion to Hirschman's review in *A Bias for Hope* is also useful in explaining the methodological approach I use in this chapter to address the Colombian paradox. In addition to refuting Payne's thesis, Hirschman addresses several criticisms of Payne's "cognitive approach"—that is, the relationship between theory and evidence, what we now call "methodology" (Burawoy 1991). Indeed, Hirschman presents Payne's work as a sign of the "tendency toward compulsive and mindless theorizing"—that is, the methodological vice of formulating grand theoretical narratives that seek to fully explain complex phenomena, based on very general empirical evidence. This obsessive "search for paradigms" was, to Hirschman, a barrier to understanding social phenomena as powerful "as the spread of mindless number work in the social sciences" (Hirschman 1971: 342), thus leading to his stern conclusion regarding the book's cognitive style: "Payne's book . . . obviously explains too much and thereby succeeds only in provoking the reader's resistance and incredulity; the only curiosity it provokes is about the kind of social science that made an obviously gifted young man go so wrong" (344).

As Portes (2004) has shown, this orientation to major theories has also been common in Latin American sociology and has presented a barrier to understanding complex phenomena such as the Colombian paradox. Hence the present project has focused on creating thick ethnographies of specific institutions in Latin America rather than a comprehensive theory of the institutions or national and regional institutional changes, as discussed in chapters 1 and 2. Given the interest in formulating a thesis that can be empirically contrasted by means of detailed studies, this "thick institutionalism" is pitched at a medium level of abstraction, that is, that of Mertonian "middle-range" concepts (Portes 2004).

The discussion of the Colombian paradox offered in this chapter occurs on this level. Thus I seek to bring together the empirical findings of the five case studies with the analytic puzzle raised by the Colombian paradox. Pointing to this intermediate area has a twofold goal. First, I compare the evidence from the case studies to inductively extract some general features that serve as hypotheses about the features of Colombian institutions and their impact on development. The goal of the comparison is to move from the evidential level of each institution to a more general discussion about what the set of case studies tells us about institutions and development in Colombia. Second, I seek to apply the dominant view in the literature on the Colombian institutions (which offers various alternative responses to the above paradox) to the empirical scrutiny of the case study data. The purpose of this summary analysis of the literature is to expose it to the detailed ethnographic evidence of these case studies. To my knowledge, this type of evidence has not been used in the discussion of the subject, which has operated only with generic quantitative and qualitative data.[4]

Therefore, this chapter has a dual nature. On the one hand, it is a synthetic discussion of case studies and an attempt at generalization based on them. On the other hand, it represents an intervention in the discussion of Colombian institutions from the point of view of thick institutionalism and thus takes as its target the leitmotiv of this discussion: the Colombian paradox.

The chapter is divided into three parts. First, I summarize and discuss the case study findings and extract the general features that emerge from the comparison of cases. For this comparison I rely on the central variables used in the collective comparative project. In the second part, I use the institutional features that emerge from the empirical review to discuss the Colombian paradox and the various explanations of it. In doing so, I use evidence from the case studies to attempt a more precise characterization of the paradox, as well as an interpretation of it that differs from those dominant in the literature. I argue that the ethnographic evidence of the project and data from other studies suggest that the Colombian institutional field represents neither a case of "institutional collapse" nor a model of stability and rationality. Instead, it is a hybrid situation characterized by institutional strength in niches of excellence and institutional uncertainty in the rest of the field. In the last section, I recapitulate and offer a conclusion.

THE OPERATION OF COLOMBIAN INSTITUTIONS: EVIDENCE FROM THE CASE STUDIES

The Institutions Studied

For reasons noted in chapter 2, five institutions that meet critical economic and social functions were analyzed: the stock market, the tax administration, the airport and air safety administration, the public health system, and the national postal service. To understand the findings of these case studies, it is necessary to first take a quick look at the characteristics and trajectories of these institutions, which in the Colombian context can be divided into three groups. First, we have institutions that have undergone rapid technological and organizational modernization, induced by external pressure. In this group are the Colombian stock exchange (Bolsa de Valores de Colombia [BVC]) and the civil aviation administration (Aerocivil). Second, the study included two declining institutions that were, in fact, in liquidation at the time of the study and recently disappeared. This category includes the Social Security Institute (Instituto de Seguros Sociales, ISS), which was for decades the entity responsible for administering the public health system, and the national postal administration (Adpostal). In an intermediate category is the National Tax and Customs Agency (Dirección de Impuestos y Aduanas Nacionales [DIAN]), which has been subject, simultaneously, to powerful pressures to strengthen and modernize and to pressures to maintain itself as a cronyist institution susceptible to corruption. Let us look at the outlines of the case studies based on this classification.

In the first group of institutions, the stock exchange is the clearest example of institutional transformation and strengthening of the sample. As documented in the case study (Rodríguez-Garavito 2009), the process that led to the consolidation of Colombia's regional stock exchanges into the BVC in 2001, as well as its subsequent technological and organizational updating, can be described as the change from a "gentlemen's club" to a global electronic trading platform. It is thus a case of institutional reinvention that has gradually replaced the mutualist model—in which the stock exchange was an exclusive area of interaction between social and economic elites—with a more open and anonymous market model. This has involved not only the entry of new members into the BVC (including financial players such as pension funds) but also the diversification of the instruments traded, to include, in addition to government bonds (which still occupy much of the transaction volume) and stocks, new instruments such as derivatives. In all these processes, the motivating forces have been competitive pressure from other players seeking to provide the same services as the BVC and the globalization of stock markets, which has accelerated the dissemination of technologies and organizational practices.

A similar shift, although more gradual and ambiguous, is evident in the case study of Aerocivil, the civil aviation administration (Hernández 2009). Given the pressure of international risk level ratings, Aerocivil has adapted its internal structure and protocols to follow international practices. An example is the strengthening of staff training through the creation of the Center for Aeronautical Studies in the mid-1990s. Hernández's ethnography and surveys show, however, that institutional change has been much more limited in terms of its airport management function, as illustrated by Aerocivil's chaotic management of the bidding and construction of the country's main airport in Bogotá.

In stark contrast to these two cases, the study of Adpostal, the national postal administration, is, as the author puts it, the story of the institution's "life, passion, and death" (Díaz 2009). It could be called a slow but sure death because, since its inception in the 1920s, the postal administration has faced a rival that its equivalents in most Latin American countries have not: the challenges of Colombian geography. Hence, from the beginning, Adpostal had to literally use mules to reach the most difficult parts of the country, while profitable market segments were occupied early on by private airlines. Dedicated to providing a monopoly "social mail" service that reached remote areas and zones affected by political violence, which private companies were not interested in serving, Adpostal became a pachyderm organization, resistant to subsequent attempts at modernization. Without a profitable business and with a stagnant bureaucracy and unsustainable pension liabilities, Adpostal succumbed to private competition and a wave of state reforms in the 1990s. It was finally liquidated in 2006.

The case study of the Social Security Institute is also an obituary, as suggested by Díaz's (2008) García Marquezian description, the "chronicle of a death foretold," of this institution. The history of the ISS's decline follows the mold of many public service institutions in the neoliberal era in Latin America. By the early nineties, the ISS, despite having several excellent hospitals (such as San Pedro Claver Clinic, the focus of Díaz's ethnography), had accumulated substantial losses and pension liabilities. Because of this, it was one of the favorite targets of the wave of privatizations and reforms undertaken by the government of President César Gaviria. In 1993, with legislation establishing a new health system (Law 100), the ISS was faced with competition from private companies, which quickly occupied the most lucrative segments of the health insurance market. To the problems of bureaucracy and stagnation that the ISS already had, these developments added increasing insolvency, which ultimately led to the liquidation of the agency in 2010.

Finally, the study of the National Tax and Customs Agency shows an intermediate scenario, oscillating between modernization and patronage (Rodríguez-Garavito and Rodríguez Franco 2008). Regarding the process of modernization, the DIAN itself was created through the merger of two entities as part of the institutional reforms that marked the turning of the Colombian state and economy toward the Washington Consensus in the early nineties (Edwards and Steiner 2008). Since then, it has gone through processes of profound technological and cultural transformation. On the technological front, DIAN has automated its procedures and methods of detecting tax evasion. Culturally, it has promoted an internal change, from viewing the citizen as a potential tax evader to viewing the citizen as a "customer," as well as an external transformation (through media campaigns against tax evasion). Despite progress on these fronts, the case study shows that modernization in the DIAN is still accompanied by entrenched patterns of corruption and cronyism, which are fed by massive inflows of legal and illegal money related to the major task of the institution, which is the control of evasion and smuggling.

With this overview as the backdrop, in the following pages I focus on the issues of interest to this book and attempt a systematic comparison of the results of the case studies. In line with the volume's analytic framework (see chapter 2), in order to explain the two outcomes of interest—the correlation between an organization's institutional rules and practice on the one hand and the institution's contribution to national development on the other—it is necessary to consider both internal and external independent variables. In addition to serving as a map of the empirical work on each of the institutions, these variables provide an axis of comparison and the means for synthesizing the findings from the case studies. This is the task undertaken in this section, in which I discuss the evidence and trends that arise from the comparison of the institutions. Tables 2.2 and 2.3, above, report the scores of the six independent variables and the two dependent variables for the Colombian institutions.

Meritocracy

The empirical findings show a tendency toward the absence of meritocratic mechanisms in Colombian institutions. In fact, three of the five institutions studied—the

ISS, the DIAN, and Adpostal—scored 2 (of 5) on the continuous scale and 0 (absence) on the binary scale. In the studies of ISS and Adpostal, Díaz (2008, 2009) collected numerous testimonies that point to a need for "political friends in high places" in order to be appointed or promoted. Furthermore, a former director of DIAN, writing her memoirs after leaving the institution, vividly portrayed the influence of patronage in the appointment and promotion of officials:

> To get congressional support, the government invented the diabolical figure of the temporary employees ("supernumeraries") of the DIAN, which were fixed-term positions distributed among politicians. They started with 300 temps, and after my three years there, there were 2,000 of them spread across the country. There are freely appointed and removable officials that have become indispensable to the administration of the organization, but their appointment is polluted by the politicking. Many of them helped, learned, and wanted to stay but after a year were rotated out for someone else with backing from some politician. Those were the positions that politicians had their eyes on, because the Ministry of Finance no longer had anything interesting to distribute. (Kertzman 2007: 138)

This trend contrasts with data from the studies of Aerocivil and the BVC. The former had high levels of meritocracy (4 of 5) because of its setup as a classic Weberian public bureaucracy with detailed rules for compensation and promotion (Hernández 2009). The same level of meritocracy is found in the BVC but for different reasons related to the private nature of the institution. Although the BVC's rules are informal, the performance and the external image of the entity's management corroborate what was said by the officials interviewed, that is, that technical competence is a central criterion of hiring and promotion. For example, in the words of its president, relating to bureaucratic matters, "the stock exchange works as a private company. It has competitive wages and, due to its current visibility, it is not difficult to get good people" with the necessary qualifications to fill vacancies (Rodríguez-Garavito 2009: 22).

Immunity to Corruption

The immunity to corruption variable repeats the previous trend: the same three institutions (DIAN, Adpostal, and ISS) are highly permeable (2 of 5) to corruption, whereas the BVC and Aerocivil are relatively immune. However, the latter two—with a score of 3 of 5—are less immune to corruption than they are meritocratic, making the average of this variable lower than the previous one. In fact, this variable has the second lowest average in the analysis (2.3), suggesting that permeability of Colombian institutions to various forms of corruption is a substantial problem.

Indeed, the comparison of the three institutions permeated by corruption reveals an interesting fact: each is captured by different combinations of the legal and illegal forces that meddle in Colombian institutions. The DIAN has been infiltrated by political sectors that use it for patronage and by intermediaries who, having worked there, conduct illegal activities and make "arrangements" to eliminate and evade sanctions and investigations (Rodríguez-Garavito and Rodríguez Franco 2008). Meanwhile, the ISS has been exposed to a combination of political patronage, capture by illegal armed actors (especially right-wing paramilitary groups, which have tended to control health systems in the vast territories they have controlled), and internal corruption of officials and union members (Díaz 2008). The postal service became victim of a combination of patronage and crimes committed by its own employees, as evidenced by Díaz´s (2009) telling finding on the internal looting of packages and letters by officials.

Absence of "Islands of Power"

The clear trend of the Colombian institutions surveyed is the absence of internal power structures or "cliques" that may impede their operation and divert institutional objectives. Indeed, four of five organizations received acceptable scores (3–4) in this variable. The exception is the DIAN, which is controlled by two groups of this type. The first are career officials who have special contractual arrangements and therefore cannot be dismissed but rather are constantly repositioned in the face of acts of venality and inefficiency. The other are members of the Legal Office, who exercise considerable power through their judgment of individual cases using their discretion to define the meaning of the labyrinthine Colombian tax code.

Proactivity

From the work of Evans (1989, 1995) on developmental states in Southeast Asia in contrast to Latin American and African states, the consensus in the sociology of development is that the internal mechanisms of an ideal Weberian bureaucracy are not sufficient to drive the process of national development. In fact, a unique conclusion of this project is that, of all the variables analyzed, proactivity seems to be the key factor for an institution to contribute to national development (see Portes and Smith 2010).

In this sense, it is noteworthy that this is precisely the variable in which the Colombian organizations obtained the lowest average (2.2). With the exception of the DIAN (which barely got an acceptable 3 of 5 rating), all the organizations analyzed were below the threshold that would qualify them as proactive. Colombian organizations are characterized by their tendency to look inward, either because their ties with society at large are weak and marked by patronage (as in the case of Adpostal and the public health system) or because there is not an organizational strategy of cooperation with relevant actors (as in the cases of BVC and Aerocivil), which makes them reactive and limits their contribution to development.

Technological Flexibility

The clear movement of the organizations studied is toward technological and managerial innovation, largely as a form of adaptation to national and international competitive pressures. For example, four of the five organizations surveyed obtained a 1 on the binary scale and between 3 and 5 on the continuous scale, making flexibility and innovation the variable with the highest average (3.6). BVC and Aerocivil both obtained relatively high scores, as did the ISS, which, despite its organizational decline, continued to incorporate new technologies into high-performing hospitals. The only exception to the trend is Adpostal, whose long-standing failure to modernize was accentuated in the period before its liquidation (Díaz 2009).

BVC and Aerocivil are the most evident examples of the innovative trend. As noted, in the past decade the BVC has become a global platform for trading financial instruments, and in the words of its former commercial vice president, it "has been able to reinvent itself" in a short time and on several fronts simultaneously (Rodríguez-Garavito 2009: 11). Meanwhile, Aerocivil showed a tendency to continuously update its physical capital and staff training, in large part to meet international standards governing the certification of officials and airports (Hernández 2009).

External Allies

In relation to the last independent variable, the clear trend of the organizations studied is the absence of external allies. In fact, most of them (Adpostal, DIAN, and Aerocivil) operate in the midst of a fragmented state apparatus that provides no reliable allies. This is particularly visible in the case of the DIAN, for whom the Ministry of Finance, its potential support within the state apparatus, has been a fickle ally.

The ISS is the only institution that has an acceptable external counterbalance, largely due to the support that national trade unions provide to the entity's unions on issues such as opposing liquidation of the organization. Again, the BVC is the exception to the rule, in large part because powerful outside agencies and groups, from the Finance Ministry to the financial sector itself, have an interest in its proper operation.

CORRESPONDENCE BETWEEN ORGANIZATIONAL OPERATION AND INSTITUTIONAL GOALS

The first outcome of interest is how close organizations are to their stated mission and rules. The evidence reinforces the division of the organizations studied into two groups. On the one hand, the BVC and Aerocivil again receive scores indicating that, in practice, they generally comply with their own rules. In that sense, for these two organizations, there is clear correspondence with their respective institutional blueprints. This is possible because, as Hernández (2009) notes, at Aerocivil there is widespread awareness among its staff about the organizational structures of the institution, and the staff closely follows the agency's governing rules.

On the other hand, we again have the underperforming group DIAN, Adpostal, and the ISS. DIAN's failure to execute its institutional expectations is mainly due to the slow progress of organizational modernization and the integration of its tax and customs functions, which maintain its status as a hybrid organization in limbo between modernization and clientelism. For Adpostal and ISS, the low value of this variable is not surprising given that these organizations were in a process of terminal decline, as shown by the telling quote of an Adpostal regional manager on first joining the organization: "I found a dead company, a dump, with the sad spectacle of a culture of waste. . . . [T]here was no business vision, no evaluation of results, no quality of service. . . . Officials were tired and inflexible, and these are factors that make a company stagnate" (quoted in Díaz 2009: 309).

DRAWING CONCLUSIONS FROM THE CASE STUDIES: A TYPOLOGY OF COLOMBIAN INSTITUTIONS AND THEIR CONTRIBUTION TO DEVELOPMENT

Beyond correspondence between the institutional blueprints and organizational realities, the key outcome of interest is whether organizations contribute to development in their economic and social field. The results of the Colombian case studies in this regard are unequivocal: none of the organizations—not even those with acceptable scores on the other variables—contributed to development.

Given the results on other variables, this conclusion is predictable for the group of less Weberian and proactive institutions (DIAN, ISS, and Adpostal). However, the conclusion requires additional explanation in the cases of the other two institutions. The evidence on the stock exchange is illustrative. Although the BVC can be characterized as a Weberian organization, it makes a negligible contribution to development insofar as it continues to promote only a modest stock market and corporate bonds market that include few publicly listed firms. Taking into account that in 2006 only ten of the one hundred largest companies in the country traded their shares on the stock exchange, it can be concluded that the BVC has yet to fulfill its mission of contributing to development "by channeling savings into productive investment" (Rodríguez-Garavito 2009: 253). The contribution of this institution, therefore, consists mainly in the circulation of public bonds, which contributes to the financing of public spending but has no clear positive impact on development itself.

If this conclusion for the BVC is taken together with evidence from the other Weberian institution in the sample, Aerocivil, an interesting corollary can be drawn: although the two generally correspond to the ideal type of rational bureaucracy, they also have in common that they are reactive in relations with actors in their field. In other words, the lack of proactivity is the common feature that prevents them from contributing to development. Therefore, the Colombian cases analyzed provide evidence for the general conclusion of the project in relation to proactivity as the essential determinant of developmental outcomes.

This finding has broader implications, which have been discussed in other studies in the sociology of development. Especially relevant is Evans's (1989, 1995) well-known thesis of the combination of bureaucratic rationality and proactivity—what he calls "embedded autonomy"—as a requirement for a developmental institution. I propose, then, to use and adapt this thesis to generate a typology that allows us to pinpoint the Colombian institutions and draw preliminary conclusions from the findings.

This typology arises from the two analytic axes proposed by Evans—bureaucratic rationality and proactivity—which are directly associated, respectively, with the internal and external variables examined in the previous section. On the one hand, the internal variables (meritocracy, immunity to corruption, and lack of islands of power) indicate the degree of bureaucratic rationality of the institution. As noted by Wright (1996) in his review of Evans's work, these are the Weberian features of the typology. On the other hand, the external variables (especially proactivity and the presence of external allies) have to do with the degree of institutional embeddedness in the power structure. As suggested by Wright (1996) again, these bring into the discussion Marxian insight about the importance of the class structure.

Table 5.1 combines these analytic categories to clarify the typology proposed by Evans and to adjust it to the analysis of case studies. In doing so, I adopt the modification proposed by Portes (2006) and call the external variable "proactivity," rather than "embeddedness," to avoid confusing it with the Granovetter's (1985) use of the term.

As shown in table 5.1, in order for an institution to contribute to national development, it must have a rational bureaucracy and be proactive in dealing with actors in its field. The opposite situation is that of a "predatory" institution that hinders development by lacking a modern bureaucracy and being isolated from its surroundings. The two intermediate cases—clientelist and reactive institutions—yield, at best, modest contributions to development and, at worst, institutional drags on development. The scores assigned to each institution (see tables 2.2 and 2.3, above) in the variables of bureaucratic rationality (A–C) and in the proactivity variable (D) allow us to locate the Colombian organizations in this conceptual space. Starting at the bottom left and going counterclockwise, the first issue

TABLE 5.1 Evans's Institutional Typology

		Bureaucratic Rationality	
		HIGH	LOW
Proactivity	HIGH	Developmentalist Institution	Clientelistic Institution (DIAN)
	LOW	Reactive Institution (BVC, Aerocivil)	Predatory Institution (ISS, Adpostal)

SOURCE: Adapted from Evans 1989, 1995.

that the typology helps clarify is the nature of the two institutions that, despite conforming to the Weberian ideal type, do not make significant contributions to national development due to their lack of proactivity. As mentioned, these institutions are the BVC and Aerocivil, which, in the proposed classification, fit the ideal type of *reactive institutions.*

The reverse case is DIAN, the only proactive institution in the sample, which nevertheless lacks the rules and structures of a Weberian organization. Evans's conceptual framework identifies the DIAN as a *clientelistic institution* whose proactivity is muddled by the pervasiveness of biased and even corrupt ties, typical of a political patronage system. Finally, the cases of the ISS and Adpostal fit neatly into the category of *predatory institutions,* which lack both bureaucratic rationality and proactivity. In fact, the case studies of the two entities, carried out during institutional decline and liquidation, show extreme situations of graft and lawlessness. No example can be given for the category of *developmentalist institutions.* Therefore, the study suggests that the combination of bureaucratic rationality and proactivity seems quite elusive in Colombia.

Our case studies offer detailed evidence of the Colombian paradox while also complicating it. In the next section, I turn to considering what the empirical findings tell us about this central theme of the ongoing academic and political social science discussion on Colombian developments.

THE COLOMBIAN PARADOX IN LIGHT OF THICK INSTITUTIONALISM

Is There a Paradox?

Unlike the vast majority of the literature on Colombian institutions, the case studies discussed here offer detailed evidence on individual organizations.[5] With these data in hand, how should we view existing characterizations and explanations of the Colombian paradox? Does the new evidence sustain, dissolve, or transform the paradox? To answer this question, let us begin by briefly recalling how the paradox has been characterized in the literature. Pizarro (2004), picking up the discussion on the subject, has formulated the paradox synthetically, in terms of the coexistence of three features. First, by Latin American standards, Colombia has exceptional macroeconomic stability and stable economic management institutions. Second, democratic institutions are also remarkably stable. Third, in contrast to the factors above, Colombia has one of the highest levels of violence in the world.

The first two features presuppose the existence of relatively stable and functional institutions, at least compared to the rest of the region. It is a widely shared assumption in Colombia, as suggested by Hirschman's cited defense of the Colombian technocracy or by Malcolm Deas's (1993: 207) argument that Colombian institutions have enabled "more elections, under more systems (central and federal, direct and indirect, hegemonic and proportional) and with greater consequences, than any other American or European country."

How does this widespread perception of high quality and the positive effects of Colombian institutions fit with the far less flattering portrait that emerges from the case studies? There are at least three answers to this question. The first holds that this perception has no empirical support and that, in fact, the country's institutions are more precarious than scholars of Colombia (and Colombians) have imagined. This line of explanation has recent support from the batteries of international indicators that have been developed to measure the quality of institutions: from the World Bank Good Governance Index (Kaufman, Kraay, and Mastuzzi 2009) to various indices of "failed states" developed by institutions such as *Foreign Policy* magazine[6] and the Interstate Conflict Program at Harvard University (Rotberg 2003). The most critical scenario is drawn by the indicators of failed states. In the most well known scenario (*Foreign Policy*'s), Colombia appeared in 2010 as the Latin American country with the highest score on the "state failure" scale and was ranked 40 globally, only behind Haiti in the hemisphere. Among the five countries included in our comparative study, only Colombia qualified as "at risk" of failure.

This same conclusion has been advocated by several political scientists, who classify Colombia as a "state on route towards failure" (Mason 2000). This conclusion is supported by other evidence, such as the World Bank index measuring "political stability" as a component of "good government," which places Colombia at the bottom of the regional group.[7]

These indices have been rightly criticized for their prescriptive bias and for arbitrarily combining diverse data sources.[8] In fact, in terms of methodology, these indices are the antithesis of the kind of careful empirical work that thick institutionalism proposes. I allude to them, however, because they have become influential in the debate on institutions and because they point to the first alternative explanation for the poor performance of Colombia in the case studies—that the Colombian institutions are actually much less solid than has been believed.

A second explanation is that the image of institutional uncertainty arising from the case studies is due to the specific sample of organizations analyzed. One could argue that the sample selected, by including two institutions that were in liquidation (Adpostal and ISS), introduced a bias in the results that does not reflect the general, more favorable, situation of institutions in the country. In support of this view, there are also quantitative data extracted from the battery of institutional indicators that contrast with the figures in our case studies. For example, according to Transparency International's Corruption Perception Index, among the sample countries, Colombia has the second best score, beating Mexico, the Dominican Republic, and Argentina.[9] Colombia also compares favorably with most of the other countries on indicators of rule of law, regulatory quality, and government effectiveness that contribute to the World Bank's Good Governance Index.[10] These indicators again support the existence of the Colombian paradox.

Bejarano and Pizarro (2004) have proposed an intermediate characterization of state institutions in Colombia, which offers a third alternative explanation for the results of our case studies. For them, Colombian institutions do not represent a collective collapse or a model of rationality and capacity. They argue that in Colombia there has been a situation of "partial collapse of the state," in which "institutions cracked" from the double war against guerrillas and drug trafficking but that this outcome has coexisted with other institutions that "have preserved remarkable strength and stability" (Pizarro 2004: 215).

In my view, this intermediate thesis best explains the mixed evidence of the case studies and of international measures of institutional quality. For example, as seen in table 5.1, alongside predatory institutions such as the ISS and Adpostal, there are Weberian institutions like the BVC and Aerocivil, as well as clientelist institutions, like DIAN. Furthermore, the scores of the controversial international indices show dissimilarities between, for example, the weakness of institutions such as the police and the strength of institutions such as the high courts or the banks.

The thesis of the partial collapse of the state, however, falls short both analytically and descriptively. In analytic terms, it supports the coexistence of weak institutions and strong ones without explaining exactly what this phenomenon is and why it occurs. In descriptive terms, the thesis adopts the political science emphasis on state institutions and, therefore, does not tell us much about the fate of social institutions (from voluntary associations to the stock market) in the midst of the "double war" in Colombia. The tools of thick institutionalism can help fill these gaps. Thick institutionalism can help clarify what the collapse of institutions means, and in what sense it is partial, by providing detailed evidence of the operation of institutions (both state and nonstate).

In the next section, I use the findings of the current study to address these gaps. I argue that the coexistence of organizational strength and precariousness is due to the profound differences between the center and the periphery in the Colombian institutional field, allowing even a single institution to be "Weberian" in the center and "predatory" in the periphery. It is thus a quite uneven institutional field, with niches of excellence in political and economic centers connected to a network of highly unstable peripheral ones. I close the analysis with a brief reference to the factors that help explain this cleavage.

The Asymmetry of Colombian Institutions

The ethnographies of the organizations studied illustrate in detail the division between center and periphery. The most obvious case is the stock market, whose sphere of action is limited to a small capital market and confined to urban areas of the country's legal economy. Even in these centers, the BVC is relevant only to a small number of economic actors who issue or trade shares. In fact, a recurring comment by interviewees was that the market served by the BVC is very small and that there is deep reluctance, even among companies in large urban centers, to issue publicly traded shares (Rodríguez-Garavito 2009). Therefore, the strongest organization in the Colombian study—the one with clear Weberian traits, openness to innovation, and external allies—is a good example of the asymmetry of the Colombian institutional field: a combination of excellence in a geographic niche and irrelevance in the majority of the country.

Among organizations with national presence, those that most vividly illustrate this inequality between center and periphery are Adpostal and the DIAN. The conclusion of the ethnography on Adpostal is telling: "the Colombian public postal service had no role in the process of unifying the nation" (Díaz 2009: 292). Since its inception in the 1920s, the postal service split, closely following the boundary lines between center and periphery. As cities and central markets were served by private companies that provided efficient service, remote areas and the areas in the midst of armed conflict were covered by the state's "social mail." This division of labor and territory condemned Adpostal financially, so that the wave of privatizations of the nineties arrived without there being a public postal service to defend. The case of Adpostal is particularly informative because it is a service that in many other countries has been the symbol of national territorial integration. Moreover, it shows that the Colombian institutional asymmetry is not a new phenomenon but lies in the very origins of the institutions of the state and modern society.

The case of the DIAN is equally revealing. In fact, it embodies the institutional hybridity of clientelism—which connects and oscillates between Weberianness and looting, between center and periphery—which, I argue, is the dominant form in Colombia and gives shape to the idea of the partial collapse of institutions. The ethnography of the DIAN shows that it is an organization permeated by two contradictory forces. On the one hand, it is undergoing a modernization process that involves profound technological transformation, as well as a cultural reinvention in the direction of customer service and the promotion of a fiscal civic culture. On the other hand, it has been subject to capture by internal and external mafias made up of powerful actors—from politicians who demand their cut of the agency's payroll to former officials who act as intermediaries to promote illegal "fixes" to highly organized criminal groups. As stated by a former director of the organization who was interviewed for this study, "The problem is very serious because the tax and customs institution is a favorite prey, not only of criminals, but of businessmen."[11]

Thus the DIAN is an icon of the clientelist hybridity of Colombian institutions and of their territorial asymmetry. Anyone who comes to one of its offices in cities like Bogotá, Medellín, or Cali will find modern facilities and efficient service protocols designed for customer service. However, those with access to the contraband checkpoints will find the typical practices and culture of the border areas, where, as García and his collaborators (2009a) have recently shown, corruption is rife and opportunism normative. In view of this, the analytic question is, what is the dividing line between the institutional center and the periphery? As suggested by the case studies and related research, the center-periphery boundary does *not* mechanically follow other conventional divisions, such as that between urban and rural areas. This is mainly due to the geography of drug trafficking and armed conflict, whose contours cross the urban-rural divide and generate their own logic.

Indeed, while Colombian institutions operated in the first half of the twentieth century at the pace of a coffee economy (Berquist 1986), beginning in the seventies they evolved under the growing influence of the mining and cocaine economies (Gutiérrez 2007). This shift coincided with the strategy adopted by guerrilla groups in the early eighties—which had traditionally operated in scarcely populated areas where the state never had a significant presence—to make a leap toward economic regions where the mining and coca booms had occurred. In these new areas, guerilla groups began extracting large incomes through direct involvement in the business of blackmailing producers (Pizarro 2004). Hence, as Echandía (1999) has proven, guerrilla expansion since then has taken place in regions that produce gold, coca, coal, oil, and bananas.

This economic shift overlapped with the expansion of right-wing paramilitary groups—private armies funded by drug traffickers and landowners who disputed territories and economic niches with the guerrillas, often in alliance with political elites and the military (Gutiérrez and Barón 2006; Romero 2002). These developments were central in the composition of the current center-periphery structure. Although there is no accurate map of this geography, a good proxy is electoral risk maps, drawn on reliable data from across the country. For the purposes of this chapter, these maps are useful because (1) they trace threats against a specific institution, the electoral system, which plays a key societal and political role; and (2) they examine risks associated both with corrupt practices (e.g., vote buying) and patterns of violence (e.g., presence of guerrilla armies, paramilitaries, and/or the mafia). The maps, therefore, offer an approximation of the risks of capture faced by other public institutions.

Figure 5.1 presents this map, prepared prior to the 2011 elections for mayors and governors. The map shows a capillary geography traversed by elements of crime and violence, with "blood vessels" running through most of the country. The territories at risk (medium, high, or extreme) include not only remote areas where the state and institutions of the legal economy have little historical presence (such as the Amazon region and the northern Pacific Coast) but also thriving urban areas where generators of corruption and violence exercise influence on a large scale (e.g., cities like Medellín, Montería, and Santa Marta, where mafia groups act like states within the state).

In the specific realm of the electoral system, the map reveals the contrast between a few centers of institutional strength (where there are not significant risks and free voting is common) and extensive peripheries of institutional uncertainty (where the risks are considerable and vote patronage and forced voting are abundant). In the latter, institutional weakness and the illegal and criminal economies feed on each other, with profound implications for the performance of organizations. Congress is the most visible example of this combination. In the 2006 elections the mixture of political patronage and illegal power—commonly referred to as armed clientelism—led to the election of a Congress in which 40 percent of its members ultimately were investigated, prosecuted, or convicted by the Supreme Court on charges of links with paramilitary groups (*Semana* 2009).

A similar map can be drawn for other institutional fields, such as those discussed in our case studies. A particularly revealing one is the public health system, whose budget became the favorite bankroll of armed clientelism, with disastrous consequences for organizational performance and service delivery. As documented by Díaz in her ethnography:

> The country has always known that health system money was one of the most desirable bankrolls of paramilitaries in their zones of influence, to the extent that some leaders were sort of "shadow administrators" [of the health system]. . . . In the Eastern Plains, [a health company controlled by the paramilitaries] reached 24,000 members between 2002 and 2005, and at least 12% of the proceeds of the area went to the main paramilitary organization, the United Self-Defense Forces of Colombia [AUC]. Given this situation, the emphasis on patients, especially those with high-cost illnesses, suffered greatly. (2008: 25)

The case studies and other investigations provide evidence of similar patterns in other institutions. For example, the DIAN, as we observed, is highly susceptible to corruption in geographic and economic frontier regions. The incidents of corruption in Aerocivil are associated with bribes paid by drug traffickers to ensure

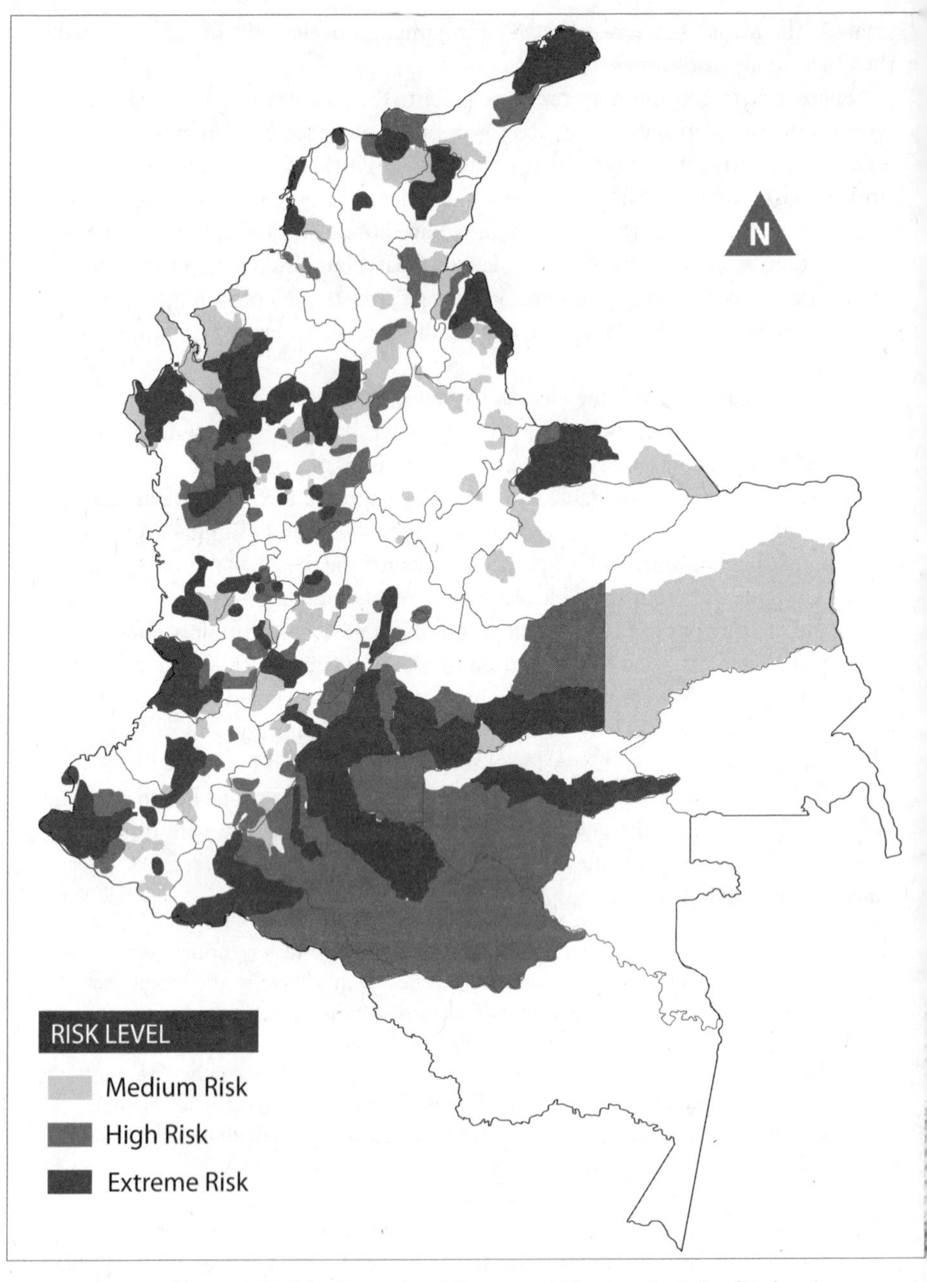

FIGURE 5.1. Electoral Risk for Mayors' and Governors' Elections in Colombia (2011). Source: Misión de Observación Electoral (2011).

that officials do not report flights originating in the areas of narcotics cultivation and processing. In addition, sociological research on the judicial system has shown the coexistence of highly competent and independent courts (located in the light-colored areas of the institutional map) with judges without state support operating in the "red zones" and at the mercy of local de facto powers (García 2009b).

In sum, the Colombian institutional field is marked by a noticeable asymmetry stemming from the combination of five factors. First, the country's complex geography has encouraged the formation of different economies and institutional practices. As documented by historians (Safford and Palacio 2001) and illustrated by Díaz's (2009) ethnography of Adpostal, the three Andean mountain ranges that begin in the south and cross the entire country and the extensive wilderness areas have been formidable barriers to communication and to building a national economy and an institutional apparatus. Second, the Colombian state has never had the monopoly of force throughout the territory. State institutions, therefore, have coexisted or have been superseded by other armed bureaucracies (guerrillas, paramilitaries, drug and emerald traffickers, settler gangs in frontier zones, etc.) that have historically controlled large parts of the territory.

Third, in the past four decades, the economic and cultural logic of drug trafficking has permeated many social institutions, from the political parties to the family, the economy, the media, and the legal system. Fourth, the tradition of patronage of political parties, which has remained stable since the nineteenth century, has left its mark in the modus operandi not only of state institutions such as the ISS, the DIAN, Aerocivil, and Adpostal but also of Colombian society at large. Finally, Colombia is characterized by high and persistent socioeconomic inequality, with a Gini coefficient of 0.59 in 2008, thus ranking as the second most unequal country in Latin America after Brazil (ECLAC 2010). In this context, institutional asymmetry is both a determinant and a result of gaps among classes and regions. If this characterization of Colombian institutions is correct, what are the effects on national development? I close the analysis by addressing this question and formulating a hypothesis about the relationship between institutions and development in the country.

Solving the Paradox? Clientelism as Institutional Equilibrium in Colombia

The sociology of development provides a useful theoretical framework to analyze this relationship from the perspective of thick institutionalism (Evans 1995; Portes 2006). I return to the typology in table 5.1, which classifies institutions according to their degree of bureaucratic rationality and proactivity and distinguishes four categories of institutions: developmentalist, reactive, clientelistic, and predatory. While institutions of the first type make a clear contribution to development, those fitting the last category are powerful obstacles to that end. The effect of intermediate categories (reactive and clientelistic institutions) is less clear, ranging from a modest boost to the hampering of economic and social development.

In light of the characterization made in the previous section, what kind of institution predominates in Colombia? I argue that the empirical evidence accumulated in studies of various institutions, not just those analyzed in this project, but also other studies such as those on political parties (Gutiérrez 2007) and the judicial system (García 2009b), point to *clientelism* as the dominant institutional form. In this regard, the combination found in the DIAN—proactivity and lack of bureaucratic rationality—seems to be the one that best fits the characteristics of the asymmetrical institutional field in Colombia. I thus hypothesize that future thick institutionalist ethnographies will repeatedly find the same modality in different social fields.

This argument finds support in quantitative analyses that have characterized Colombian institutions against the backdrop of other Latin American countries. Carey and Shugart (1995) have shown that Colombian institutions (specifically the electoral system) are the closest to the clientelistic model of all the countries in the region. And a host of other studies have reached a similar conclusion with regard to the political system as a whole (Deas 1993; Duarte 2003; Leal and Dávila 1990; Martz 1997). The hypothesis regarding clientelism as the dominant institutional arrangement also finds particularly strong support in Robinson's (2007) work addressing the question of the relationship between institutions and economic development in Colombia and comparing it to the developmental trajectories of other Latin American countries. In examining the historical data, Robinson concludes that Colombia is a "normal Latin American country," as its economic performance with regard to key indicators (e.g., GDP per capita and income distribution) has been very close to the regional average. Aware of the Colombian paradox, he also highlights the exceptional macroeconomic stability of the country and the absence of populist episodes throughout the nation's history.

How is the "normal" related to the "exceptional" in Colombia's economic and institutional trajectory? Robinson's answer is that clientelism has provided a functional equivalent to the role that populism has played in other Latin American countries. Clientelism embodies an institutional equilibrium that reconciles the interests of elites and those of citizens, at the cost of producing inefficiency in the provision of "micro public goods" (health care, tax collection, education, roads, etc.). By working through well-established patron-client networks (within political parties, community organizations, state agencies, etc.), clientelism redistributes wealth piecemeal from the elite to the citizens while ensuring the continuing dominance of the former. Populism also achieves an institutional equilibrium between citizens' and the elite's interests but does it so through macroeconomic measures (e.g., price controls, manipulation of the exchange rate, and salary raises) that redistribute income to key political constituencies. Thus it generates inefficiency in the provision of "macro public goods" (price stability, prudent debt policy, etc.). Both clientelism and populism are socially wasteful but offer institutional arrangements that can be stable and attractive for elites and citizens (Robinson 2007).

Why has clientelism taken root in Colombia while populism has predominated elsewhere in Latin America? Robinson offers a plausible hypothesis: the long endurance of the Colombian two-party system (which reigned supreme for 150 years, from the mid-nineteenth century through the turn of the twenty-first century) and the capacity of elites to control and co-opt dissidents led to the growth of extensive social networks for delivering patronage. Building such networks takes time and money on the part of elites. Thus they are unavailable to dissident parties and political newcomers—like those that have emerged in other countries in the region where party systems have been more volatile. Under the latter circumstances, populism, which does not require extensive social networks and can be put in motion by macroeconomic policies established by decree, becomes a politically attractive strategy for political elites to gain citizen support.

Robinson's work offers a useful analytic framework and a convincing case for the characterization of the Colombian institutions that I have extracted from the case studies and the literature on the sociology of development. However, given its analytic focus, it fails to address two key sets of questions that emerge from the discussion in this chapter. First, how is clientelism related to the asymmetry we have observed in Colombian institutions? How does it help explain the fact that they operate differently in the center and the peripheries of the institutional field? Second, how does electoral clientelism affect the operation of other institutions? How do they permeate other public and private organizations given the extensiveness and endurance of patron-client networks?

With regard to the first set of questions, data from the case studies and other ethnographies point to a connection between clientelism and institutional asymmetry. I argue that patron-client ties function not only as the coordinating mechanism of actors and interests in the red zones of highest institutional precariousness (e.g., those where patronage voting predominates), but as a coordination mechanism *between* central and peripheral areas of the institutional field. As shown by Gutiérrez (2007) in his study of the Liberal Party, this is the way the most powerful party in Colombian politics has operated. Through patronage networks, the party has connected a "decent elite" of modern, technocratic politicians from the urban aristocracy and a "gangster elite" of electoral barons in the Colombian periphery in charge of obtaining the required votes through corrupt practices. We observed a similar pattern in the quintessential clientelistic institution in our sample, the DIAN, whose core staff includes both a specialized technocracy and political appointees embedded in the same clientelistic networks that dominate the organization in the periphery. Thus clientelistic networks constitute the organizational infrastructure that allows for the coexistence of and connection between markedly different institutional realities in the center and the periphery.

As for the second set of questions, the case studies suggest that clientelistic networks indeed reach beyond electoral institutions (e.g., political parties) and that they influence the operational logic of organizations in different social fields, from firms to community associations. Most of the institutional ethnographies offer evidence of the existence of such networks in state agencies, ranging from the postal service (where "having friends in high places" was key to securing a position) to numerous pockets of clientelism within the DIAN and the public health system. Given that there was only one private institution in the sample (the stock exchange) and that the literature is lacking in ethnographies of other private organizations, the hypothesized impact of clientelism in the private sector has yet to be fully examined.

Finally, Robinson's explanation of the predominance of clientelism in Colombia is challenged by recent developments in Colombian politics, which are worth addressing briefly. If the reason for clientelism is the endurance of the two-party system, will this institutional equilibrium be destabilized by the recent crisis of this system? Beginning in the 1990s and taking earnest hold in the 2002 elections, the qualitative shift in Colombian politics has been the success of "transitional" candidates, that is, those who made a career in the traditional parties but left them to run as independents or establish a new party (Gutiérrez 2007; Rodríguez-Garavito 2008). The key transitional figure is former President Álvaro Uribe, who won the 2002 elections as a dissident from the Liberal Party and managed to get a constitutional amendment passed to get reelected in 2006. In addition to shattering the two-party system, the Uribe government implemented aggressive security policies that extended the presence of the military to some of the areas of the country that had hitherto remained under the control of the guerrillas. In so doing, the political right partially countered one of the above-mentioned conditions that underlie institutional asymmetry in the country, that is, the lack of territorial control by the state.

In light of the argument advanced in this chapter and of Robinson's explanation, it stands to reason that in the face of the erosion of these two conditions (a closed two-party system and limited state control over the territory), institutional asymmetry and clientelism would also be undermined. In practice, however, the results of these qualitative shifts have been (again) paradoxical: they have reinforced, rather than weakened, clientelistic practices. Instead of replacing clientelism with another institutional equilibrium (e.g., populism), transitional politicians and parties have become more deeply embedded in and dependent on regional clientelistic networks. These are now influenced or controlled by right-wing paramilitary groups or mafia gangs that extract generous rents from the frontier economies and drug trafficking (Gutiérrez 2010). As developments in the Uribe administrations

(2002–8) bear witness, the outcome has been the expansion and consolidation of clientelism, both through the growing capture of key national institutions by the newly empowered regional mafias (from Congress[12] to the national intelligence agency [DAS])[13] and through "armed clientelism" in the periphery (Romero 2007).

CONCLUSION

In this chapter I have tried to bring into dialogue the findings of five case studies of specific institutions with the broader discussion on institutions and development in Colombia. To do so, I have used the theoretical and methodological tools of thick institutionalism, which offer a perspective that is simultaneously conceptually broader and empirically richer than the prevailing studies of institutions in other disciplines. For this reason, I have included in the analysis not only state institutions (as political science studies often do) but also institutions, such as the stock exchange, that operate in other social fields but have a direct impact on economic development.

With these tools, I sought to answer three questions: What characterizes Colombian institutions? What effect have they had on economic development? What do answers to these questions tell us about the "Colombian paradox" that dominates the literature? Regarding the first question, I have argued that the evidence shows that asymmetry is the defining feature of the Colombian institutional field, which combines small niches of excellence in the center and large areas of instability in the periphery. This hybridity can be seen in action within single institutions, as shown by the contrast between the modern face of the tax administration, the postal service, and the judiciary in the institutional centers and the precariousness of the same organizations in the periphery. I also argued that this asymmetry stems from a combination of social, economic, and political factors: the complex national geography, the economy's transition to resource extraction and drug trafficking, the existence of territories controlled by nonstate armed groups, political patronage, and socioeconomic inequality.

Regarding the relationship of this institutional landscape with economic development, and based on Evans's (1995) typology, I argued that the dominant institutional type in Colombia is clientelism: a combination of proactivity and lack of bureaucratic rationality that, although not corresponding to predatory or "failed" institutions, has contributed to the modest performance of the Colombian economy. Based on this argument, I hypothesize that future thick institutionalist analysis will find clientelistic patterns similar to those documented in the case study of the DIAN.

Finally, in relation to the Colombian paradox, I offered an intermediate response. Against the strong version of this paradox, which states that the Colombian institutions are of exceptional quality and stability in the Latin American context, I have offered evidence that in fact they are more precarious than scholars and Colombians themselves have imagined. Against the opposite view, which holds that Colombia is a "failed state" with collapsed institutions, I have shown that there are strong institutional niches embedded in transnational processes of managerial and technological modernization. In the middle, and in line with the institutional asymmetry thesis, I have shown that Colombian organizations are simultaneously solid in the institutional centers and precarious in the economic, political, and social peripheries. In addition, I have argued that clientelism serves as a form of suboptimal equilibrium that sustains and reproduces this asymmetry. It is a resilient equilibrium indeed, as shown by its remarkable stability in the face of qualitative changes in Colombian politics, economy, and society at the beginning of the century. Herein lies another Colombian paradox to decipher.

APPENDIX 5.1: INSTITUTIONAL STUDIES IN COLOMBIA

The reports on which this chapter is based are listed below with English translation of the original Spanish titles. The individual studies can be downloaded from the webpage of the Center for Migration and Development, Princeton University: http://cmd.princeton.edu.

Díaz, Luz Marina. "The Health Social Security System of Colombia."
———. "Life, Passion, and Death of the National Postal Administration of Colombia."
Hernández, Iván. "Institutional Analysis of Aerocivil in Colombia."
Rodríguez-Garavito, César. "From Gentlemen's Club to Electronic Market: An Institutional Analysis of the Stock Exchange of Colombia."
Rodríguez-Garavito, César, and Diana Rodríguez Franco. "Between Clientelism and Modernization: An Institutional Ethnography of Tax Administration in Colombia."

NOTES

1. Hirschman had a particular admiration for Carlos Lleras Restrepo, president of Colombia between 1966 and 1970. In 1963 he dedicated his book *Journeys towards Progress* to Lleras and Celso Furtado, calling them "master reformmongers." For Hirschman's experience in Colombia, see Caballero 2008.

2. The countries included in the project are Argentina, Chile, Colombia, Mexico, and the Dominican Republic.

3. The other countries were Mexico, Costa Rica, and Venezuela.

4. See, e.g., Kalmanovitz 2001; Pizarro 2004.

5. The most notable exception to this trend in the literature is Gutiérrez´s (2007) painstaking study of one of the key Colombian institutions, the Liberal Party. Gutiérrez combines historical research with qualitative and quantitative methods to produce a detailed institutional radiography with theoretical implications.

6. For more on this index, see www.foreignpolicy.com/chapters/2009/06/22/the_2009_failed_states_index.

7. See http://info.worldbank.org/governance/wgi/mc_chart.asp.

8. For criticisms of these and other similar indices, see Clapham 2004; Herbst 2004. See Tokatlián 2008 for an excellent critique of applying the concept to the Colombian case.

9. See www.transparency.org/news_room/in_focus/2008/cpi2008/espanol.

10. See http://info.worldbank.org/governance/wgi/mc_chart.asp.

11. Interview with Horacio Ayala (former director general of DIAN, May 12, 2008), quoted in Rodríguez-Garavito and Rodríguez Franco 2008.

12. It is estimated that in the 2006 elections, 33 senators (of 100) and 50 representatives of the Lower House (of 165) were elected in regions of the institutional periphery controlled by paramilitary groups (*Semana* 2009).

13. At the time of this writing, three former DAS directors were under judicial investigation based on abundant evidence that DAS had been captured by paramilitary groups and that it had orchestrated a multiyear campaign of espionage and defamation against independent journalists, opposition politicians, NGOs, union leaders, U.N. officials visiting the country, and numerous other political targets (*El Espectador* 2010).

REFERENCES

Avella, Mauricio. 2007. "El acceso de Colombia al financiamiento externo durante el siglo XX." In *Economía colombiana del siglo XX: Un análisis cuantitativo,* edited by J. Robinson and M. Urrutia, 518–84. Bogotá: Banco de la República and Fondo de Cultura Económica.

Bejarano, Ana María, and Eduardo Pizarro. 2004. "Colombia: The Partial Collapse of the State and the Emergence of Aspiring State-Makers." In *States within States: Incipient Political Entities in the Post-Cold World Era,* edited by P. Kingston and I. Spears, 99–118. New York: Palgrave.

Berquist, Charles. 1986. *Coffee and Conflict in Colombia, 1886–1910.* Durham: Duke University Press.

Burawoy, Michael. 1991. "The Extended Case Method." In *Ethnography Unbound: Power and Resistance in the Modern Metropolis,* edited by M. Burawoy, 271–85. Berkeley: University of California Press.

Caballero Argáez, Carlos. 2008. "Albert Hirschman en Colombia y la planeación del desarrollo." *Desarrollo y Sociedad* 62: 165–99.

Carey, John M., and Mathew S. Shugart. 1995. "Incentives to Cultivate a Personal Vote: A Rank-Ordering of Electoral Formulas." *Electoral Studies* 14: 417–39.

Clapham, Christopher. 2004. "The Global-Local Politics of State Decay." In *When States Fail: Causes and Consequences,* edited by R. Rotberg, 77–93. Princeton: Princeton University Press.

Deas, Malcom. 1993. *Del poder y la gramática, y otros ensayos sobre historia, política y literatura colombiana.* Bogotá: Tercer Mundo.

Díaz, Luz Marina. 2008. "La seguridad social en salud en Colombia." Final report to the project *Latin American Institutions and Development: A Comparative Analysis.*

———. 2009. "Vida, pasión y muerte de la Administración Postal Nacional Colombiana." In *Las instituciones en el desarrollo latinoamericano: Un estudio comparado,* edited by A. Portes, 292–316. Mexico City: Siglo XXI.

Duarte, Jesús. 2003. *Educación pública y clientelismo en Colombia.* Medellín: Universidad de Antioquia.

Echandía, Camilo. 1999. *El conflicto armado y las manifestaciones de violencia en las regiones de Colombia.* Bogotá: Presidencia de la República, Oficina del Alto Comisionado para la Paz.

Economic Commission on Latin America and the Caribbean (ECLAC). 2010. *La hora de la igualdad: Brechas por cerrar, caminos por abrir.* Santiago: ECLAC.

Edwards, Sebastián, and Roberto Steiner. 2008. *La revolución incompleta: Las reformas de Gaviria.* Bogotá: Grupo Editorial Norma.

El Espectador. 2010. "En la mira por las 'chuzadas.'" February 22.

Evans, Peter. 1989. "Predatory, Developmental, and Other Apparatuses: A Comparative Political Economy Perspective on the Third World State." *Sociological Forum* 4: 561–87.

———. 1995. *Embedded Autonomy: States and Industrial Transformation.* Princeton: Princeton University Press.

García, Mauricio. 2009a. *Jueces sin estado: La justicia colombiana en zonas de conflicto armado.* Bogotá: Dejusticia and Siglo del Hombre.

———, ed. 2009b. *Normas de papel: La cultura del incumplimiento de reglas.* Bogotá: Dejusticia and Siglo del Hombre.

Granovetter, Mark. 1985. "Economic Action and Social Structure: The Problem of Embeddedness." *American Journal of Sociology* 91: 481–510.

Gutiérrez, Francisco. 2007. *¿Lo que el viento se llevó? Los partidos políticos y la democracia en Colombia, 1958–2002.* Bogotá: Grupo Editorial Norma.

———. 2010. "Extreme Inequality: A Political Consideration. Rural Policies in Colombia (2002–2009)." In *Distributive Justice in Transitions,* edited by M. Bergsmo, C. Rodríguez-Garavito, P. Kalmanovitz, and M. P. Saffon. Oslo: Torkel Opsahl Academic Publisher.

Gutiérrez, Francisco, and Mauricio Barón. 2006. "Estado, control territorial paramilitar y orden político en Colombia." In *Nuestra tierra sin nombre: Transformaciones del conflicto en Colombia,* edited by F. Gutiérrez, M. E. Wills, and G. Sánchez, 267–309. Bogotá: IEPRI, Grupo Editorial Norma, and Universidad Nacional de Colombia.

Herbst, Jeffrey. 2004. "Let Them Fail: State Failure in Theory and Practice: Implications for Policy." In *When States Fail: Causes and Consequences,* edited by R. Rotberg, 302–18. Princeton: Princeton University Press.

Hernández, Iván. 2009. "Análisis institucional de la Aerocivil de Colombia." In *Las instituciones en el desarrollo latinoamericano: Un estudio comparado,* edited by A. Portes, 268–91. Mexico City: Siglo XXI.

Hirschman, Albert O. 1971. "The Search for Paradigms as a Hindrance to Understanding." In *A Bias for Hope: Essays on Development and Latin America,* 342–60. New Haven: Yale University Press.

Kalmanovitz, Salomón. 2001. *Las instituciones y el desarrollo económico en Colombia.* Bogotá: Grupo Editorial Norma.
Kaufman, Daniel, Aart Kraay, and Massimo Mastuzzi. 2009. *Governance Matters VIII: Individual and Aggregate Governance Indicators.* Washington, DC: World Bank.
Kerztman, Fanny. 2007. *Soltaron los perros: En la intimidad del poder.* Bogotá: Grupo Editorial Norma.
Leal, Francisco, and Andrés Dávila. 1990. *Clientelismo en Colombia: El sistema político y su expresión regional.* Bogotá: Tercer Mundo.
Martz, John. 1997. *The Politics of Clientelism: Democracy and the State in Colombia.* New Brunswick, NJ: Transaction.
Mason, Ann. 2000. "La crisis de seguridad en Colombia: Causas y consecuencias internacionales de un estado en vía de fracaso." *Colombia Internacional,* no. 49–50: 82–102.
Misión de Observación Electoral. 2011. *Mapas y factores de riesgo electoral: elecciones de autoridades locales Colombia 2011.* Bogotá: MOE.
Payne, James. 1968. *Patterns of Conflict in Colombia.* New Haven: Yale University Press.
Pizarro, Eduardo. 2004. *Una democracia asediada: Balance y perspectivas del conflicto armado en Colombia.* Bogotá: Grupo Editorial Norma.
Portes, Alejandro. 2004. "La sociología en el hemisferio: Convergencias pasadas y una nueva agenda de alcance intermedio." In *El desarrollo futuro de América Latina,* 113–47. Bogotá: Ilsa.
———. 2006. "Institutions and Development: A Conceptual Re-analysis." *Population and Development Review* 32: 233–62.
Portes, Alejandro, and Lori D. Smith. 2010. "Institutions and National Development in Latin America: A Comparative Study." *Socio-Economic Review* 8: 585–621.
Robinson, James. 2007. "Un típico país latinoamericano? Una perspectiva sobre el desarrollo de Colombia." In *Economía colombiana del siglo XX: Un análisis cuantitativo,* edited by J. Robinson and M. Urrutia, 639–74. Bogotá: Banco de la República and Fondo de Cultura Económica.
Rodríguez-Garavito, César. 2008. "Colombia: The New Latin American Left: Origins, Trajectory, and Prospects." In *The New Latin American Left,* edited by P. Barrett, D. Chavez, and C. Rodríguez-Garavito, 129–57. London: Pluto Press.
———. 2009. "De club de caballeros a mercado electrónico: Un análisis institucional de la Bolsa de Valores de Colombia." In *Las instituciones en el desarrollo latinoamericano: Un estudio comparado,* edited by A. Portes, 238–67. Mexico City: Siglo XXI.
Rodríguez-Garavito, César, and Diana Rodríguez Franco. 2008. "Entre el clientelismo y la modernización: Una etnografía institucional de la Administración de Impuestos de Colombia." Final report to the project *Latin American Institutions and Development: A Comparative Analysis.*
Romero, Mauricio. 2002. *Paramilitares y autodefensas, 1982–2003.* Bogotá: IEPRI-Planeta.
———. 2007. *Parapolítica: La ruta de la expansión paramilitar y los acuerdos políticos.* Bogotá: CEREC–Corporación Nuevo Arco Iris.
Rotberg, Robert. 2003. "The Failure and Collapse of Nation-States: Breakdown, Prevention and Repair." In *When States Fail: Causes and Consequences,* edited by R. Rotberg, 1–50. Princeton: Princeton University Press.

Safford, Frank, and Marco Palacio. 2001. *Colombia: Fragmented Land, Divided Society.* Oxford: Oxford University Press.

Sánchez, Fabio, Andrés Hernández, and Armando Armenta. 2010. "A Monetary History of Colombia in the Twentieth Century" In *The Colombian Economy in the 20th Century: A Quantitative Analysis,* edited by J. Robinson and M. Urrutia. Cambridge, MA: Harvard University Press.

Semana. 2007. "Eleonora Pineda." May 14.

———. 2009. "La Corte contraataca." September 7.

Tokatlián, Juan. 2008. "La construcción de un 'estado fallido' en la política mundial: El caso de las relaciones entre los Estados Unidos y Colombia." *Análisis Político* 64: 67–104.

Urrutia, Miguel. 1991. "On the Absence of Economic Populism in Colombia." In *The Macroeconomics of Populism in América Latina,* edited by R. Dornbusch and S. Edwards, 369–91. Chicago: University of Chicago Press.

Wright, Erik Olin. 1996. Review of Peter Evans, *Embedded Autonomy. Contemporary Sociology* 25 (2): 176–79.

6

Development Opportunities

Politics, the State, and Institutions in the Dominican Republic in the Twenty-First Century

Wilfredo Lozano

This chapter summarizes the principal findings of the studies on institutions and development in the Dominican Republic. In the Dominican case, the institutions studied were civil aviation, the postal service, the public health system, and the internal taxation system.[1] In addition to being exposed to the currents of global changes, the institutions under consideration represent fundamental axes for national development. Thus civil aviation is key to the articulation of the country with the global economy, internal taxes define the potential for the generation of financial capacity for development of the national economy, and the health institutions are a cornerstone of the welfare of the population (Sen 1999). The postal service is a traditional institution undergoing a profound transformation in the new framework of globalization. This agency represents a paradox: while in the developed world it persists and serves the increasing needs for information exchange, in many developing countries it has disappeared or gone into crisis (Portes 2006a).

This chapter first analyzes the conditions of national development that define the institutional cases studied. This is followed by an analysis of experiences in the specific domains. Third, the experiences of institutional change are analyzed highlighting the role of the state as a central actor, as well as the interventions of other strategic actors. Finally, institutional change is discussed as a complex product that articulates historical opportunities, the action of development actors, and the internal framework. This framework is defined by the hypothesized determinants discussed in chapter 2.

Titles and authors of individual reports on which this chapter is based are found in Appendix 6.1.

NATIONAL DEVELOPMENT AND INSTITUTIONS: THE DOMINICAN EXPERIENCE

The Context of Institutional Change: The Transformations of the Economy and the State since the 1990s

As in all of Latin America, in the Dominican Republic the 1990s were a period of significant economic growth. Beyond the gross domestic product (GDP), there were profound structural changes both in the institutional order and in the role of the state (Stiglitz 2002, 2003). In the Dominican Republic, processes of economic change occurred simultaneously with political change, yielding a new scenario in which the country transformed itself into a service economy and the state lost the capacity to guide society. There were, however, changes that strengthened sectors such as the justice system and Congress (CEPAL 2000). Axes of change were concentrated in two points. The first was economic modernization, following which the country evolved from an export economy based on sugar and low-technology manufacturers to an exporter of services. The new lead sectors of the economy were free trade zones, tourism, and remittances.[2]

The second axis was institutional, leading to a wholesale opening up of the economy, reorienting the dynamics of circuits of production and consumption toward nontraditional areas. On the whole, this meant a change in the role of the state in the economy, giving more freedom to the private sector (CEPAL 2000). To this should be added a new framework of tax collection, which transformed the sources of fiscal income away from traditional custom duties to internal taxation (table 6.1). The monetary policy strategy gradually liberalized finances, producing a new unified adjustment mechanism and certificates of participation from the Central Bank, which came to constitute the principal mechanism for monetary control. Interest rates were liberalized, and incentives for the financial integration to multiple banking were generated (CEPAL 2000.)

In addition to these changes came others in labor policies, whose most noteworthy aspect was labor flexibility, specifically with regard to salaries. The new regime stimulated a dynamic rotation of the labor force—especially in high labor demand sectors, such as the free trade zones, facilitating the informalization of the labor force as a whole (Lozano 2002).

In less than twenty years, a significant reorientation of the international trade structure of the Dominican Republic took place. Sugar exports were displaced by service exports (above all free trade zones and tourism). In 1991 the free trade zones already represented 5 percent of GDP. Henceforth they maintained their relative weight in the GDP but duplicated their size by 2007. The tourism sector at the beginning of the period represented 5 percent of GDP, but in 2007 it had quadrupled in size and increased its relative proportion of GDP to 7 percent (table 6.2). According to the U.N. Economic Commission for Latin America (CEPAL),

TABLE 6.1 Composition of the Income of the Central Government

Year	Customs, %	Internal taxes, %	National Treasury, %	Total, %
1998	35.1	42.5	21.6	99.2
1999	34.1	41.3	12.9	88.3
2000	34.8	43.6	10.7	88.8
2001	23.1	46.9	13.8	83.8
2002	23.9	44.7	17.6	86.2
2003	20.2	44.3	30.6	95.1
2004	33.8	48.5	13.4	95.7
2005	33.7	42.6	11.9	98.2
2006	27.0	59.1	12.1	98.3
2007	22.4	62.9	13.0	98.3
2008	23.5	64.7	11.2	99.5
2009	21.6	67.2	10.5	99.3

SOURCE: National Treasury/Directorate of Internal Taxes (DGII) 2010 figures.

TABLE 6.2 Participation of Tourism in the Economy

Year	GDP (*in millions of RD$ of 1991*)	Available Rooms (*units*)	Rate of Hotel Occupation (%)	Income from Tourism (*US$ millions*)	Employment Generated by Hotel Activity (*persons*)		
					DIRECT	INDIRECT	TOTAL
1990	...	19,043	68.8	817.6	28,564	59,985	88,549
1991	5,763	21,510	64.5	840.4	27,963	69,908	97,871
1992	7,047	24,410	69.3	1,007.1	31,733	79,333	111,066
1993	8,394	26,801	74.7	1,223.7	32,161	80,403	112,564
1994	9,096	29,243	72.1	1,428.8	35,092	87,729	122,821
1995	10,602	32,846	76.8	1,570.8	36,131	90,327	126,458
1996	11,393	36,273	72.6	1,780.5	36,273	90,683	126,956
1997	13,200	40,453	76.2	2,099.4	44,498	111,246	155,744
1998	13,170	44,665	69.7	2,153.1	44,665	111,663	156,328
1999	14,093	49,623	66.9	2,524.0	45,653	114,133	159,786
2000	15,364	51,916	70.2	2,860.2	47,763	119,407	167,170
2001	15,141	54,034	66.33	2,798.2	44,031	110,075	154,106
2002	15,560	54,730	62.78	2,730.4	44,968	112,420	157,388
2003	17,683	56,378	72.68	3,127.9	47,055	117,639	164,694
2004	18,241	58,932	74.20	3,151.6	48,994	122,484	171,478
2005	19,881	59,870	73.90	3,518.3	49,176	122,940	172,116
2006	20,853	63,206	73.00	3,792.2	53,797	134,492	188,289

SOURCE: Central Bank of the Dominican Republic.

free trade zones represented 83.1 percent of exports in 2000. And whereas in 1980 they constituted only 2.7 percent of the manufacturing sector, in 2005 they accounted for 15.1 percent. In 1990 just $817.6 million were generated by tourism; sixteen years later, the figure had quadrupled, to $3,792.2 million.

To this increase in the export of services and trade was added a rapid process of urbanization that in less than twenty years (1970–80) transformed the country into an urban society, with about 60 percent of the population in towns. In the 1990s the capital city of Santo Domingo accounted for about one-third of the population in the country (Lozano 2002). This rapid urbanization made construction one of the most dynamic sectors of the economy. In 1980 this sector accounted for 6.6 percent of GDP; by 2005, 10.4 percent (Lozano 2002).

The changes experienced by the Dominican economy and society generated pressures for institutional change that, however, did not always produce modernizing results. The institutional change was not always "successful" in terms of creating more effective agencies capable of making a sustained contribution to development. I review next the experiences of the sectors included in our institutional studies.

Reform of the Public Health System

The institutional study of the public health system privileged the analysis of the normative framework since the beginning of the twenty-first century.[3] In this case, perhaps the most relevant aspect is the importance acquired by the conflict of interests among numerous actors in the health sector: doctors, private insurers, the state bureaucracy, international organizations, Congress, lobbyists, trade unions, and business groups (Castellanos 2008). The reform of the health sector in the Dominican Republic took place in the context of sustained growth of the economy (CEPAL 2000). The end goal was greater equity, reducing levels of exclusion in the health field and universalizing medical attention.

As a result of this reform, there has been an important decrease in negative general indicators, such as mortality and morbidity (Castellanos 2008; Lizardo 2005, 2008). There has also been an effort to construct establishments that increase coverage and access to health services. However, maternal mortality continues to be high. This reflects the poverty of the population but also the low quality of service, affected by low funding (Lizardo 2005). Reform of the health sector took place in the framework of institutional weakness. The latter is reflected in the scarcity of management capacity, in finances, and in human resources, as a consequence of the absence of an administrative career option. This weakness impedes the strategic design of policies and the regulatory control of different agents. In addition, there are different levels of authority, which do not always converge in common actions. This has implied a number of distortions (Castellanos 2008).[4]

In the Dominican health sector, a clinical model predominates that prioritizes hospital attention over ambulatory and primary care. A large concentration of resources in the principal provincial hospital centers overvalues individual care relative to the efforts of teams engaging in collective action (Castellanos 2008). There is a need to strengthen the model of primary attention and the establishment of rural clinics. In 1981, in recognition of hospital deficiencies, the first proposal was formulated for a new policy. The private sector began to constitute itself as a powerful actor. Political parties also began to produce program proposals for standardizing public management. By 1991 the first integrated and operative program of health sector reform was launched.

Henceforth, a new actor intervened: international development organizations. The first such agency to introduce a proposal for health sector reform was the Inter-American Development Bank (IADB). Subsequently the United Nations Programme for Development (UNDP) introduced a proposal for a model based on the equity and solidarity approach pioneered in Costa Rica. With some reservations, this initiative was supported by the National Association of Private Clinics (ANDECLIP). For its part, the National Council of Private Business (CNHE) also introduced a project based on a neoliberal design for the health sector. The political parties themselves were forced to include health reform in their programs.

This debate culminated in a legislative proposal, and, in consequence, the discussion was transferred to Congress. In this scenario, the debates intensified and lobbying of Congress became important for diverse interest groups. The congressional health commission was backed by international development organizations such as the IADB and the World Bank. In 2000 the first agreement was reached. The Dominican Medical Association (AMD) proposed that the health system should be subordinated to social security. From then on, two poles of interest emerged. On the one hand, the National Confederation of Enterprises (CONEP) and other business sectors came to defend the need to approve a unified project; on the other, the AMD and other unions as well as citizen organizations defended the modification of this proposal.[5]

While the Ministry for Public Health and Social Assistance (SESPAS) continued to direct the health system, other decentralized organisms acquired importance. Above all, the new law established that the system should operate in agreement with civil society. This was clearly expressed in the new schema of services organized as a decentralized network, while the idea of "collective health" came to privilege an extensive preventive health model. This model depended on an interactive scheme between service and solidarity networks (Castellanos 2007, 2008).

Henceforth, the new system defined three social security and health regimes: contributory (with contributions from the employers and the workers), contributory-subsidized (with contributions from the worker and a state subsidy), and subsidized (only with state contributions). After almost a decade, with seven of the ten transitional years having elapsed, there appears to be consensus that the reform is at a standstill. Experts have generally evaluated this process of reform negatively.

The Postal Service

The study of the Dominican postal service focused on the route taken by the process of institutional change faced with a leadership vacuum and direct pressure from private postal services (Sánchez 2008). After 1965 and the fall of the Trujillo dictatorship there were timid atttempts at institutional reform (Lozano 2004). It was not until much later, however, that there was a vigorous attempt at reform emphasizing meritocratic principles. The results were disappointing: in 2005 only some 1,292 employees had been incorporated into the career civil service; by 2006 the figure had barely reached 27,717, or less than 8 percent of the total number of state employees. According to Echebarría (2006) the Dominican Republic is one of the worst performing states in Latin America, with rampant clientelism severely affecting the quality of administrative performance.

Since the 1970s the public postal service has been exposed to competition from the private sector. In the search for efficiency, the postal service was transformed into an autonomous public business with its own budget, such that the state shifted its role from management to regulation (Sánchez 2008). The new entity, the Dominican Postal Institute (IMPOSDOM), was established in 1985. The enabling law indicated that the service would be organized according to business logic, based on the supposition that this would make the service more efficient and improve the quality of its employees. The new agency explicitly modeled itself after the U.S. and Canadian postal services.

However, the reorganization took place without business guidance and without the necessary investment. By 2000 there were fifteen private businesses competing with IMPOSDOM and making up around 80 percent of the market. In that year, some 3 million pieces of correspondence were transported at a value of some 15 million pesos monthly. International couriers had also entered the scene. Today IMPOSDOM has 168 offices in 383 municipalities and municipal districts; there are only 350 mail carriers, and these are concentrated in the large towns (Sánchez 2008). The principal weakness in the reorganization of the institution has been the lack of continuity in management and technical personnel. Another key element is pervasive corruption. In response, there have been new attempts since 2004 to reorganize management operations. These attempts have been accompanied by the signing of agreements with private and public firms and the restoration of messenger services, particularly those serving the expatriate community in New York.

Despite these efforts, IMPOSDOM can be characterized as a failed institution. It reflects the general weakness of the Dominican state in terms of lack of professionalism and vulnerability to corruption. A clear sign of the failure of the public service is that it turned to private operators to organize its own delivery system, thereby further weakening the agency. The latter has been trapped in a vicious circle, with no positive end in sight.

The Tax Service

In the case of the tax system, the central point of institutional reform was the need to produce an efficient framework of taxation given the new conditions imposed by trade liberalization. This urgent need gave rise to an efficient bureaucratic leadership, at the price of redefining relations with the business sector and generating important changes in the bureaucratic apparatus of the state. From the 1960s to the mid-1990s the Dominican economy grew slowly. In consequence, the principal objective was to reactivate the economy. The increase in public spending demanded by this effort exceeded the tax collection capacity of the state and thus demanded greater resources. This led to the substitution of customs duties by internal taxes as the main source of state income. In this context, the subject of tax evasion came to the fore.

Reform of this institution started in 1997 with the merger of the Office of Internal Taxes with the Office of Income Taxes, adopting the name General Management of Internal Taxes (DGII). The new institution was placed under the Ministry of Finance. This meant that the majority of its resources and its administrative decisions would be subject to the discretion of the ministry. Subsequently, those who wanted the DGII to operate using private management criteria pressed for autonomy. Since its creation, the DGII sought to increase tax collection independently of the final destination of these resources. In pursuit of this goal, the institution finally acquired operational autonomy in 2004. Collection efficiency, the reduction of evasion, and accountability became normative within the institution, which also adopted a hierarchical form of organization (Guzmán 2008).

The changes experienced by the DGII have, to a large extent, reflected a new paradigm defined by the privatization of the state and the opening of the economy. The overall aims are to strengthen the tax collection capacity of the state and to achieve greater clarity and accountability in relation to taxpayers. This change may have been the product of an implicit pact between the economic and social elites in the country. Instead of massive fraud or evasion, powerful groups sought to reduce their tax payments via formal agreements with the authorities. The struggles between different interest groups were subsequently played out within a formal framework, through legislation and negotiations (Guzmán 2008).

In the DGII, as in other agencies of the central government, the old practice persists of employment being subordinate to the electoral cycle of politics. In short, the institution has of two types of staff positions: those based on "trust," without benefit of meritocratic competition, and those that are part of the regular career service. For both types, average wages are higher than the median in the public sector, and "islands of excellence" have predictably emerged. There has been a noteworthy improvement in the auditing process, which has strengthened fiscal control. The overall view of outside experts is that the agency's administration is generally honest but with a strong tendency to interpret rules and take discretionary action; this tendency ends up facilitating agreements in favor of the most important and powerful taxpayers (Guzmán 2008).

The public image of the DGII is acceptable: there is a significant degree of satisfaction with its performance within and outside the government. The current director general understands that the success of tax collection depends on the generation of reliable information, which has led, in turn, to important technological innovations. DGII allies in its process of institutional modernization have been mainly economic agencies within the government, but the institution has also found significant support in the business sector.

Civil Aviation

The process of change and modernization of the Dominican civil aviation strengthened a technocratic nucleus inside the organization in response to external and internal pressures. These come from the market, transnational capital, supervisory agencies, pilots, and internal controllers. The reform required internal leadership and strong presidential support. Broad economic changes made the improvement of civil aeronautics a requisite for competitiveness in the new service economy, centered on tourism. Politically, the reform was enabled by a strengthened new ethos in the civil administration following the collapse of military power.

Law 505, which came into force in November 1969, was the first instrument for the regulation and ordering of civil aviation in the country (Tobal 2001). With this law, a new schema of effective control of civil aviation began to be articulated. The law established the Junta of Civil Aviation (JAC) and a general director for civil aeronautics.[6]

Nevertheless, this law maintained the military's hold on civil aviation. Following this model, a national security vision predominated that subordinated the function of control and regulation of civil aviation to military interests. In this context, the institutionalization of a system of control, order, and regulation of civil aviation was strongly subordinated to the regional geopolitics of the Cold War.

The civil aviation Law 491 of 1996 defined a new juridical framework in which there was a clear interest to connect the institutional order with the demands for development and those of the international community. The new law emphasized in its introductory considerations support for a service economy. In the design of this law, international regulatory institutions intervened directly, above all the Federal Aviation Agency (FAA) of the United States. Law 491 established the

Dominican Institute of Civil Aviation (IDAC), with specific responsibilities: fiscalization of the aeronautic sector, security of navigation, guarantee of the operational security of civil aviation and oversight. IDAC is financially autonomous and, as such, has its own budget, but its execution is reviewed by the JAC.

The functions of the director of IDAC are wide-ranging. He is directly responsible for achievement of the goals of its agency and, therefore, has control of all the personnel whom he appoints. He can create autonomously the rules demanded by control, navigation, security, and other requirements of civil aviation, without having to await JAC approval. The institutional blueprint of IDAC defines as its central aim the security of flights, aircraft, and personnel. By contrast, for airport administration the state adopted a private business approach in which efficiency was defined by the market. From the viewpoint of the state, in its pursuit of an open and export-oriented service economy, the airports' privatization represented a functional response not only to the need to reduce costs of civil aviation but also to raise standards of global competitiveness.

In March 1993 the Dominican Republic was dropped to Category 3 in the FAA ranking. This closed North American airspace to Dominican airlines, leading to the demise of the flagship airline, Compañía Dominicana de Aviación.[7] This situation generated serious difficulties for Dominican civil aviation and strong pressures on the state by powerful actors who controlled the tourism business at the local and international levels. Exclusion from the FAA's Category 1 revealed the inefficiency of the system of inspection and control of aircraft with national licenses, and it laid bare the power of local airline operators over the regulatory agencies of the state. Similarly, it made clear that military predominance, with its authoritarian control of the system, was not a guarantee of security and efficiency. It denoted exactly the contrary: a system of exchange of favors, trafficking of influence, and the presence of corporate islands of power inside those organizations responsible for security and civil navigation.

By the beginning of the twenty-first century relations between IDAC and other civil institutional actors had strengthened. This weakened the military and led to its gradual replacement by civilian staff. Airport privatization introduced an element of discipline inside the aviation and airport system that obliged those responsible for flight safety to respond to the new modernizing pressures (Lozano 2008). A small airport may be managed with a certain degree of deficiencies in terms of the controls of flights, but it is impossible to do so in airports that are annually transporting millions of persons.

Predictive Variables and Institutional Change

The case studies present a very clear bifurcation of the institutions under review, considered in terms of their contribution to development. In the analysis of the Dominican case, according to the truth table presented in chapter 2, civil aviation and the tax authority are adequate institutionally and contribute significantly to national development; the public health system and the postal service do not. It should be highlighted that the tax authority contributes to development, despite its not being immune to corruption and lacking proper meritocracy logic in its organizational structure. If the same variables are considered on a scale of diffuse values (see table 2.3 above), there are nuances worth noting: the postal service and the public health service continue to have very little institutional capacity. In the postal service, this incapacity is accentuated especially in the absence of meritocracy and a high degree of corruption; in public health, low institutional capacity is due, above all, to the significant presence of internal islands of power and the absence of strong external allies. The most interesting cases, however, are those of civil aviation and the tax authority. In civil aviation, institutional adequacy and potential contribution to development are high, principally because of a strong proactive bureaucracy and the strategic role of external allies. In the case of the DGII, its potential is a product of a large capacity for technological flexibility, although proactivity and strategic external allies have also been important.

It is worth discussing briefly the reasons given by each investigator for assigning these sets of scores. In the case of public health, Castellanos (2008) notes that hiring and promotion in the bureaucratic apparatus respond, above all, to the discretion of the authorities; in terms of integrity, the system is vulnerable to interest groups, as many islands of power exist. In relation to proactivity, he indicates that the system often takes action in accordance with the needs and interests of particular groups. To be sure, there are possibilities for innovation, but what predominates is resistance to change and lack of strategic management.[8]

In the case of civil aviation (IDAC), security of passengers and aircraft constitutes a key institutional value. There is a clear hierarchy of human resources: an executive body, a technical body, and administrative personnel. This latter is the most exposed to political influences, but the technical body has meritocratic competences, although they are weaker in management. The loss of power of the military has made the system more accountable.[9] One notes that under the civilian administration the aerial navigation system depends less on corporative groups, with technical staff acquiring greater decision-making power. Undoubtedly, the capacity to generate proactive competences is strongly conditioned by the institutional ethos that each organization possesses, at least in its leadership nucleus; in civil aviation it is very strong. Once IDAC adopted a model reliant on resources and technical capacities, decision making had to take into account the specialized personnel and, therefore, move to a less top-down management model than previously. Proactivity is impossible without a certain number of external allies, and this has been an essential factor in the institutional redesign of IDAC.

In the case of the tax authority (DGII), we note that although there is not a culture of meritocracy proper, there is a technical nucleus with strong meritocratic capacities that the management takes into account and protects. Although there are not, properly speaking, islands of power, the great power of the executive director generates in practice consequences similar to those situations. It appears that there is considerable immunity to corruption, in part because of the model of efficient tax collection imposed by central management but also as a result of the new pattern of negotiation and the resolution of differences between the business community and the government. The importance of the DGII for the central government has enhanced its capacity for innovation and technological flexibility. Finally, it is clear that in this institution the strong support received by management from the central political power (the presidency) and its negotiating power with the business sector give it powerful external allies to pursue its basic institutional objectives.

In the postal service, there has never been an effective model of meritocracy, and this has decisively affected its bureaucracy. This is related to the weak control of corruption, which has been significant in the past. It is true that there have been certain modernizing efforts regarding especially the diversification of services, but the institution has not had powerful external allies. This has prevented the creation of internal competences that could have made it resistant to corruption and more able to compete with private operators who have in the end predominated.

STATE, DEVELOPMENT ACTORS, AND INSTITUTIONAL CHANGE

If we limit the analysis to each individual institution and its immediate environs it would be difficult to appreciate the potential for institutional change and the institutions' contribution to development, since the latter is a process articulated by a unifying entity, namely the state.

The State as Development Agent

In the four cases under review, the state defines the field of articulations around which successful institutional change can take place. In the case of internal taxes, this field was established by the relation between the most powerful taxpayers and the tax collection bureaucracy. In the case of civil aviation, it was established around the relationship between pilots, air controllers, and high-level bureaucrats, including international actors such as the FAA. In the case of the health sector, the field was articulated around the doctors' union, the medical bureaucracy, insurance agents, and international development agencies. In the case of the postal service, it was established by the relation between clients, the government bureaucracy, and private couriers.

In all these instances, we note the presence of the state bureaucracy but also of institutional leadership as a condition for producing change. In the more successful cases (internal taxation and civil aviation), the state recognized and supported clear leadership: in internal taxes, in the person of their director; in civil aviation, in the team of executive civil servants led by a director. In both cases, the two leaders had direct access to the president of the country. In the other cases, public health and the postal service, state action was also important, but the leadership was diffuse, not well articulated, and, above all, subject to multiple pressures and lacking a minimum level of support from the president or Congress. Where the leadership is not well articulated, possibilities for successful institutional development are very limited.

What we have pointed out enables us to recognize that the state may certainly constitute itself as a stimulus for change, but it also may be a limiting factor. In both cases, everything depends on key conditions, crucial among which are the past performance of the institution, the team of relevant actors, and the structure and ethos of the organization. Of the cases studied, the most unfavorable performance was that of the postal service, not because conditions for change were not present, but because, in this case, three unfavorable conditions intervened: first, the absence of effective institutional leadership; second, lack of access to the president or other figures with political power; and third, lack of effective external allies. Thus, while modernizing pressures on the institution were real, there was little chance of articulating a functional response to them. The result is that the service, whether intentionally or not, was abandoned to the vagaries of the market.[10]

Internal taxation represents a diametrically opposite case. Guzmán (2008) shows that the DGII organized itself from the beginning with the support of an effective institutional leadership, which was not so much connected to the political leadership of the party in power but rather to the president himself. In contrast to the postal service, the DGII was seen by the state as a strategic actor in the face of the economic transformation the country has undergone since the 1990s. It became indispensable for the success of the institutional redesign of tax collection to reach an agreement with the business sector. This obliged the state and in particular the DGII's management to make their conduct more efficient and to create a policy of maintaining allies within the business elite. In the postal service, this did not happen since it was not deemed a strategic institution by the president or his political and economic teams.

In the case of civil aviation, the success of the reform was a product of two combined forces. One of these was pressures brought by business interests—airlines, tourism operators, and hotel chains—to modernize airport security in order to make the tourist sector more competitive. These pressures were initially heterogeneous and diffuse, but what unified them eventually was their influence over the aviation system. A first product of these pressures was the privatization of airport administration through AERODOM (Dominican Airports), a consortium in which private Dominican capital and international capital participated. Although

AERODOM did not have anything to do with the management of civil aviation security, it became a factor conditioning it. This was so because of the complexity of the demand for airport services, the increase in the volume of passengers, and, naturally, the increase in the influence of this corporation over the civil aviation authorities. The second of the forces for reform is civil aviation personnel themselves. In this case, a pressure group composed of air controllers, pilots, and technical personnel managed to come together based on a bureaucratic ethos that involved lobbying the political elite. A central aspect of this process was the gradual decrease in the power and influence of the military.

In the health sector, what was distinctive was the heterogeneity of interest groups converging around the reform process and the complexity of the conflict of interests. To be sure, institutional reform took place, but bounded as it was by an old clientelist system, it has produced inefficiency and dispersion. Thus we have a situation of clientelist blockage of institutional efficiency, not because of a clash of interests among different actors, but because none of them have the power to impose their views. The result has been a kind of balkanization of the system that pushes it in one direction or another depending on the temporary sway of one of these main actors: the medical bureaucracy, the doctors' union, and the private clinics. The problems for institutional reform have not been, therefore, the exclusive result of an incompetent medical bureaucracy without an ethos or vocation for service.

Actors and Institutions

All this brings us to the subject of actors and institutions, as the final subject to consider in the analysis of relations between the state and institutional change. We consider two types of actors: the business sector and international development actors.

The business sector has had a clear presence in almost all the previous scenarios. In the case of civil aviation, they pressed for reform of the mechanisms of airport control, as well as the safety of civil aviation. It was the FAA excluding the Dominican Republic from a Category 1 ranking that generated this pressure on the part of business interests. The situation benefits the hegemony of the U.S. airlines but, in the long run, would have produced a serious problem for the image of the country as a tourist destination. The result of this pressure was a new civil aviation law and the institutional reform of the system.

In the case of internal taxes, the leadership for institutional change was not a bureaucracy convinced of the need for a new model of tax collection. What was essential here was the force of the state promoting a new economic model that in turn modified the logic of tax collection. The concrete form assumed by this structural pressure is important: it led to a leadership well situated politically vis-à-vis the president as well as the business sector. All this led to the articulation of a new institutional design and to an increase in the amount of taxes collected, as a new schema of negotiation between the business sector and the state replaced the old pattern of fiscal evasion.

In the unsuccessful cases of institutional change, one notes a kind of bipolar model with similar consequences. In the postal service, it was the absence of internal leadership. In this case, one notes reform action, to be sure, but without any institutional coherence. Nor can one recognize systematic support by the powers that be. The result was that the market trumped institutional development, with private operators substituting in practice for the public service. In the case of health, we find the opposite situation: it was the existence of a hypertrophied bureaucracy inside the state and multiple groups of private and public interests that, when converging, blocked effective reform. Thus we see that social actors, independently of their local, international, or other status, have played a crucial role in reform, in some cases by strengthening the competences that end up defining a successful route and in others by creating the conditions for their failure and the effective end of institutional modernization.

CONCLUDING REMARKS

The topic of institutional strengthening and, more concretely, of its contribution to national development cannot be approached only by looking at the predictive variables employed above to identify "developmental institutions." The analysis needs to locate these variables in historical terms. Thus, as the proposal by Portes (2006a) had foreseen, the institutional trajectories assume considerable importance. In the Dominican case, we have seen how large changes in the economy during the 1990s reoriented productive activities toward a service economy of exports, opening up markets and reorganizing institutional rules along the axes of flexibility and informalization of labor markets. This context, however, did not give sufficient impetus to institutional reform since that process was also conditioned by path dependence. As we know (Campbell 2004), path dependence not only implies accumulated experience but also the values and symbols that unify an institution and create an internal identity, a sense of belonging and coherence. And it is here that diverse trajectories inside the framework of common structural change produced successful reforms in some cases and in others not.

Modernizing ideology is a powerful tool for the articulation of institutional reforms, but, as we have seen, all reform requires, beyond the idea and the values, cohesive groups that push for change and political conditions enabling it. Among the truly crucial conditions are effective external allies and the recognition of the need for change by these allies. In the Dominican Republic, three routes for innovation and institutional change have been delineated. The first route is that of leadership and charisma as a necessary condition for motivating innovative groups to push the process from the inside. This is clear in the cases of internal taxation and civil aviation. The second route refers to the existence of groups within the institution for which meritocracy constitutes a weapon to achieve protection against privilege. This is the case with the groups of air controllers and pilots who not only organized themselves corporatively to defend themselves from the military but also achieved alliances with political elites who had "voice."

The third route is through the power of external allies who are so interested in change that they manage to strengthen internal actors within the institution in order to produce it. This was the case of the DGII, whose mission was defined by the urgent need of the central power to generate sufficient tax resources to enable it to manage the turn of the Dominican economy. The combination of possibilities to which the model presented in chapter 2 refers certainly constitutes a potent instrument for understanding institutional change, but we should not forget that all institutional reform is embedded in specific historical conditions that, among other things, make the state a fundamental instrument to orient the sense of change and articulate its possibilities, with its actions conditioned, in turn, by the political context and institutional path dependence.

APPENDIX 6.1: INSTITUTIONAL STUDIES IN THE DOMINICAN REPUBLIC

The reports on which this chapter is based are listed below with English translation of the original Spanish titles. The individual studies can be downloaded from the webpage of the Center for Migration and Development, Princeton University: http://cmd.princeton.edu.

Castellanos, Pedro Luis. "The Reform of the Public Health Sector in the Dominican Republic."

Guzmán, Rolando. "Tax Proceedings and Development: An Institutional Analysis of the Revenue Authority of the Dominican Republic."

Lozano, Wilfredo. "Civil Aviation and Development in the Dominican Republic."

Sánchez, Julio. "The Postal Service of the Dominican Republic: A Paraplegic System."

NOTES

1. At variance with the experiences in other countries, the stock exchange does not have significant weight in the Dominican Republic.

2. The transformations produced by tourism are arguably the most significant. In 1980 the sector hardly constituted 1.2 percent of GDP, whereas in 2005 it constituted 6.4 percent. Similarly, the contribution of the sector in terms of balance of payments represented 81.6 million pesos in 1990 prices; by 2006, it had increased to 392.2 million pesos (CEPAL 2000).

3. The normative framework of the Dominican health sector is based in the following legislation: the General Health Law (42–01) and the Law of the Dominican system of Social Security (87–01): Decree 1522–04 (Castellanos 2008).

4. Recently there have been strong pressures toward decentralization that are reflected in the increasing importance of local government in matters affecting specific communities. Many factors converge in this situation, among which is the importance that a growing expatriate population has had on municipal life through remittances and financial support to their home communities. This new phenomenon is a daily reality in towns such as Baní in the south and San Francisco de Macorís in the north (Lizardo 2005).

5. For a vision of the general argument of CONEP, see their 2008 development proposal.

6. In the framework of this law, the JAC constitutes an advisory organ of the executive branch. The director of civil aeronautics presides over it; the deputy director is the civil servant who replaces him in his absence. In addition to these two functionaries, the JAC is composed of an official from the Dominican Air Force (FAD), the director general of tourism, two experts in the area, and a lawyer designated by the executive.

7. If a country does not have a Category 1 ranking, its airlines cannot carry passengers to the United States. This does not, however, prevent commercial flights from transporting goods. Following the exclusion of the Dominican Republic from Category 1, more than fourteen national airlines were suspended. See Tobal 2001.

8. The institutional trajectory of the health sector was a decisive factor for the process of reform; interest groups conditioned the action of the state to a point where they virtually blocked any significant change.

9. According to the new law, IDAC is an autonomous entity that draws up its own budget and disperses it with resources from the airport (rates, taxes, etc.) under the supervision of the JAC. A second type of control comes from JAC's obligation to open itself to audits by the Chamber of Accounting; this mechanism, however, operates only in specific circumstances. A third control mechanism is the general comptroller of the republic, who has the authority to intervene in budget execution.

10. The state cannot be thought of as a monolithic entity. It constitutes rather a field of power relations articulated institutionally around the legitimate monopoly of force, the management of order, and the production of a sense of identity in the people. Obviously this is organized around class interests, which, in many respects, implies conflict. The state not only administers the mechanisms to control this conflict but also may resolve it in alliance with a heterogeneous collection of interests. Above all, the state assures the continuity and the legitimacy of the social order. For a debate on these issues, see Poulantzas 1979; Evans, Rueschemeyer, and Skocpol 1985.

REFERENCES

Campbell, J. L. 2004. *Institutional Change and Globalization.* Princeton: Princeton University Press.

Castellanos, Pedro. 2007. "Hacia un nuevo sistema nacional de salud: Por qué es necesaria una reforma del sector salud." Report. Pontificia Santo Domingo Universidad Católica Madre y Maestra.

———. 2008. "La reforma del sistema público de salud en la República Dominicana." Final report to the project *Latin American Institutions and Development: A Comparative Analysis.*

Echebarría, K. 2006. *Informe sobre la situación del servicio civil en América Latina*. Washington, DC: Inter-American Development Bank.

Evans, Peter, Dietrich Rueschemeyer, and Theda Skocpol. 1985. *Bringing the State Back In*. New York: Cambridge University Press.

Guzmán, Rolando. 2008. "Recaudación y desarrollo: Un análisis institucional de una entidad tributaria en la República Dominicana." Final report to the project *Latin American Institutions and Development: A Comparative Analysis*.

Lizardo, Jefrey. 2005. "El gasto social en la República Dominicana, 1995–2005: Tendencias y desafíos." Report. Unidad de Análisis Económico, Secretariado Técnico de la Presidencia (June).

———. 2008. *Financiación pública del sector salud y la seguridad social en la República Dominicana antes y después de la reforma*. Santiago: Pontificia Universidad Católica Madre y Maestra.

Lozano, Wilfredo. 2004. *Después de los caudillos*. Santo Domingo: Editorial Manatí.

———. 2008. "Aviación civil y desarrollo en la República Dominicana." Final report to the project *Latin American Institutions and Development: A Comparative Analysis*.

Portes, Alejandro. 2006a. "Instituciones y desarrollo: Una revisión conceptual." *Cuadernos de Economía* 45: 13–52.

———. 2006b. "Institutions and Development in Latin America: A Comparative Study." Research Proposal. Center for Migration and Development, Princeton University.

Poulantzas, Nicos. 1979. *Estado, poder y socialismo*. Mexico City: Siglo XXI.

Sánchez, Julio. 2008. "El servicio postal público en la República Dominicana: ¿Un sistema parapléjico y sin dolientes?" Final report to the project *Latin American Institutions and Development: A Comparative Analysis*.

Sen, Amartya. 1999. *Development as Freedom*. New York: Knopf.

Stiglitz, Joseph. 2002. *El malestar en la globalización*. Bogotá: Taurus.

———. 2003. *Los felices noventa: La semilla de la destrucción*. Bogotá: Taurus.

Tobal, Vinicio. 2001. *Compendio de derecho aeronáutico*. Santo Domingo: Editora Alfa y Omega.

United Nations Economic Commission for Latin America (CEPAL). 2000. *Desarrollo económico y social en la República Dominicana: Los últimos 20 años y perspectivas para el siglo XXI*. Proyecto BT-DOM-1999, LC/MEX/R.760.

7

The Uneven and Paradoxical Development of Mexico's Institutions

José Luis Velasco

Among developing countries, Mexico seems quite rich. With a per capita income of almost $10,000, it is close to the top of the upper-middle income category, as defined by the World Bank. Its total output makes it the world's fourteenth economy (World Bank 2010). Moreover, its political system was stable for most of the twentieth century, which facilitated the establishment and consolidation of its institutions. The economic and political transformations of the late twentieth century brought new members to this institutional apparatus, some of them notably efficient and legitimate. To this, one should add the effects of the North American Free Trade Agreement (NAFTA), which, since 1994, has provided additional stimulus for institutional development, at least in the economic field.

Bearing these and similar facts in mind, one should expect Mexico's institutions to be fairly advanced. But the social context in which these institutions are embedded also includes important negative features. In 2008 almost one in every two Mexicans lived in poverty. Inequality was a leading cause of this situation: with a Gini coefficient of 0.53, Mexico was a full member of the world's most unequal region (Latin America). The growth of the economy, notably its manufacturing sector, has failed to create jobs for large numbers of people, many of whom have been pushed into some form of illegality (the informal economy, illegal migration, or criminal activities). In the first years of the twentieth century, a growing crisis in public security weakened or even destroyed many institutions, especially those related to law enforcement. Institutional innovation has thus gone hand in hand with institutional decay.

Titles and authors of individual reports on which this chapter is based are found in Appendix 7.1.

In this contradictory context, the development of institutions and the contribution of institutions to development are full of paradoxes. As shown below, efforts to set up "Weberian" bureaucracies ended up weakening the social links that had facilitated the functioning of a specialized institution like the civil aviation authority. The stock exchange modernized its administrative and technical processes and became more profitable and better integrated into global capital markets, but it remained under the tight control of a small number of firms owned by a few families. Even as its own budget has been seriously reduced, the tax authority has been able to extract greater resources for the state, but it is unable or unwilling to effectively tax the highest and the lowest economic sectors. An ambitious attempt to resuscitate the public postal service through the appointment of a powerful leader achieved impressive goals, but it was subsequently derailed by an unrelated conflict within the bureaucratic and economic elite. Twenty national or regional hospitals offer first-rate health care for the uninsured population, but the country's health indicators remain significantly below those of nations at similar levels of economic development.

This chapter, which summarizes the five Mexican institutional studies, describes and explains these and similar paradoxes.[1] It does so by analyzing similarities and differences among the five institutions and by reflecting on what these cases reveal about the general institutional situation in Mexico.

Institutions studied were the civil aviation authority (Dirección General de Aeronáutica Civil, DGAC), the public mail service (SEPOMEX or Correos de México), the Manuel Gea González General Hospital (HGMGG, taken here as illustrative of the national health care system), the tax authority (Servicio de Administración Tributaria, SAT), and the stock exchange (Bolsa Mexicana de Valores, BMV).

The first four institutions are part of the federal government. This entails a limitation of their representativeness, for federal institutions tend to be more developed than their subnational counterparts. Yet each of the selected institutions is either the only one in its field or the largest and most developed. Therefore, one may say that they are representative of the best institutions that Mexico has in the respective sectors. Something similar can be said about the single private institution, the stock exchange. In sum, these five cases, although not good representatives of the diversity of Mexican institutions, are at the forefront of the country's developmental efforts.

The five institutions are relatively old and well established. The youngest of them, SAT, was set up as an independent agency in 1997, but by then it already had a long history within the Ministry of Finance. Two of these institutions, SAT and SEPOMEX, are large; together, they employ more than 56,000 people, approximately 1 of every 12 people working in the federal government. In contrast, HGMGG and DGAC are quite small, each with less than 2,000 employees. We do not have an estimation of the number of people working for BMV, but this institution should be better gauged by its sheer economic importance.

A GLANCE AT THE LITERATURE

The recent literature about Mexican institutions is voluminous. This literature has analyzed fundamental aspects of Mexican society but has neglected other, equally important, if less visible, aspects. The present chapter may contribute to filling out some of these analytic voids.

By far the preferred topic in the existing literature has been the impact of democratization and economic reforms on the institutions of the country. Much attention has been paid to the creation or reform of entities like the Federal Electoral Institute, the Electoral Tribunal, the Supreme Court, the Central Bank, and the Freedom of Information Institute. Similarly, scholars have often analyzed the institutional transformations related to political and governmental decentralization, changing executive-legislative relations, reforms of fiscal federalism, privatization of state-owned enterprises, and the establishment of new forms of economic regulation.[2] This focus is, of course, entirely justified. The broad political and economic changes that took place at the turn of the century largely reorganized Mexico's institutional environment.

Less abundant but still ample is the literature about institutions related to social development and poverty alleviation. Here, interest has centered on such phenomena as the reform of the pensions system, the creation of the Ministry of Social Development, the successive design of three major antipoverty programs (Solidaridad, Progresa, and Oportunidades), the enactment of the Law for Social Development and the establishment of organisms charged with measuring poverty and evaluating social policies.[3] Again, the attention given to these institutions is obviously justified: recent political and economic transformations have renewed the interest in poverty and economic inequality, acute ills from which the country seems unable to cure itself.

It would be unwise to attempt even a cursory review of this literature. The variety of themes, approaches, and findings is staggering. But four quick remarks about it will put in context the analysis presented in the following sections of this chapter. The first relates to institutional continuity. As already stated, the institutional changes that Mexico underwent at the turn of the century were broad and deep. But the institutional structure of the country suffered no major collapse or wholesale restructuration. "Reform of the state" has been a catchy phrase in several political and academic circles, but changes have been introduced incrementally. There has been nothing comparable to the constitutional assemblies that revamped the basic institutions of the Andean countries between 1991 and 2008, or to the massive changes that military dictatorships, civil wars, and democratic transitions provoked in other parts of Latin America. As one author has pointed out, institutional continuity is noticeable in virtually any area of Mexican life: "Even beyond the political parties, many of the same institutional actors remain largely in place. Despite extensive privatization in the eighties and nineties, many state industries like PEMEX, NAFIN, BANOBRAS, and others remain. Many of the major corporatist labor unions like the CTM continue to survive, though some with far less political influence than in the past, and others, like the teachers union (SNTE), with significant political clout" (Morris 2010: 186).

A second point is that many institutions, typically associated with the old system of political and economic governance, have survived, interacting with the new rules and organizations. This has widened even more the traditionally large gaps between the formal and informal institutions of the country.[4] Old, publicly discredited forms of political mobilization like clientelism or state-sponsored corporatism intermingle with competitive electoral institutions and new associative models (Montambeault 2011; Samstad 2002). Old forms of corruption have been fitted into new economic and political frameworks (Bailey and Paras 2006; Morris 2010). Powerful oligopolies, tightly controlled by a few families, continue to flourish under formally competitive market rules (Levy and Walton 2009). As will be seen in the following sections, disrupting these and similar forms of coexistence may have unexpected consequences.

Third, even if it has suffered no institutional collapse or wholesale institutional replacement, the country has experienced notorious processes of deinstitutionalization. As defined by Claus Offe (2006: 26), deinstitutionalization happens when "rules are being abandoned *without* being replaced by some alternative institutional pattern" (original emphasis).[5] This has been particularly evident in the field of public security, where institutions seem caught in a peculiar balance of power: the state cannot impose its rules on belligerent criminals, while the latter, for obvious reasons, are unable to create their own, publicly defendable sets of rules. Aware that their actions are not achieving their declared aims, the authorities have devoted considerable energy to creating, reforming, and eliminating institutions and laws. This at first sight may look like a positive sign of dynamism and flexibility. In reality, it is a serious obstacle to real institutional development. The pattern is very similar to the one that, according to Jean-Jacques Rousseau (1772), characterized Polish legislation: "Whenever an abuse was noticed, a law was made to remedy it. From this law arose further abuses, which had in turn to be corrected. This way of acting is endless, and leads to the most terrible of all abuses, which is to deprive all laws of their force by dint of multiplying their number."

But Mexico's deinstitutionalization is not confined to public security. It is an important, if often neglected, consequence of the dismantling of many formal and informal rules that used to give stability to the postrevolutionary regime (Grayson 2010: 2–4).

Finally, Mexico's "new institutionalism" has paid little attention to the concrete workings of institutions, especially those far from the spotlights of economic and political change. How formal and informal institutions interact; how institutional innovation deals with rigid power configurations; how the praiseworthy aims of formal public institutions compete with other, less commendable but decisive ends; how institutions recruit and train their personnel, modernize their technological resources, and update their procedures under severe budgetary constraints; how people who occupy the commanding positions in institutionally defined hierarchies react to the often contradictory incentives coming from the context in which their institutions operate—questions like these have received less attention than they evidently deserve. The case studies summarized in this chapter address these and similar issues. By so doing, they contribute to improving our understanding of the complex, often contradictory institutional arrangements that both facilitate and hinder Mexico's development.

THE CONTEXT

To know how Mexico has developed in the last years and the contributions that institutions studied here have made to such development would require a lengthy investigation, a task that cannot be carried out here. But no amount of subtlety and complexity is likely to blur certain basic trends, which we keep in mind when trying to understand the performance of these five institutions.

Development is understood here as sustainable, meaningful, and equitable growth. The first fact to notice in this respect is that from 1990 to 2008 Mexico's per capita economic output grew at an average yearly rate of 1.5 percent, quite a respectable figure. It should be noted, however, that this rate was lower than the comparable figure for Latin America as a whole (1.8 percent). As figure 7.1 shows, economic growth in Mexico was more volatile than that in the entire region. Mexico seems to be more vulnerable to economic shocks than the average Latin American country, as was confirmed by the effects of the 2008 recession. In sum, there has been important growth in Mexico, but such growth does not look solid enough.

With regard to fairness and social wellbeing, figure 7.2 shows that poverty decreased from 1992 to 2008. But it is difficult to assert whether this improvement is sustainable. The evolution of poverty seems too dependent on the economic cycle, with poverty decreasing when the economy grows and increasing in times of crisis (as in 1996 and 2008). As shown in figure 7.3, the gains against inequality, as measured by the Gini coefficient, were less impressive and seem even less stable. Even at its best moment, the Gini coefficient did not drop below 0.51. Throughout the period, Mexico remained a typical, highly unequal Latin American country.

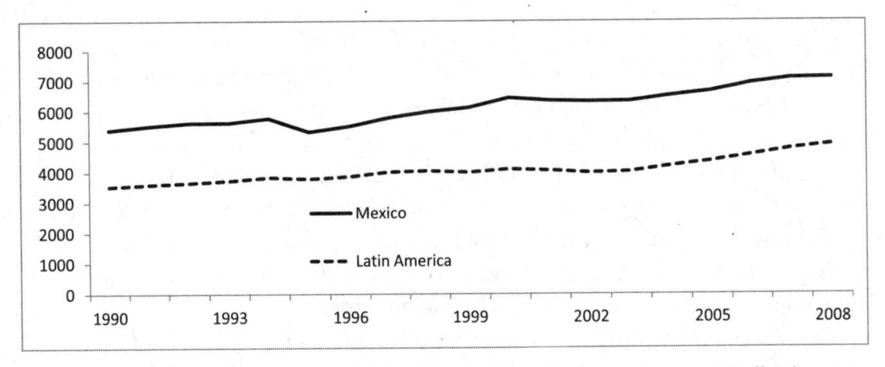

FIGURE 7.1. Per Capita GDR in Mexico and Latin America (2000 Constant Dollars). Source: ECLAC (2010).

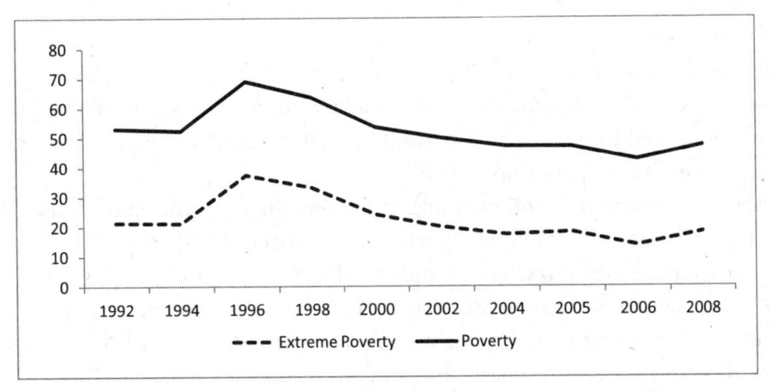

FIGURE 7.2. Percentage of People in Poverty in Mexico. Source: Consejo Nacional de Evaluación de la Política de Desarrollo Social (Coneval 2009).

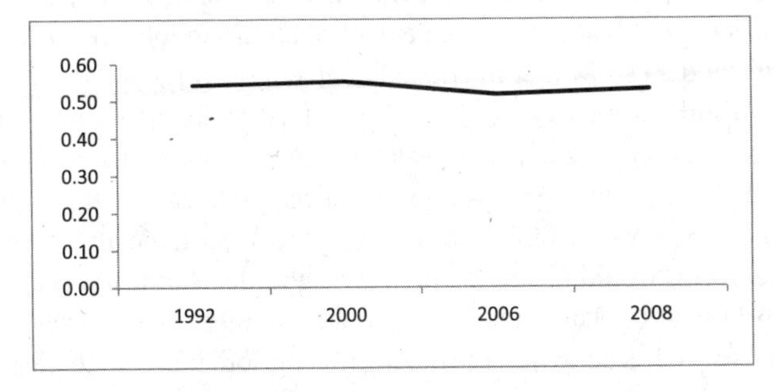

FIGURE 7.3. Income Inequality in Mexico: Gini Coefficient. Source: Coneval (2009).

An indicator of the productive capacity of the country—and of the social factors that underlie and surround it—is the growth of exports. In 2008 Mexico's non-oil exports, measured in current dollars, were seven times as great as in 1991. A similar trend was visible in most of Latin America. What sets Mexico apart from other countries in the region is the importance of manufacturing exports: in 1980 these accounted for 60 percent of total non-oil exports; by 1991 that share had grown to 91 percent, and in 2008 it amounted to 96 percent (INEGI 2010).[6] Together, these trends suggest an increase of productive capacity—particularly in the industrial sector—and openness to foreign trade.

But development also implies improving the situation of a country in the international power structure. A country that is truly developing should become more autonomous and influential in the world. However, in the last decades, Mexico has become more, not less, dependent on foreign technology, investment, and markets, especially from the United States. From 1993 to 2009, 92 percent of all Mexican exports went to the United States. From this country came 54 percent of all the foreign direct investment that Mexico received in 1999–2009 (SE 2010). The United States is also the source of virtually all remittances by Mexican immigrants, which amounted to more than 2 percent of GDP in 2008 and which has a major impact on millions of poor households.

Another important component of development is the creation of decent, productive, and reasonably well paid jobs. In this respect, the Mexican record is dismaying. In spite of the growth of the industrial sector, its capacity to provide formal jobs has remained stagnant. In the year 2000, industry accounted for 28 percent of all employment in the country; in 2009 this share dropped to 24 percent. The situation of agriculture is particularly dramatic: according to official data, from 1991 to 2008 the absolute number of people working in the agricultural sector decreased from 8.2 million to 5.7 million (INEGI 2010).

The alternative for vast numbers of people has been informality and (mostly illegal) migration to the United States. The International Labor Organization (ILO 2008: 20) calculated that in 2005, 55 percent of all urban jobs in Mexico were informal. Official data show that in 2009, 64 percent of workers did not have social security or health care coverage (INEGI 2010). According to a much cited estimation (Passel 2005), in 2004 there were 5.9 million Mexicans illegally living in the United States. On average, 485,000 new illegal Mexican migrants entered the United States every year from 2000 to 2004. The great majority of these people were workers. This would mean that of every eight Mexican workers almost one is illegally working in the United States. It would also mean that of every ten people who entered the Mexican workforce during that period, four had to illegally search for a job in the United States.

Apart from its strictly economic effects, the lack of formal jobs for at least half the working population has obvious implications for social justice, for effective citizenship, and even for the rule of law.[7] It also has specific consequences for the institutions analyzed here, especially for health care and tax administration.

In short, the balance seems mixed. In the last decades, Mexico experienced notable economic growth, as well as important reductions in poverty and small gains against inequality. But the sustainability of these achievements seems uncertain. At the same time, the economy of the country became more dependent and painfully unable to provide stable and well-paid jobs for the majority of workers. Such is the context that one should keep in mind when assessing the developmental performance of our five institutions.

INSTITUTIONAL ADEQUACY AND CONTRIBUTION TO DEVELOPMENT

Tables 2.2 and 2.3, above, present the scores that these institutions were given in the two outcomes of interest for the study: institutional adequacy (the degree to which the really existing organization functions in accordance with its formal goals and norms) and contribution to development (the degree to which the institution makes a significant contribution to development in its area of specialization).

The five institutions analyzed have worthy missions, at least on paper, and are ostensibly designed to accomplish them. Fieldwork done for this project shows that, roughly speaking, most of them live up to those ideals, the only exception being the postal service. In contrast, their capacities to make specific contributions to development show more variation. But even in the worst case, these institutions can make at least a minimum contribution.

Our case studies can be sorted into two subsets. The first consists of BMV, HGMG, and SAT—the best-performing institutions, according to both outcome variables. With respect to BMV's institutional adequacy, the main observation made in the case study is that, acting in a market that it is constantly evolving, the stock exchange "continuously re-creates itself and, in that process, establishes structures and designs manuals with such a speed that it is impossible to dissociate practices from ideals. Frequently, manuals do not precede structures, but vice versa" (Gómez Fonseca 2009: 85).

During its current stage, initiated in 1975, BMV has undergone important changes. As a consequence of the nationalization of banks in 1982, securities brokers, or *casas de bolsa*, became the only private agents doing financial transactions. This gave an extraordinary push to the securities market in general and to BMV in particular. The number of very large firms participating in the market grew substantially, but the most visible change was the inclusion (for the first and only time in Mexican history) of myriad small, middle-class investors. The ensuing bubble burst in 1987, coinciding with the infamous global Black Monday. The consequences were asymmetrical: small investors were wiped out, but very large speculators reinforced their control over the market.[8] The neoliberal reforms implemented during the Salinas government (1988–94) further accelerated this process of concentration.

After the financial crisis of 1995, BMV made a series of institutional changes. One of them was the automation of transactions, with the creation of the so-called Sentra systems (1995–99). This not only made BMV transactions more fluid; it also improved the integration of Mexico into the international markets. It was in these years that the BMV holding company started to create specialized firms for information, technology, custody, derivatives, and so on. The latest large change was the process of demutualization, that is, the transformation of BMV from a mutual company (fully owned by its customers—the securities brokers) into a joint stock company whose shares are traded in the market.

While experiencing all these changes, BMV has shown its capacity to transform both its institutional design and its organizational structure. At the same time, it has also been able to increase its contribution to the functioning of Mexican capitalism. Among the benefits resulting from the operation of the stock exchange, the case study underlines the following: "a greater number of financial instruments, activation of domestic financing and preservation of foreign financing, debts with longer maturities, the creation of investment companies, and the inclusion of pension funds that are beginning to participate in the securities market" (Gómez Fonseca 2009: 73).

However, Mexico's securities market has serious limitations. Perhaps the most important of these is its low penetration. Figure 7.4 compares Mexico's market capitalization (as a percentage of GDP) with those of two relatively well developed Latin American countries and with that of the United States for 1990 through 2008. Throughout the period, Mexico's securities market remained quite thin. At the beginning of the period, it was comparatively greater than Brazil's, but this relation was reversed by 1999. The low penetration of Mexico's securities market is related to its elitism: six brokerage firms managed more than 50 percent of the total value traded in 2008; and the stocks of seven large companies—most of them owned or controlled by a few families—concentrated 64 percent of total value traded (BMV 2008: 13).[9] In sum, BMV has facilitated financial operations in the country. It has done little, however, to democratize access to the securities market, which has remained thin and elitist.

HGMGG is another relatively bright story. This general hospital is emblematic of the national public health care system not in the sense of being typical but rather of being exemplary, of being a model worthy of imitation by the rest of the system. Mexico's public health system has two branches: social security and

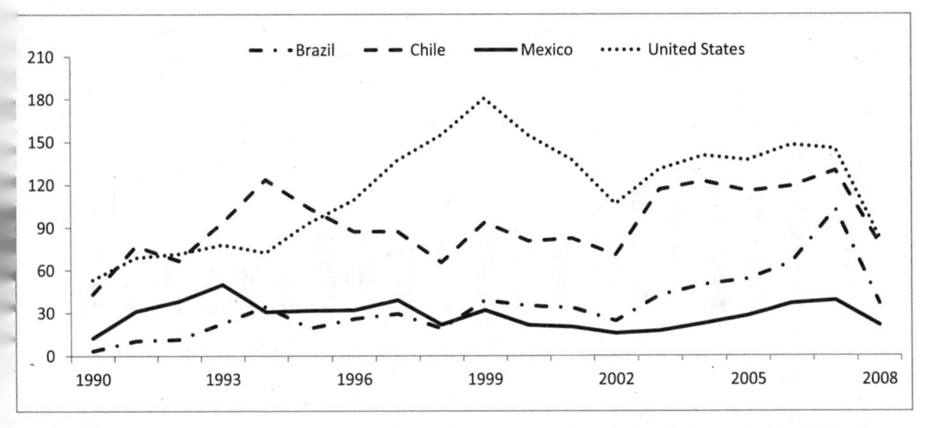

FIGURE 7.4. Market Capitalization of Listed Companies (% of GDP). Source: World Bank (2010).

"public assistance" (which serves the noninsured population, otherwise known as the "open population"). HGMGG is part of the latter branch.[10]

Efforts to decentralize the public health care service for the open population began in the early 1980s. After long and complicated efforts, the process culminated in the National Decentralizing Accord, signed in 1996. The bulk of the service was transferred to state governments. The federal government, through the Health Ministry (Secretaría de Salud, SA), retained leadership of the entire system and the direct administration of twenty elite hospitals: ten national health institutes, five high-specialty regional hospitals, and five general reference hospitals.[11]

HGMGG is one of the five general hospitals directly operated by the Health Ministry. It provides specialty service to patients referred by a primary health care institution who live in southern Mexico City or in the states of Morelos, Guerrero, Oaxaca, and Chiapas (the first is adjacent to Mexico City; the other three are very poor states). HGMGG classifies its patients according to a seven-level socioeconomic table. All services to patients in category 1x (poorest) are free of charge. But the fees for even the richest category are quite low compared to those charged by most private institutions.

In 2004–6 only approximately 3 percent of all HGMGG patients were classified in the poorest, nonpaying category. This number seems too small if one recalls that, according to the official data shown in figure 7.2, more than 18 percent of the Mexican people were in extreme poverty in 2005. About 80 percent of HGMGG patients were placed in categories 1 and 2 (second and third poorest, respectively); and only slightly above 1 percent were classified in the two richest categories (Gómez Fonseca and Ruiz 2008: 5).

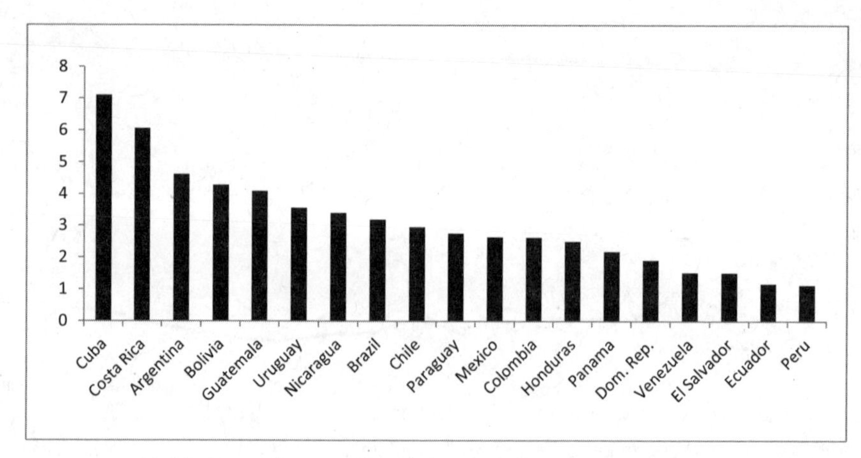

FIGURE 7.5. Public Expenditure on Health (% of GDP), 2000–2008. Source: ECLAC (2010).

A single example would help one assess how accessible the services provided by HGMGG are. In 2010 a first-time consultation cost 94 pesos and each subsequent consultation 64 pesos, for patients at any socioeconomic level except the lowest (HGMGG 2010). Such figures amounted, respectively, to 1.6 and 1.1 daily minimal wages, which may seem insignificant to someone at the highest socioeconomic level—but surely not to a person in extreme poverty. On balance, while more accessible than most private hospitals, HGMGG imposes considerable costs on its patients—especially those in poverty and extreme poverty.

Apart from its main objective—providing specialty medical service—HGMGG also prepares specialists and conducts medical research. Its list of "strategic objectives" includes a fourth one: to have an efficient and transparent administration. Fieldwork done for this research showed that HGMGG fulfills its objectives and complies with its norms reasonably well. The hospital provides about 175,000 medical consultations, performs more than 1,250,000 clinical analyses, and accepts more than 18,000 hospitalizations per year. In these and related items, its performance has improved in the past years. According to surveys done by hospital personnel, patient satisfaction with services is high.

Being directly operated by the Health Ministry, HGMGG is free from the financial and administrative obstacles that affect the great majority of hospitals operated by state governments. And, as explained in the following section, because of its partial autonomy, this hospital is also free from the powerful influence of the national union of health care workers.

HGMGG (together with the other nineteen elite public hospitals) is, relatively speaking, an "island of excellence" within a far more troubled sea of public health

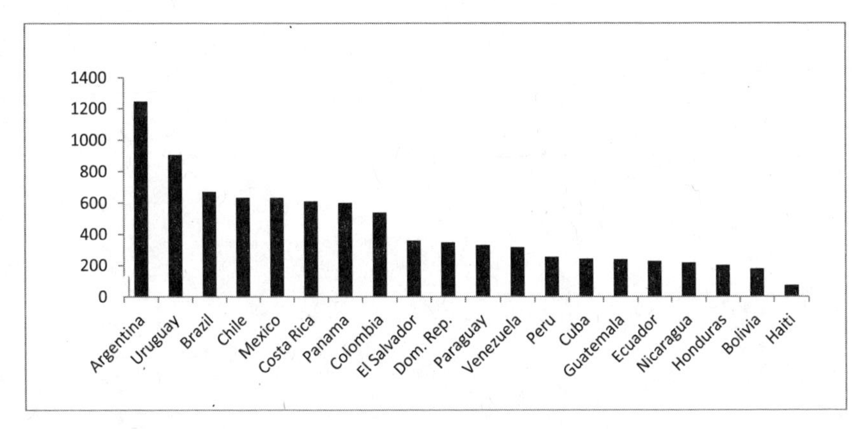

FIGURE 7.6. Per Capita Total Expenditure on Health (PPP int. $), 2000–2006. Source: WHO (2010).

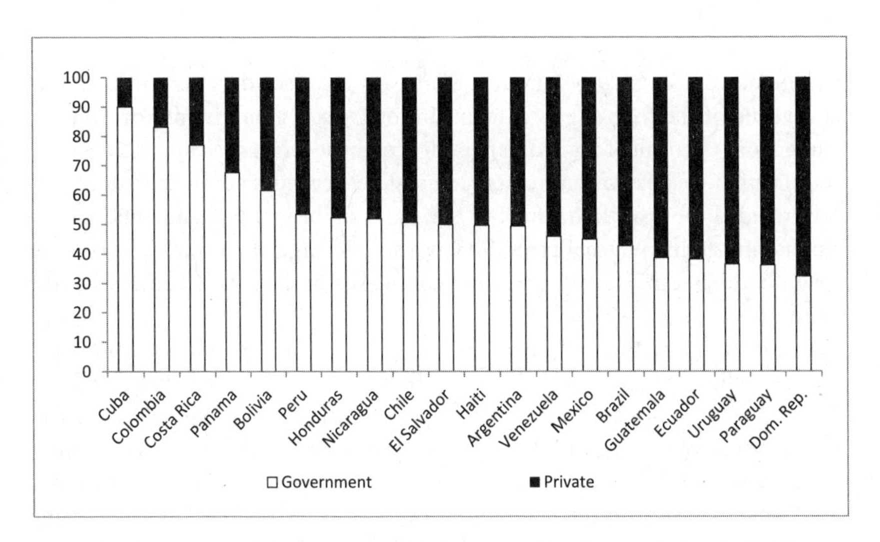

FIGURE 7.7. Government and Private Contributions to Total Expenditure on Health, 2000–2006. Source: WHO (2010).

care service. Figures 7.5, 7.6, and 7.7 give a summary idea of these troubles. Mexico's public expenditure on health care is low, even by the obviously low Latin American standards. Its total (public and private) per capita expenditure on health is mediocre, by similar standards. And the contribution that public expenditure makes to total expenditure in Mexico (45 percent) is significantly smaller than the respective Latin American average (53 percent).

The third relatively bright story is SAT. To realize the importance of this

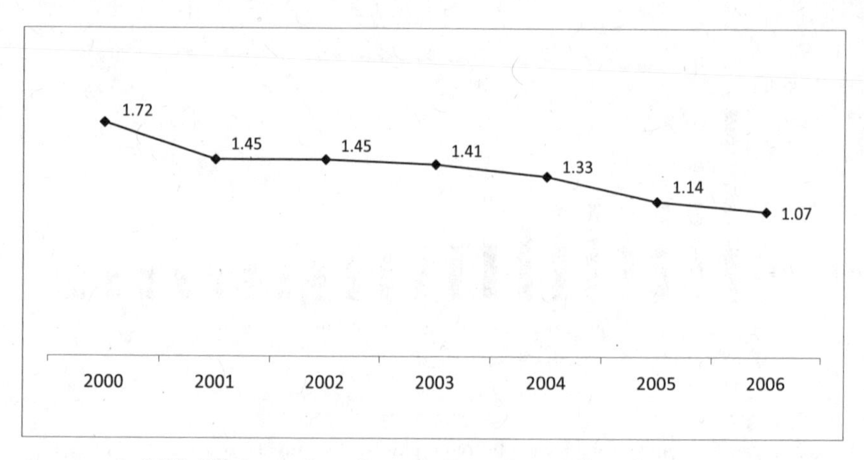

FIGURE 7.8. SAT's Efficiency: Cents Spent for Every Peso Collected. Source: SAT (2007:103) and SAT (2008).

institution, we need only point out that in 2005 it collected 95 percent of all the tax revenue of the federal government. In total, taxes administered by SAT accounted for 55 percent of the ordinary budget of the federal government. Given the centralization of Mexico's entire taxation system, revenues administered by SAT also provided most of the income of state and municipal governments.[12] Apart from administering internal taxes, SAT is also in charge of customs and taxes to foreign trade (but this function was not considered in the detailed analysis of the institution).

In several senses, the performance of SAT was admirable. As shown in figure 7.8, SAT's efficiency, as measured by the productivity of the taxes that it collects, improved significantly in recent years. In part, this might be simply an effect of the economic cycle. The correlation between the evolution of the revenues administered by SAT and the evolution of GDP is almost perfect (0.99).[13] Even so, it is remarkable that SAT's productivity grew even as its own budget was decreasing (from 2000 to 2006, this budget decreased 13 percent in constant pesos). As a result of this double trend, SAT's efficiency grew notably: in 2000 SAT spent 1.7 cents for each peso that it collected; by 2006 it spent only 1.07 cents.

Other, more specific indicators point in the same direction. From 2004 to 2007 the "cost of compliance" (the cost of paperwork and related expenses that a taxpayer incurs when complying with his, her, or its tax obligations) slightly decreased for both individuals and corporations.[14] From 2000 to 2007 the number of registered taxpayers (individuals and corporations) grew 22 percent.[15] "Fiscal presence" (defined as the percentage of taxpayers whose transactions are audited by the tax authority) remained low in 2000–2007 (1.1 percent);[16] but its productivity (the revenue generated by these audits) increased notably.[17]

But SAT's performance has two grave faults. One is a big incongruence between SAT's norms and its practices. Since its inception, SAT was defined as a meritocratic institution, endowed with a civil service system. This definition was engraved in SAT's law. However, attempts to implement such a system have repeatedly failed. Specific reasons for each of these failures were variegated, but they all seem to come down to two causes: deficiencies in the training, evaluation, and certification of tax functionaries and budgetary restrictions. When fieldwork for this research was conducted (mid-2008), the civil service meritocratic system was yet to be implemented.

The other fault is even graver. It affects SAT's capacity to collect money from all taxpayers in an equitable way. SAT is more efficient at collecting the most regressive taxes than at collecting the more progressive ones. A good indicator in this respect is the size and distribution of "tax gaps" (the potential revenue that the authority fails to collect). According to a study commissioned by SAT itself, the gaps for income tax on wage earnings and for value-added tax (VAT) are reasonably low: 15 and 20 percent, respectively; but the gap is much larger for personal income tax on business earnings, 80 percent, and the gap for corporate income tax is moderate, 26 percent (Samaniego Breach et al. 2006).

The unfairness of taxation is also evident in the "fiscal credits" (amounts that taxpayers unduly failed to pay, as determined by the audits conducted by the authority). For 2000–2005, the fiscal debts of taxpayers officially defined as "large" amounted to a third of all the standing debts. However, less than 2 percent of the total amount recovered by SAT during that period came from large taxpayers; the rest came from small and middle-level ones. Differences within the group of large taxpayers are perhaps greater. By the end of 2005, three banks had fiscal debts equivalent to 28 billion pesos—a sum "larger than the annual federal budget for public security, social development or healthcare" (ASF 2007: 189). All of this justifies the opinion expressed by the auditing entity of Congress (ASF, the equivalent of the U.S. Government Accounting Office): large taxpayers "are, at the same time, the big fiscal debtors" (ASF 2007: 182). Similar imbalances exist in the outcomes of legal controversies between the authority and taxpayers.[18]

In sum, SAT can control and even terrorize small and middle-size taxpayers, but it looks much weaker when facing the economic elite.[19] These inequalities not only render the tax system unfair; they also imply severe reductions in the revenues of the state. In this context, it comes as no surprise that Mexico's tax burden is excessively light: for 2000–2006, Mexico's tax revenue amounted, on average, to only 10.4 percent of GDP—the fifth lowest tax burden among nineteen Latin American countries (ECLAC 2010).

The two remaining institutions—the postal service and the civil aviation authority—are less fortunate. The main problem with DGAC is its limited capacity to make significant contributions to Mexican development. This is chiefly due to the small stature of the institution. In Mexico there is no organism comparable, in resources and competences, to the Federal Aviation Authority of the United States. The civil aeronautic and airport authority is distributed among several agencies, among which DGAC occupies a special place not because it is the most powerful but because it is the only one exclusively devoted to performing functions within the field. In other words, all that falls within the purview of DGAC does not exhaust the functions required by Mexico's civil aviation.

DGAC—a third-level agency within the Ministry of Communication and Transportation—shares the authority to regulate and oversee civil aviation with the minister whose "nontransferable competences" include two critical functions: directing the aeronautic and airport authority and granting or canceling concessions to administer airports and provide commercial air transportation. It also shares the authority with the vice-minister of transportation, who is entitled to direct the administration and operation of private and public aviation services. Finally, DGAC shares its authority with three specialized agencies: the National Center for Aviation Medicine (CENMA), Services to Navigation in Mexico's Air Space (SENEAM), and Airports and Auxiliary Services (ASA).

Hence it is clear that the strategic and more general functions of the civil aviation authority, as well as some specialized competences, are placed out of reach of the DGAC. The internal norms of the Ministry of Communication and Transportation give DGAC the following main functions: verify that airports and airplanes comply with all the relevant regulations, especially those concerning the safety of operations; grant permissions, licenses, and certificates to relevant firms, people, and products (e.g., pilots, aircraft, and flight schools); compile and process statistical databases on civil aviation; investigate aviation accidents and coordinate rescue operations; and serve as liaison with relevant international organisms. But interviews with DGAC people revealed that the agency's main concerns are those related to the safety of airports and flights. The coordination of the different authorities (customs, migration, police, etc.) and service providers that operate in airports also figures among DGAC main practical tasks.

The formal mission of DGAC seems grandiose: "Ensure that air transportation contributes to sustainable growth, social well-being, regional development and the creation of jobs, thereby contributing to the establishment of a better integrated and communicated society." But, as said above, its real competences are far more modest. An authority with these real characteristics may have been functional until the mid-1980s, when the civil aviation market was much smaller and dominated by state-owned firms. But since the early 1990s, there have been three broad changes. First, the market became larger and more diverse, with more domestic and international passengers, a larger number of international flights, a larger number of Mexican cities served, and more participation of foreign airlines. Second, air transportation was privatized and deregulated, especially visible in the problematic privatization of the two main airlines (Aeroméxico and Mexicana).[20] Third, airport administration was selectively privatized, a process that is still incomplete.[21] To these trends one should add the continuous technological changes that the worldwide aviation industry has experienced and the equally important transformations in the environment in which civil aviation operates (with, among other things, greater concerns with safety and security).

DGAC personnel interviewed for our study apparently feel that they are satisfactorily performing their limited functions. Yet they also fear that their resources—human and technological—may prove insufficient for the new challenges. And they also believe that their contribution to the development of Mexico's air transportation market is seriously limited. They all seemed to long for an autonomous and better-equipped agency.

The case of the postal service is even more dramatic. Correos de México is an institution in crisis, which can be illustrated with a few figures. The number of offices (service points) that it maintains throughout the country decreased by 20 percent from 2004 to 2008. SEPOMEX's financial deficit, measured in constant pesos, grew 303 percent from 2004 to 2008.[22] The total number of pieces delivered grew 7.1 percent from 2000 to 2008, a very modest increase considering the expansion of the potential market. In 2008 only 44 percent of the country's 29,974 localities with more than 250 inhabitants had postal service; 45 percent of people living in rural areas had no access to the service. In 2008, according to an estimation made by ASF, 27 percent of the postal pieces managed by SEPOMEX were delivered with delay.[23]

Four main problems seem at the roots of the crisis. The first is financial. The postal service has been in deficit for most of its modern history. This is a consequence of its very nature: rather than a commercial entity, it is a provider of a public service. Its own revenues are insufficient for these tasks. Therefore, it depends on government subsidies, which have been too low in the last decades, as shown in the following section. The second problem is closely associated with the first: the postal service has not been able to keep up with recent technological changes. Its technology is obsolete, for the most part. The third problem is the growing competition from private firms, which, since the late 1980s, began to monopolize the most lucrative segments of the market. The operation of these firms is at odds with the Mexican Constitution: article 28 defines the postal service as a strategic function exclusively reserved to the state. Finally, the agency is mandated to provide free postal service to the judiciary power, the federal congress, the Federal Electoral Institute, and political parties. According to SEPOMEX, the cost of these services (known as "postal franchises") accounted for 10 percent of the financial deficit accumulated in 2004–8.

Fieldwork for this study coincided with the appointment (in April 2007) of a new director of the postal service, Purificación Carpinteyro. A friend of President

Felipe Calderón, the new director had had a brilliant career in the private sector. As soon as she came to the position, she announced an ambitious "Transformation Plan" that included changes in the leadership of the institution, new relations with workers, acquisition of new technology, more aggressive commercial methods, a new image (including a reversal to the traditional name of the institution), and even new uniforms for postmen. When Carpinteyro was promoted to vice-minister of communication, the transformation plan apparently received a new push. But then she entered into a heated conflict with her boss, the minister of communication and transportation, largely fueled by disputes between powerful telecommunication companies (especially Telmex and Televisa). She was dismissed in February 2009, and the reform that she had championed lost momentum.

This coincidence between fieldwork for this study and the reform process largely explains the apparently anomalous scores that SEPOMEX received in table 7.1. The really existing organization deviates, in several respects, from its own norms and ends. Perhaps the greatest incongruence derives from its inability to exert the state's exclusive rights on postal services. Infringements on the legally mandated inviolability of mail pieces and the circulation of prohibited items are other important deviations. Nonetheless, the transformations of 2007–8 seemed to open the possibility of a renaissance of the agency; in any case, they showed that the public postal service can still survive. And, for all its failures, this service is still the only one accessible to most people in Mexico.

INSTITUTIONAL DETERMINANTS

The second step in our analysis is to look for the potential causes of the developmental outcomes discussed above. Tables 2.2 and 2.3, above, present the scores that our five institutions received in each of the six determinants. Below is a summary description of the situation of each institution with regard to those potential causes.

Meritocracy

The first potential cause is meritocratic recruitment and promotion. Three cases received considerably high marks on this determinant: the civil aviation authority, the stock exchange, and HGMGG. BMV's human resources methods are not so much meritocratic as they are competitive. Three methods are particularly important. The first is the use of performance-based payment for operative personnel and performance-based promotion for nonoperative personnel. Employees strenuously vie with each other for promotion and bonuses. This, of course, increases the risks of opportunistic or dishonest behavior. In response, government regulators at CNBV (Comisión Nacional Bancaria y de Valores, or National Banking and Securities Commission) have set tougher sanctions, including fines and public disclosure—an important punishment in a milieu where reputation is decisive. A consequence of this competitive regime is high personnel turnover at the operative level; most line workers are forty years old or less.

The second expedient is personnel training, which is offered by the professional association of securities intermediaries and by higher-education institutions. The third, related method is the certification of personnel, which is carried out by BMV itself. People interviewed for this study explained that certification has become less demanding, but it is now accessible to more people. Finally, since the 1990s the position of BMV's CEO ceased to be an honorary appointment. The chief of BMV, as well as the directors of subordinated firms, is a person with demonstrable professional qualifications.

HGMGG recruits new doctors mainly from the specialists that it trains. Entrance to the specialization programs that HGMGG offers is very competitive. And the recently graduated specialists hired by the hospital have to pass through a selection process that takes into account their academic credentials and the recommendations of senior doctors. That is why our case study concludes that recruitment depends both on the merits of the candidate and on his or her social and professional ties. Recruitment of other medical personnel—nurses, social workers, and stretcher bearers—also requires examinations. In contrast, hiring of nonmedical personnel is highly influenced by the labor union, and preference is given to relatives of retired workers. Appointment as HGMGG general director is made by the governing board, "on the indications" of the nation's executive power. But, according to the established rules, the candidate must be a prestigious specialist.

Recruitment at state-run hospitals is much less meritocratic, as illustrated by Mexico City hospitals. In these cases, the union of national health workers in effect appoints 50 percent of all new employees—and being recruited through the union is the safest and quickest path to tenure. In contrast, employees at HGMGG are not affiliated with the national union but with an independent one that does not interfere a great deal with recruitment and promotion.

The situation of the civil aviation authority is curious. Like the rest of the ordinary federal bureaucracy (and unlike the other institutions studied, which are independent organisms), DGAC was submitted to a daring experiment to quickly establish a professional civil service. This attempt to create a "Weberian" bureaucracy by decree began in 2003. Although DGAC people seemed to recognize the need for a more professional bureaucracy, they all regretted the consequences of the experiment. The new rules have complicated the hiring of personnel to fill vacancies in critical areas. People with good technical qualifications are eliminated at the beginning of the new selection process, often because they do not appear to have the "DNA of a good functionary" (which includes general knowledge about government functions and a set of desired moral principles).[24] In contrast, the people who make it to the final stage of the selection process often have doubtful technical credentials or have a notorious reputation in the civil aviation community.

One lesson that this Weberian experiment leaves is that, in a small community of specialists where technical reputation and interpersonal trust are important, the sudden introduction of impersonal mechanisms for recruitment and promotion may be counterproductive. To these problems we should add the consequences of severe personnel cuts mandated by the federal government at the beginning of the decade, which left many voids in the DGAC organizational chart. The leaders of the institution interviewed for this study believed that it was necessary to increase the workforce by at least 50 percent. This problem is compounded by the low level of salaries—which are uncompetitive not only when compared to those of relevant private firms but also vis-à-vis the salaries paid by other government institutions in the civil aviation sector.

In contrast to the preceding cases, SAT and SEPOMEX received low ratings in meritocracy. Compared to those of other Mexican institutions, SAT's sins against meritocracy may look rather venial. But when measured by SAT's own standards—and by the requirements of an institution that must extract resources from an uncooperative population and particularly from a powerful and often hostile economic elite—those failures seem far more serious.[25] As mentioned above, the most flagrant failure is the nonimplementation of the civil service rules established since the inception of the institution. Nonetheless, the hiring of new employees seems to be well regulated: job openings are publicly offered, and new candidates are submitted to a three-stage evaluation process (psychometric tests, review of their professional and educational credentials, and an interview to assess their technical competences).

Promotion, however, seems much less structured. Since 2007 SAT employees have been submitted to ambitious "360° evaluations." But by the time our fieldwork was conducted, there was no system to sanction or reward employees according to their performance. Compared to those of other government institutions, SAT's salaries are highly competitive, but they look rather meager when measured against those of the business sector. Therefore, talented people tend to remain only a few years in the service and then move to the business sector, where their knowledge of tax matters is highly valued and rewarded.[26] According to people interviewed, these problems have two main causes: the "rigid" regulations about government salaries and bonuses and the insufficient budget of the institution—a problem to which we will return below.

The case of SEPOMEX is even graver. According to its own norms, SEPOMEX should recruit its personnel through its Recruitment and Selection Office (which is part of the Human Resources Direction), following strict and detailed meritocratic criteria. In practice, however, hiring occurs through two basic channels. High-level personnel enter the institution at the discretion of the general director or some of his or her close subordinates or by the "recommendation" of some influential person. These employees are bitterly criticized by the rank-and-file workers on the ground that they are either "traditional bureaucrats" or alien to the institution. In contrast, the hiring of rank-and-file employees is largely influenced by the labor union.[27] It is virtually impossible for these workers to accede to high-level positions, which generates great resentment and demoralization. Low salaries and very limited career opportunities are the usual lot of these workers. In compensation, they enjoy such "privileges" as short working hours and reduced responsibilities.

Immunity to Corruption

It is generally easy to suspect the existence of corruption, but it is hard to prove it. What seems reasonably certain is that the institutions that we studied have made important efforts against corruption—with some visible success. While it has obviously not disappeared, corruption in these institutions has apparently become more subtle and more selective. As shown in table 2.2, except for SEPOMEX, these institutions seem to have at least a barely satisfactory score in this respect.

This is partly a result of several anticorruption efforts that have been made in Mexico—at least at the federal level. One of them was the creation, in the early 1980s, of the Ministry of the Government Comptroller (now known as the Ministry of the Public Function). Another important development was the creation of the auditing arm of the Chamber of Deputies (ASF) in the year 2000, which conducts meticulous evaluations of the federal bureaucracy. Similarly significant were the promulgation of the federal freedom of information law and the creation of a specialized institute in this area in 2002.

The best-ranked institution on immunity to corruption was SAT. Opinion surveys conducted by SAT itself show that taxpayers' perception of corruption within the institution has decreased significantly in recent years.[28] By itself, this indicator may be misleading. But interviews with people who ordinarily interact with the tax administration confirm that corruption is now less massive. To reduce the risk of corruption, SAT adopted a very centralized structure since its creation. Its sixty-six local offices are internally segmented, with each segment directly connected to the respective central authority; in none of these offices is there a local authority that coordinates the different segments.

SAT's efforts against corruption seem sincere. They are obviously related to the strategic function that SAT performs for the Mexican state: corruption in this institution provokes direct damage to public finances, and, therefore, the country's top authorities are very interested in preventing it. However, extreme centralization and related administrative measures may be quite successful at controlling small- and middle-level corruption, but its effects at the top are more doubtful. According to our interviews, people who interact with SAT think that corruption has become more selective, benefiting the very large taxpayers. In addition, there have been some notorious allegations of corruption in SAT's purchases of goods and services. Even more serious have been the accusations of conflict of interest concerning people at the highest levels of the Finance Ministry.[29]

The situation of DGAC with respect to corruption seems paradoxical. There have been at least partially credible accusations of corruption in civil aviation, especially in the privatization and rescue of airlines, in the privatization of airport administration, in the granting of concessions to new commercial airlines, and even in the imposition of sanctions on airlines that supposedly violate safety regulations. Yet, except for the last point, these matters are not in the hands of DGAC but in those of its superiors. In most of these cases, perhaps the greatest problem is not so much corruption proper as the very strong influence exerted by the economic elite or, more exactly, the close relationship between top business groups and some segments of the political elite. Thanks to its subordinated nature, which places it far below the economic and political elites, DGAC has been mostly immune to large-scale corruption.

There was virtual consensus among people interviewed for this study that BMV had become less vulnerable to corruption. The training of employees (on both technical and ethical matters) and the sanctions imposed by government regulators are often cited as the main causes for this improvement. But, on the other hand, the very existence of these sanctions and BMV's constant efforts to instill ethical values in its employees are indications that corruption, especially in the form of opportunistic or predatory behavior, is continuously lurking in the stock exchange.

Fieldwork on HGMGG did not detect major cases of corruption that specifically involved this hospital. The clearer instance was the illegal sale of appointment tickets to first-time patients. This violation, committed by members of the private security firms that work for the hospital, has proved difficult to eradicate despite the efforts of the authorities. Another form of misconduct happens when patients give false information regarding their place of residence or their economic situation in order to unduly get access to this prestigious hospital or to pay less than they should according to the regulations.

But these are minor problems; their basic cause is the paucity of good medical facilities accessible to most of the population. Far more critical is the fact that the hospital is immersed in a milieu where allegations of large-scale fraud and other forms of corruption are recurrent. Mexico is the ninth market in medical drugs, and the first in Latin America. Pharmaceutical companies are always tempted to bribe the medical authorities to illegally improve their access to this market. The existence of an illicit market for medical drugs is another structural problem. Large-scale cases of corruption have also been documented in the selection of doctors applying to specialization programs in Mexican hospitals. Last, another important factor is the existence of an undemocratic national union of health care workers, which illegally—but with the toleration of authorities—interferes with the administration of the public health care system. As mentioned above, HGMGG personnel are not affiliated with that national union.

The ratings of HGMGG, DGAC, SAT, and BMV on immunity to corruption are roughly similar. These institutions seem to enjoy at least an acceptable level in this dimension. Such is not the case with SEPOMEX. In the last decades, there have been numerous denunciations of corruption in the postal service. The stealing of letters and parcels, allegedly committed by SEPOMEX personnel, has been one of the most notorious crimes. In 2007 the press reported the discovery, in Ciudad Juárez, of what seemed to be the largest postal theft in Mexican history—about ten metric tons of letters from the United States, from which checks, money orders, and other valuable documents had been removed. Another form of corruption that has been publicly denounced is the misuse of the postal franchise (free postal service privileges), especially by legislators who have sent millions of letters for political purposes. Finally there have also been abundant denunciations of corruption at the highest level. Directors of SEPOMEX have been accused of different kinds of fraud (especially in the purchase of goods and services from private firms). The prolonged tenure of Gonzalo Alarcón Osorio as SEPOMEX general director (1988–2007) was particularly notorious in that respect.[30]

Absence of "Islands of Power"

Except for SEPOMEX, all our institutions are reasonably free from entrenched cliques capable of subverting institutional rules for their private benefit. In this respect, the best rated institution was SAT, closely followed by HGMGG and DGAC. Fieldwork on SAT could not detect any significant segment of the institution controlled by external agents or used to pursue ends different from those of the tax administration. SAT's extremely centralized structure, as well as the direct supervision by the finance minister and, more indirectly, by the president, are obvious causes of this integrity. Legally mandated oversight by Congress and, indirectly, by state authorities also contribute to this end.[31]

In the HGMGG, the rules about meritocracy described above, the periodic circulation of people at the executive levels, and the demanding professional qualifications that general directors must have all contribute to the integrity of this hospital. The situation of the national health system is sadly different, as illustrated by the excessive influence of the national union of health care workers.

The Mexican securities market has grown, in terms of both operations and participants. People interviewed for this study believed that this expansion has somewhat curbed the capacity of powerful actors to exert a decisive influence within BMV. But they also feel that this process has only gone half the way. The elitist nature of the Mexican securities market and the competitive methods for human resources management, described above, obviously contribute to BMV's integrity. It would be very difficult for a clique to invade and colonize such an elitist and competitive institution. In fact, we could say that BMV's immunity to islands of power is largely due to the fact that BMV itself is an island of power within Mexican society—a stronghold of the business elite.

As already noted, because of its very weakness, DGAC has remained alien to the conflicts and alliances among members of the political and economic elites, the main forces that could capture or corrupt it. To use a metaphor, big predators have not considered DGAC a worthy prey; and given the highly specialized area in which it operates, these are the only hunters with the capacity to capture it. In addition, interviews with DGAC leaders suggested that the labor union does not unduly interfere with the functioning of the institution.

Sepomex is, once again, the deviant case. Especially before the 2007–8 reform attempts, the institution seemed seriously weakened by cliques operating at both its highest and lowest echelons. Indeed, it would not be unreasonable to suspect that the long tenure of Alarcón Osorio at the helm of SEPOMEX was part of a plan to deliberately tarnish the image of the institution, making it intolerably inefficient and corrupt in order to justify its privatization. Alarcón Osorio's tenure coincided with the expansion of private courier companies; it was also in this period that the hiring of private companies to take care of SEPOMEX deliveries became common; and it was also in this period that critical structures designed to preserve the integrity of the institution were dismantled.[32]

At the lower echelons, there was evidence that some groups of workers conspired to steal correspondence and commit other illegal acts.[33] The official labor union has also been accused (especially by the independent union) of operating as a particularistic clique within the institution. As noted, it has certainly interfered with recruitment and promotion policies. Surprisingly, however, the official union endorsed Carpinteyro's "Transformation Plan," which, among other things, called for greater productivity and less corruption.

Proactivity

Four of our five institutions were credited with having at least a moderate ability to involve themselves with their clients, users, and other relevant actors. This time, the exception was DGAC, not SEPOMEX. In the last decades, the Ministry of Health implemented a new model of quality management, which has been backed by powerful international organisms and is inspired by neoliberal ideas. This model sees patients as "clients" and promotes three strategies: opinion surveys as the means to know patients' satisfaction with the service, medical arbitration to solve patient-doctor disputes, and impersonal universalistic channels for receiving patients' complaints and suggestions. Major innovations in this respect include the National Commission of Medical Arbitration, created in 1996, and periodic national surveys aimed at measuring satisfaction with health care services.

HGMGG has adopted this model since at least 2003, when it set up the Quality Management Department. Specific measures that the hospital has implemented include the following: periodic surveys to obtain the opinions of discharged patients, publication of "letters of commitment" through which the hospital promises to improve its services, and establishment of two channels for receiving patients' complaints and suggestions. Even before these measures, HGMGG's performance standards were above national averages (at least among public institutions). But these new measures have apparently brought several improvements, including reduced waiting times for regular medical consultation, kinder treatment of patients, quicker emergency services, and better hospitalization services. According to HGMGG employees interviewed for our study, improvement in waiting times have gone as far as the available human and physical resources allow; further improvements would, in their opinion, jeopardize the quality of services.

As noted, in spite of its diminishing budget, SAT took advantage of economic growth to increase the yield of the taxes that it administers. To accomplish this, it adopted new strategies, better adapted to the characteristics of its normally reluctant "clients" (taxpayers). These strategies include the implementation of risk management techniques (especially useful for deciding which taxpayers to audit); the creation of the Large Taxpayers Unit (one of the main recommendations of tax administration experts); the creation and later reinforcement of a taxpayer assistance unit to promote voluntary compliance; and the outsourcing of services. Although these measures have enhanced SAT's overall efficiency, they have done little to improve its capacity to penetrate the informal economy or to overcome the resistance of the economic elite.

As suggested in the previous section, BMV has been able to seize opportunities in the Mexican economy, or even to create those opportunities. It has also been successful at interacting with relevant international actors. However, its proactivity has not gone as far as to make the securities market more inclusive. This market remains, in effect, closed to most of the middle class and even to many large business firms.

For the best part of the past twenty-five years, SEPOMEX has been a passive, decaying institution. But the ambitious transformations projected and partially executed since 2007 infused it with new vitality. The new reformist director lobbied legislators, made numerous public appearances, signed collaboration agreements with the U.S. Postal Service and the Federal Electoral Institute, and introduced the innovative concept of "multiservice postal offices" (fully equipped with information technology and providing access to several government services). This activism explains the relatively optimistic evaluation of SEPOMEX's proactivity. It remains to be seen, however, if the institution will be able to maintain that vitality.

From what has been said above about DGAC—its subordinated nature, its limited competences, its insufficient personnel—one can hardly expect it to be a proactive institution. When fieldwork for this study was conducted, the institution seemed able to discharge its rather modest duties, but it looked unprepared to actively seek and successfully confront new challenges.

Technological Flexibility and Openness to External Innovation

The two most successful cases of technological flexibility were the two economic institutions—BMV and SAT—the worst being, once again, SEPOMEX. All things considered, BMV seems to be the absolutely best case in this respect. Its flexibility and openness have been manifest in three areas. The first is the use of information technology, especially the establishment of automatic systems for debt and equities transactions. This technological upgrading did not necessarily imply greater independence because it largely depended on the importation of technology and the acquisition of licenses. The second area is the adoption of new organizational schemes, particularly the creation of specialized firms within the BMV holding company, and the successful process of demutualization. The third area is the seizure of new business opportunities, something that is eloquently illustrated by BMV's entry into the derivatives market in 1998 (through a specialized firm known as MexDer).

Two innovations illustrating SAT's technological flexibility and capacity for innovation have been mentioned already: the adoption of risk management techniques and the creation of new units for large taxpayers and for taxpayer assistance. Another important innovation has been automation. To cite the most visible example: according to SAT, the number of electronic operations (declarations, payments, etc.) grew from 52 percent of the total in 2004 to 67 percent in 2007. But this success created a serious problem, which illustrates the paradoxical consequences of new technologies: as they grew in volume, SAT's informatics systems became increasingly dispersed and incompatible. By 2006 SAT's information was dispersed among sixty-six databases. To solve this problem SAT created the so-called Integral Solution Platform, largely funded by a World Bank credit. But several problems (many of them attributable to the private firms to which their project was outsourced) delayed its full implementation (Flores 2007).

HGMGG has adopted new technology both in its administrative activities and in its medical specialties. By the end of the twentieth century, the hospital had a modest network of twenty computers for administrative purposes. By 2008 up to 95 percent of its administrative units had computers. In 2006, following the directives of the Ministry of Health, HGMGG adopted the so-called Integral System of Hospital Management, which has already transformed several administrative tasks. However, the automation of patient files has not been achieved, which places this hospital behind its counterparts in the social security system. In medical technology, HGMGG is reasonably updated. The hospital has high-tech equipment for endoscopy, laparoscopy, and tomography. From 2003 to 2008, its investment in medical technology grew between 74 and 103 percent. To take advantage of economies of scale, HGMGG and other hospitals in southern Mexico City have created a system for the mutual referral of patients. However, the relatively high technological capacity of HGMGG contrasts with the poor equipment of other parts of the national public health care system—in particular of its primary health care branch, where advances are mostly limited to the adoption of information technology for administrative purposes.

DGAC operates in a context in which technological innovation is not a matter of choice but of necessity. Despite its limited resources, this institution has been able to somehow keep pace with the technological progress of the civil aviation industry. The main reason for the relatively high score given to DGAC on this dimension is that technological flexibility and openness to innovation obviously refer not only to demonstrated capacities but also to attitudes. Fieldwork for this study revealed an unequivocal desire for news and more advanced technologies by the institution's staff.

SEPOMEX has clearly fallen behind its competitors, especially the transnational courier companies that have heavily invested in new technologies. The first thing that the institution needs, if it is to reduce this technological gap, is better financing. But it also needs to surmount the resistance of its largely demoralized workforce. Equally daunting is the task of upgrading the technological skills of its workers. As a worker interviewed for the study reported, "Even here, in Mexico City, some employees are afraid of computers."[34]

External Allies

The best rated institutions on this indicator are BMV and, somewhat anomalously, Sepomex. The optimistic evaluation of SEPOMEX is mostly a reflection of the juncture at which our study was done. In 2007–8, after suffering decades of government indifference, and perhaps even hostility, SEPOMEX began to enjoy the enthusiastic support of the president himself. But the dismissal of Purificación Carpinteyro in February 2009 showed, among other things, that personal sympathies—even if they come from people at the highest positions—may be unreliable if they are not backed by structural and institutional conditions.

BMV provides a useful contrast to SEPOMEX. As said above, the fact that BMV is an instrument of the economic elite is the best guarantee against its capture by hostile forces. Since the late 1970s, but particularly since the Salinas presidency (1988–94), the Mexican business elite became more independent and assertive. Today, virtually no part of the government—from whatever political party—would dare to oppose it. On the contrary; politicians seem all too eager to please business leaders. Moreover, the stock exchange also has the backing of transnational and foreign business elites. Thus, in contrast to SEPOMEX, BMV's fate does not depend on personal sympathies but on the structural strength of the business elite, on BMV's structural position within Mexican capitalism, and on the power of transnational capital.

The situations of SAT and HGMGG seem roughly equivalent. A group that exerts a powerful influence on the public health care system is the Mexican Health Foundation (known as Funsalud). This group brings together prestigious doctors, high-ranking government officials in the health care sector, and private sector groups interested in medical matters. Funsalud has been the main promoter of neoliberal health care reform in Mexico, a program that extols the virtues of market mechanisms and praises personal responsibility and individual choice. Funsalud has the support of influential international organisms but is opposed by the national union of health care workers and the traditional medical bureaucracy.

Funsalud affects HGMGG indirectly, through its general influence on the national system, and directly, through the private donations that it procures. More generally, HGMGG has the support of a part of the Mexican medical community, which is interested in the success of a hospital like this. It also has the support of the Ministry of Health, since HGMGG is one of its showcases, one of the twenty elite hospitals directly administered by the federal government. But, to be sure, the main social ally of a hospital like this is the huge portion of the Mexican population that has no access to private health care or to social security. The needs and expectations of this population are the main force behind the creation and existence of this and similar hospitals.

We can perceive here an illustrative similarity—and difference—between HGMGG and SEPOMEX. Both are clearly biased toward the poorer members of society; in fact, one can argue that SEPOMEX prices are more accessible to the poorest people.[35] But the need that public medical services satisfy is clearly more pressing, more difficult to satisfy by other means, than that to which SEPOMEX responds.

As previously explained, SAT has the decisive support of the president and the minister of finance, and, more indirectly, of state governments and federal legislators. But it also faces the opposition of taxpayers, especially those located at either extreme of the social hierarchy. Thanks to its low revenue potential, the informal sector in effect dissuades SAT from trying to tax it. And thanks to its economic power (and the legal and illegal resources that it can mobilize), the business elite is often able to neutralize the efforts of the institution. Even in the absence of corruption, SAT is forced to tacitly collaborate, or at least tolerate, the evasions and elusions at which the Mexican business elite is so adept. Finally, the only external allies of DGAC are its superiors at the Ministry of Communication and Transportation. Apparently, this support allows DGAC to perform its modest duties—but not achieve much more.

BUDGETS

Before concluding, a brief look into the financial situation of the four government institutions may be useful. The availability of funds has obvious consequences for all dimensions analyzed above. A well-funded institution may not necessarily use its money wisely, for example, to hire well-qualified personnel or to purchase new technology. But a poorly financed institution, even with the best intentions, is materially incapacitated to improve itself beyond a certain point. The direction of causality may also be reversed. For instance, an institution with powerful allies will be able to obtain larger and more reliable subsidies, but a patently inefficient institution would have trouble securing even what is strictly necessary for its survival.

The first decade of the twenty-first century was a bad period for the set of government institutions analyzed here. As shown in table 7.1, their combined 2010 budget was 8 percent lower, in constant pesos, than that of 2000. Another significant point is the overwhelming relative weight of SAT. In the entire decade, SAT's budget accounted for 88 percent of the total budget allocated to these four institutions. In fact, much of the decline in their combined funding is explained by SAT's losses, which were especially large in 2007–8.

The situation of SEPOMEX was even worse. In 2010 it registered a sizable gain but not large enough to offset the accumulated losses. SEPOMEX's average annual budget during the decade was 31 percent lower than its budget at the beginning of this period. HGMGG made modest advances during most of the decade, and, in its final years these gains became large. However, the best situation by the end of the decade was that of DGAC. Until 2007 the budget of this institution was basically stationary, but it made a major gain in 2008: DGAC's average annual funding for the entire decade was 64 percent higher than in 2000. Even after these gains, DGAC's budget was the smallest of all institutions examined, representing just 5 percent of SAT's.

CONCLUSION

In recent years Mexico experienced significant economic growth. But, for the most part, this progress has been fragile and inequitable. Large sections of the Mexican population were marginalized from this economic expansion. National development, however, also has an institutional dimension: developed societies have stronger, more coherent, and more efficient institutions. The dual change from more to less regulated markets and from a closed to a competitive political system provided a propitious environment for large institutional innovations in Mexico. Among the new or renovated institutions, the Federal Electoral Institute, the autonomous Central Bank, and the Supreme Court stand out as mostly positive instances. At the same time, other institutions, many of them devoted to providing

TABLE 7.1 Budget of the Four Government Institutions

Year	Budget in Million Dollars 2003					Index of Growth (2000 = 0)				
	DGAC	SEPOMEX	HGMGG	SAT	COMBINED BUDGET	DGAC	SEPOMEX	HGMGG	SAT	COMBINED BUDGET
2000	12.41	63.22	36.47	853.35	965.45	0	0	0	0	0
2001	15.66	22.07	38.35	854.26	930.34	26.2	-65.1	5.1	0.1	-3.6
2002	15.06	24.50	38.66	861.84	940.07	21.3	-61.2	6.0	1.0	-2.6
2003	12.61	67.01	36.19	813.70	929.50	1.6	6.0	-0.8	-4.6	-3.7
2004	12.82	53.96	38.70	775.53	881.00	3.3	-14.7	6.1	-9.1	-8.7
2005	12.08	46.93	38.89	760.25	858.15	-2.7	-25.8	6.6	-10.9	-11.1
2006	12.77	47.24	38.60	741.47	840.07	2.8	-25.3	5.8	-13.1	-13.0
2007	11.96	27.94	39.42	687.34	766.66	-3.7	-55.8	8.1	-19.5	-20.6
2008	39.87	25.94	47.24	655.91	768.95	221.2	-59.0	29.5	-23.1	-20.4
2009	40.55	31.76	40.59	724.84	837.74	226.7	-49.8	11.3	-15.1	-13.2
2010	38.54	71.64	53.13	724.47	887.79	210.5	13.3	45.7	-15.1	-8.0
Average	20.39	43.84	40.57	768.45	873.25	64.3	-30.7	11.2	-9.9	-9.6

SOURCE: SCHP. Presupuesto de Egresos de la Federación (several years). Nominal budgets were deflated with data from INEGI (2010) and converted into 2003 dollars with data from Banco de México (2010).

TABLE 7.2 Ratings by Institution across the Eight Indicators

Institution	Average[a]	Standard Deviation
Stock Exchange	3.88	0.48
Tax Agency	3.88	0.93
Health Care System	3.75	0.43
Civil Aviation	3.06	1.01
Postal Service	2.06	1.16
Average	3.33	

[a] See key to scores in Table 2.3.

TABLE 7.3 Ratings by Indicator across the Five Institutions

	Average[a]	Standard Deviation
E. Technological Flexibility	3.70	1.47
02 Contribution to Development	3.60	0.58
C. No "Islands of Power"	3.50	1.34
01 Institutional Adequacy	3.40	1.20
D. Proactivity	3.30	0.93
B. Immunity to Corruption	3.20	0.68
A. Meritocracy	3.00	1.26
F. External Allies	2.90	0.73
Average	3.33	1.10

[a] See key to scores in Table 2.3.

social services, have been dismantled or seriously damaged. The institutional crisis has been particularly evident in the area of public security.

These contradictory trends are reflected in the cases analyzed in this study. As shown in table 7.2, the notable success of the stock exchange and tax authority across the eight comparative indicators starkly contrasts with the poor situation of the postal service. And, as table 7.3 suggests, institutions are much better at acquiring and using new technology than at overcoming traditional obstacles like corruption, lack of professionalism, or elite indifference. The analysis reported in this chapter gives some clues to understanding these divergences. The first clue concerns the role of technological innovation. A comparison of SEPOMEX (which has been at death's door) with the other four cases suggests that technological upgrading is a necessary condition for the very viability of an institution. An agency incapable of absorbing new technology—especially information technology—will be approaching its end. This surely is a consequence of the rapid and profound technological changes that the world has undergone in recent decades but also of the symbolic appeal of new technologies.

TABLE 7.4 Truth Table Analysis: Causal Combinations Associated with Contribution to Development

Causal Combinations	Raw Coverage	Unique Coverage	Consistency
MERITOCRACY * IMMUNITY TO CORRUPTION * NO ISLANDS OF POWER * PROACTIVITY * TECHNOLOGICAL FLEXIBILITY * ALLIES	0.436416	0.196532	1
meritocracy * immunity to corruption*no islands of power * PROACTIVITY * technological flexibility * ALLIES	0.306358	0.182081	1

NOTES: Capital letters indicate presence of a causal condition; lowercase indicates absence. * means logical AND. "Raw coverage" refers to the proportion of cases that are explained by a given causal combination (alone or together with other combinations); "unique coverage" refers to the proportion of cases that are explained by that causal combination and by no other combination. "Consistency" is the proportion of cases that, sharing a given causal combination, also share the outcome of interest.

The second clue concerns the special importance of proactivity and external allies as causes of good institutional performance. Applying the fsQCA software to the admittedly small number of Mexican institutions analyzed here shows that there were two sure paths toward the goal of making an important contribution to development. As shown in table 7.4, the first path required good scores on all six causal determinants. The other safe path required good scores on only two causal determinants: Proactivity and External Allies.

The point can be illustrated by comparing the two extreme cases of SEPOMEX and BMV. Obviously, powerful allies are a necessary condition for good performance. But this support must not be purely personal, and therefore potentially transient, as it has been in SEPOMEX's case. But, as the BMV case illustrates, if the structural support is purely elitist, it would lead to another kind of failure: the result is likely to be an exclusionary institution, capable of achieving its own goals but making a negligible contribution to social equity. Hence, an institution that aims at both achieving its own goals and making a significant contribution to development should seek to provide a service or perform a function that is valued by a large sector of the population, not just a closed elite.

The third and final clue refers to the general qualities that a good Mexican institution should have if it is to make a real contribution to national development. Such an institution must combine several characteristics that now appear dispersed in the five institutions studied, always mixed with undesirable traits. A developmental institution should be designed with clear awareness that the country suffers from high inequality and extended poverty; it should have SEPOMEX's potential to serve even the poorest members of society, minus SEPOMEX's inefficiency, technological backwardness, and vulnerability to corruption. Such an institution must have BMV's efficiency and flexibility, minus BMV's elitism. It should provide high-quality services, at least as good as those provided by HGMGG; but it should be more accessible to the poor and have a wider reach than this elite hospital. It should imitate DGAC's technical competence but shun DGAC's smallness and powerlessness. It should have SAT's efficiency—minus the patent unfairness of the current Mexican tax system.

APPENDIX 7.1: INSTITUTIONAL STUDIES IN MEXICO

The reports on which this chapter is based are listed below with English translation of the original Spanish titles. The individual studies can be downloaded from the webpage of the Center for Migration and Development, Princeton University: http://cmd.princeton.edu.

Gómez Fonseca, Miguel Angel. "The Mexican Stock Exchange."
Gómez Fonseca, Miguel Angel, and María Teresa Ruiz. "Mexico: Public Health Services to the Open Population—The Case of the Manuel Gea González General Hospital."
Luján Ponce, Noemí. "Time Running Out: The Mexican Postal System in the Crossroads of Modernization."
Velasco, José Luis. "The Aeronautics Authority of Mexico."
———. "The Administrative Tax Service of Mexico."

NOTES

1. The case studies were conducted from 2005 to 2008, and this chapter refers mainly to that period. Whenever possible, information from published documents or statistical reports was updated.

2. Good examples of the literature on political institutions include Dominguez, Lawson, and Moreno 2009; Zamora and Cossío 2006; Eisenstadt 2007; Snyder 1999; Camp 2007: chap. 7; De Reimes 2006. On changes in economic institutions, see Bab 2001; Boylan 2001a, 2001b; Lustig 1998; Minushkin 2002; Williams 2001.

3. See, e.g., Dion 2009; Levy 2009; Williamson 2001.

4. As Scott (2008: 153) argues, formal institutions usually reflect "officially sanctioned offices and ways of conducting business," while their informal counterparts reflect the "actual patterns of behaviour and work routines."

5. "Social action that used to be governed by binding rules now becomes—and is, by some, recommended to be made—a matter of unrestrained, inventive, and unilateral ad hoc decision making, including the making of decisions on which rules (if any) are to be invoked and adopted, if perhaps only on the spot and for the time being" (Offe 2006: 26).

6. The figure for 1980 does not include the *maquiladora* sector (which was not as large as it became in the following decades).

7. As the working-age population grows and the number of formal jobs remains stagnant, criminal activities become more attractive to the most disadvantaged sectors.

8. It was at this juncture that Carlos Slim placed himself firmly on the road to the global economic elite.

9. The seven companies were América Móvil, Walmart de México, Cemex, Grupo México, Telmex, Grupo Financiero Banorte, and Televisa.

10. To have an idea of the size of the uninsured population, one should recall that 64 percent of Mexican workers do not have social security or health care coverage.

11. On this process of decentralization, see De la Fuente and López Bárcenas 2001; Fajardo Ortiz 2004.

12. From 2002 to 2006, 87.8 percent of all the revenue of state governments and two-thirds of that of municipal authorities came from federal sources (INEGI 2007).

13. This correlation was calculated with data for 1995–2004.

14. Still, this cost remained very high. According to data provided by SAT itself, to comply with its tax obligations during a year, an individual taxpayer had to spend an amount equivalent to almost eight months of the minimum wage; the cost for a corporation was equivalent to more than three years of the minimum wage.

15. Even so, in 2007 the total number of individual taxpayers amounted to only 52 percent of the working population. Here we see the obvious effect of the informal economy.

16. In the specialized literature, a fiscal presence of 1 percent or less is considered too low (Silvani and Baer 1997: 24).

17. As a percentage of all the tax revenues administered by SAT, the income generated by this "secondary collection" grew from 2.7 in 2002 to 5.1 in 2007 (SAT 2008).

18. According to SAT, the causes of these inequalities are "the legal mechanisms to which large taxpayers resort, taking advantage of holes and ambiguities in the legislation" (ASF 2007: 121).

19. In practice, SAT's willingness to tax workers in the informal economy is almost negligible. This is understandable given the doubtful revenue potential of this sector of the labor force (OECD 1999: 89).

20. The two airlines were first privatized in 1989–89, then "rescued" by the state in 1995 and privatized again in 2005 and 2007.

21. In 1998 the thirty-five main airports of Mexico (of a total of eighty-five) were organized into four "packages" that were to be gradually sold off. However, by early 2010 this privatization process remained unfinished.

22. The extraordinarily high deficit registered in 2008 may be temporary, associated with changes implemented that year. It was partly an effect of a 4.8 percent increase in the wages of operative personnel, a new productivity bonus, and several expenses associated to the "image change" of the institution.

23. Figures corresponding to 2004–8 were provided by SEPOMEX to ASF (2010). Figures for 2009 come from SEPOMEX (2010).

24. See Velasco 2009.

25. According to the 2007 Latinobarometro survey, in Mexico only 43 percent of the population believed that paying taxes was a necessary condition for citizenship; the Latin American average was 52 percent.

26. In the words of a person from SAT's human resources area: "We are a big business school. We train great tax administrators, who are then hired by private firms who offers them twice or thrice the salaries we pay them. . . . And later [when dealing with those

firms], we are knocked out by people who know our processes and our vulnerabilities." Project interview; see Velasco 2009.

27. This refers to the main union. There is, in addition, an "independent union," very critical of these practices.

28. According to those surveys, the proportion of people believing that corruption in SAT was high or very high decreased from 54 percent in 2003 to 26 percent in 2007.

29. A case in point was the minister of finance during the 2000–2006 period, a person with strong interest in the banking community who, on leaving office, was hired to lead a telephone company that SAT had allegedly benefited with tax exemptions.

30. Alarcón Osorio's removal was demanded in the Chamber of Deputies, on the grounds that his leadership at SEPOMEX had been "inadequate, illicit, and fraudulent" (see *Gaceta Parlamentaria*, Cámara de Diputados, 1484-IV, April 27, 2004).

31. By law, SAT must send detailed quarterly reports to both legislative chambers and monthly reports to the National System of Fiscal Coordination.

32. According to Purificación Carpinteyro (2008), the corps of postal inspectors (charged with supervising the adequate handling of correspondence) was virtually dismantled; its total membership was reduced from 300 to 6.

33. The Ciudad Juárez theft, mentioned above, was allegedly organized by a SEPOMEX worker with a twenty-two-year career in the institution (see *La Jornada*, February 2, 2007).

34. See Velasco 2009.

35. However, it should be noted that SEPOMEX's main clients are business enterprises. In 2008, 92 percent of the pieces delivered were classified as "commercial" (ASF 2010: 531). The most relevant difference between commercial enterprises and poorer users of the postal service is that the latter lack access to alternatives.

REFERENCES

Auditoría Superior de la Federación (ASF). 2007. *Informe del resultado de la revisión y fiscalización superior de la cuenta pública 2005*. Mexico City: ASF.

———. 2010. *Informe del resultado de la revisión y fiscalización superior de la cuenta pública 2008*. Mexico City: ASF.

Bab, Sarah. 2001. *Managing Mexico: Economists from Nationalism to Neoliberalism*. Princeton: Princeton University Press.

Bailey, John, and Pablo Paras. 2006. "Perceptions and Attitudes about Corruption and Democracy in Mexico." *Mexican Studies/Estudios Mexicanos* 22 (Winter): 57–81.

Banco de México. 2010. "Serie histórica del tipo de cambio." www.banxico.org.mx/sistema-financiero/estadisticas/mercado-cambiario/tipos-cambio.html.

Bolsa Mexicana de Valores (BMV). 2008. *Informe anual de la Bolsa Mexicana de Valores 2008*. Mexico City: BMV.

Boylan, Delia Margaret. 2001a. *Defusing Democracy: Central Bank Autonomy and the Transition from Authoritarian Rule*. Ann Arbor: University of Michigan Press.

———. 2001b. "Democratization and Institutional Change in Mexico: The Logic of Partial Insulation." *Comparative Political Studies* 34 (February): 3–29.

Camp, Roderic A. 2007. *Politics in Mexico: The Democratic Consolidation.* Oxford: Oxford University Press.

Carpinteyro, Purificación. 2008. "Comparecencia ante la Comisión de Comunicaciones y Transportes del Senado." *Milenio,* February 6.

Consejo Nacional de Evaluación de la Política de Desarrollo Social (Coneval). 2009. "Reporta Coneval cifras de pobreza por ingresos 2008." Comunicado de prensa #006/09. July 18.

De la Fuente, Juan Ramón, and Joaquín López Bárcenas. 2001. *Federalismo y salud en México: Primeros alcances de la reforma de 1995.* Mexico City: UNAM and Diana.

De Remes, Alain. 2006. "Democratization and Dispersion of Power: New Scenarios in Mexico's Federalism." *Mexican Studies/Estudios Mexicanos* 22 (Winter): 175–204.

Díaz-Cayeros, Alberto, José Antonio González, and Fernando Rojas. 2011. "Mexico's Decentralization at a Crossroads." In *Federalism and Economic Reform: International Perspectives,* edited by J. Wallack and T.N. Srinivasan, 364–406. Cambridge: Cambridge University Press.

Dion, Michelle. 2009. "Globalization, Democracy, and Mexican Welfare, 1988–2006." *Comparative Politics* 42 (October): 63–82.

Dominguez, Jorge I., Chappell Lawson, and Alejandro Moreno. 2009. *Consolidating Mexico's Democracy: The 2006 Presidential Campaign in Comparative Perspective.* Baltimore: Johns Hopkins University Press.

Economic Commission for Latin America (ECLAC). 2010. CEPALSTAT. www.eclac.org/estadisticas/.

Eisenstadt, Todd A. 2007. *Courting Democracy in Mexico: Party Strategies and Electoral Institutions.* Cambridge: Cambridge University Press.

Fajardo Ortiz, Guillermo. 2004. "La descentralización de los servicios de salud en México (1981–2000)." *Elementos: Ciencia y Cultura* 11: 45–50.

Flores, Nancy. 2007. "Oracle, rentables negocios." *Fortuna: Negocios y Finanzas.* December. www.revistafortuna.com.mx.

Gómez Fonseca, Miguel Angel. 2009. "La Bolsa Mexicana de Valores." In *Las instituciones en el desarrollo latinoamericano: Un estudio comparado,* edited by A. Portes, 57–86. Mexico City: Siglo XXI.

Gómez Fonseca, Miguel Angel, and María Teresa Ruiz. 2008. "México: Servicios públicos médicos de atención a población abierta. El caso del Hospital General Manuel Gea González." Final report to the project *Latin American Institutions and Development: A Comparative Analysis.*

Grayson, George W. 2010. *Mexico: Narco-Violence and a Failed State?* New Brunswick, NJ: Transaction.

Hospital General Dr. Manuel Gea González (HGMGG). 2010. "Tabulador de cuotas de recuperación." Retrieved February 20, 2010, from www.hospitalgea.salud.gob.mx/.

Instituto Nacional de Estadística y Geografía (INEGI). 2007. *El ingreso y el gasto público en México.* Mexico City: INEGI.

———. 2010. "Banco de Información Económica." www.inegi.org.mx/.

International Labor Organization (ILO). 2008. *Panorama laboral de América Latina y el Caribe.* Lima: ILO.

Levy, Santiago. 2009. *Good Intentions, Bad Outcomes: Social Policy, Informality, and Economic Growth in Mexico.* Washington, DC: Brookings Institution Press.

Levy, Santiago, and Michael Walton. 2009. *No Growth without Equity? Inequality, Interests, and Competition in Mexico.* Washington, DC: World Bank and Palgrave Macmillan.

Luján Ponce, Noemí. 2009. "El tiempo se acabó: El Servicio Postal de México en la encrucijada de su modernización." In *Las instituciones en el desarrollo latinoamericano: Un estudio comparado,* edited by A. Portes, 117–64. Mexico City: Siglo XXI.

Lustig, Nora. 1998. *Mexico: The Remaking of an Economy.* 2nd ed. Washington, DC: Brookings Institution Press.

Minushkin, Susan. 2002. "Banqueros and Bolseros: Structural Change and Financial Market Liberalisation in Mexico." *Journal of Latin American Studies* 34: 915–44.

Montambeault, Françoise. 2011. "Overcoming Clientelism through Local Participatory Institutions in Mexico: What Type of Participation?" *Latin American Politics and Society* 53: 91–124.

Morris, Stephen D. 2010. "Continuity and Change in Mexican Politics: The Legacies of the Mexican Revolution." *Latin Americanist* 54 (December): 183–99.

Offe, Claus. 2006. "Political Institutions and Social Power." In *Rethinking Political Institutions: The Art of the State,* edited by I. Shapiro, S. Skowronek, and D. Galvin, 9–31. New York: New York University Press.

Organization for Economic Cooperation and Development (OECD). 1999. *OECD Economic Surveys, 1998–1999: Mexico.* Paris: OECD.

Passel, Jeffrey S. 2005. "Unauthorized Migrants: Numbers and Characteristics." Background Briefing Prepared for the Task Force on Immigration and America's Future. Pew Hispanic Center, Washington, DC.

Portes, Alejandro, and Lori D. Smith. 2010. "Institutions and National Development in Latin America: A Comparative Study." *Socio-Economic Review* 8: 585–621.

Rousseau, Jean-Jacques. 1772. *Considerations on the Government of Poland and on Its Proposed Reformation.* Online edition. www.constitution.org/jjr/poland.htm.

Samaniego Breach, Ricardo, Anabel Mitsuko Endo Martínez, Vidal Mendoza Montenegro, and Francisco Marcos Zorrilla Mateos. 2006. *Medición de la evasión fiscal en México.* Vol. 2. Mexico City: ITAM.

Samstad, James G. 2002. "Corporatism and Democratic Transition: State and Labor during the Salinas and Zedillo." *Latin American Politics and Society* 44 (Winter): 1–28.

Scott, W. Richard. 2008. *Institutions and Organizations: Ideas and Interests.* 3rd ed. Los Angeles: Sage.

Secretaría de Comunicaciones y Transportes (SCT). n.d. *Manual de Organización.* Section 1.3. Mexico City: SCT.

Secretaría de Economía (SE). 2010. "Informe estadístico trimestral sobre el comportamiento de la inversión extranjera directa en México." www.economia.gob.mx/.

Secretaría de Hacienda y Crédito Público (SHCP). 2010. "Presupuesto de egresos de la federación." www.apartados.hacienda.gob.mx/presupuesto/index.html.

Servicio de Administración Tributaria (SAT). 2007. *Plan estratégico 2007–2012.* Mexico City: SAT.

———. 2008. *Informe tributario y de gestión: Primer trimestre.* Mexico City: SAT.

Servicio Postal Mexicano. 2010. "El correo en números." www.correosdemexico.gob.mx/acercadesepomex/elcorreoennumeros/Paginas/default.aspx.

Silvani, Carlos, and Katherine Baer. 1997. "Designing a Tax Administration Reform Strategy: Experiences and Guidelines." IMF Working Paper WP/97/30.

Snyder, Richard. 1999. "After Neoliberalism: The Politics of Reregulation in Mexico." *World Politics* 51 (January): 173–204.

Velasco, José Luis. 2008. "Servicio de Administración Tributaria de Mexico." Final report to the project *Latin American Institutions and Development: A Comparative Analysis.*

———. 2009. "La autoridad aeronáutica de México." In *Las instituciones en el desarrollo latinoamericano: Un estudio comparado,* edited by A. Portes, 87–116. Mexico City: Siglo XXI.

Williams, Mark Eric. 2001. *Market Reforms in Mexico: Coalitions, Institutions, and the Politics of Policy Change.* Lanham, MD: Rowman and Littlefield.

Williamson, J. B. 2001. "Privatizing Public Pension Systems: Lessons from Latin America." *Journal of Aging Studies* 15 (September): 285–302.

World Bank. 2010. *World Development Indicators Database.* www.worldbank.org/.

Zamora, Stephen, and José Ramón Cossío. 2006. "Mexican Constitutionalism after Presidencialismo." *International Journal of Constitutional Law* 4 (April): 411–37.

8

Conclusion

The Comparative Analysis of the Role of Institutions in National Development

Alejandro Portes and Lori D. Smith

Having examined in detail the character and role of institutions in each of the countries included in our study, we turn now to a systematic analysis of this evidence. For this purpose, we turn to the QCA methodology described in chapter 2 for analysis of the two outcomes of interest: (I) Institutional Adequacy, or the extent to which really existing organizations correspond to their original institutional blueprints; and (II) Contribution to Development, or the extent to which each organization makes a contribution to the socioeconomic development of the nation in its sphere of activity. Results of this analysis, based on a large sample of organizations of national scope, should provide an authoritative statement of the role of institutions in national development going beyond the assignment of single scores to individual countries, as done in prior economic and sociological research on the topic.

These results are followed by a reflection on the significance of differences encountered among institutions and among countries. The first set of differences highlights common patterns throughout the region, pointing toward the significance of external forces unleashed by the process of globalization. The second set brings forth the importance of historical antecedents, molding the form and operation of individual institutions in each country.

This chapter is partially based on a previously published article (Portes and Smith 2010).

DETERMINANTS OF INSTITUTIONAL OUTCOMES

In keeping with Ragin's (1987) original admonition, we make use of QCA methods not as an arbiter of final conclusions but as a tool for organizing the data and finding common patterns. A mechanistic application of this method without historical knowledge of the subject and careful evaluation of what results imply could yield nonsensical conclusions.

Crisp-Set Analysis

Institutional Adequacy. Rankings of our sample of twenty-three institutions on a dichotomous scale have been arranged in the truth table presented in chapter 2. Hypothesized determinants, internal and external, are identified by capital letters, A through F, and the outcomes of interest by Roman numerals I and II (see table 2.2). A perusal of the table indicates that conformity to institutional blueprints is more easily achievable than effective developmental agencies: just short of 70 percent of the studied organizations were evaluated to be "institutionally adequate," while only half (52 percent) were evaluated as making a significant contribution to development.

In a prior analysis of a subset of nine of these institutions, the determinants of institutional adequacy (IA) were reduced by Boolean minimization to the expression:

IA = ABC (I) (Portes and Smith 2008).

This result was both parsimonious and theoretically defensible, as it implied that only an autonomous organization characterized by the presence of meritocratic recruitment and promotion (A), the absence or near-absence of corrupt practices (B), and the elimination of self-serving internal groups or cliques (C) was capable of fulfilling its original institutional blueprints. No single factor led to this outcome that required the *combination* of all three internal predictors. The nine institutions that furnished the data for this earlier analysis represent a subset of those included in the present one.

With twenty-three different institutions, the process of minimization is more complex. Each of the following causal combinations leads to positive evaluation of institutional adequacy in the new sample (frequencies in parentheses):

IA = ABCDEF (4), ABCDE (2), ABCE (2), ABCD (1), BCDEF (1), BDEF (1), DBEF (1), ABCEF (1), ABDEF (1), ADEF (1). (II).

These logical combinations are known as "primitive terms." Before minimizing equation II, three points should be noted. First, in Boolean algebra, the *absence* of a cause (denoted by lowercase letters) has the same theoretical status as its presence. We omit lowercase letters from equation II for clarity and because no theory exists that predicts that absence of any of these predictors would lead to a positive result. Complete algebraic expressions for each primitive term can be reached by simply adding lowercase letters for missing predictors to any four- or five-term in equation II.

Second, the rows in table 2.2 are but a subset of all possible logical combinations of predictors and outcomes. The number of such combinations is 2^k, for k number of determinants, yielding 64 possible combinations in our case. The nonexistent 41 logical expressions in table 2.2 are known as "remainders" (Ragin 2008). They can be disregarded or can be treated as "counterfactuals" by assuming that had they existed they would lead to a positive or, alternatively, a negative outcome. The most conservative approach is to assume that nonexistent combinations would *not* produce the outcome of interest, and this is the option adopted in most of the following analysis, with exceptions noted.

Third, with a sample of institutions as sizable as the present one, several causal solutions are possible. The ultimate decision is between "complexity" and "parsimony" (Ragin 2008). Parsimonious solutions are attractive because of their simplicity, since they include only those elements common to all primitive expressions. That very simplicity may make them less theoretically appealing because they do not capture more complex combinations that actually produce the relevant outcome. In the end, the preferred solution emerges from a dialogue between results of the analysis and plausible theoretical expectations. In our case, the most parsimonious solution for Institutional Adequacy is:

IA = A+B+C (III).

This solution is similar to equation I, except that each internal predictor becomes, in this case, a sufficient condition. A perusal of table 2.2 shows that indeed all expressions leading to a positive result include either A, B, or C, with one exception. However, this solution is not satisfactory because it does not capture the more complex causal patterns observable in the data. A solution of intermediate complexity would cover all positive outcomes in the table. With some manipulation of the counterfactuals, that solution is reduced to:

IA = ABC+DEF (IV).

This solution says that an existing organization meets its original institutional mandate either when it satisfies all hypothesized internal requirements (ABC) *or* all external ones (DEF).[1] The first expression corresponds, of course, to the findings obtained previously (see equation I), pointing to the powerful effect of a meritocratic organization immune to bribery and entrenched interests. However, results highlight an alternative route through which institutional adequacy can be achieved. It consists of the combination of a proactive stance toward its external environment (D), openness to technological and organizational innovations (E), and powerful external allies (F). This alternative solution is present in two countries: Argentina and the Dominican Republic. In Argentina, three of the four positive outcomes are due to DEF; in the Dominican Republic, one of the two positives is due to the same combination.[2]

A final reduction is possible if we limit the analysis to causal expressions observed more than once. The rationale for this approach is that in a sizable sample such as this a positive combination observed only once may be due to chance and can be discarded in favor of those that display greater consistency. This approach limits causal primitives to just three terms, and Boolean minimization further reduces them to:

IA = ABCE (V).

This solution has a consistency of 1.00 and coverage of 100 percent of all repeated combinations.[3] ABCE offers a parsimonious and theoretically defensible solution that highlights the joint importance of all internal characteristics of the institution plus technological openness and flexibility. Indeed, it is difficult to conceive an agency or organization that meets the institutional goals for which it was created while adhering rigidly to traditional ways of doing things and closing itself to external innovations. ABCE accounts for the majority of positive outcomes in table 2.2; its main limitation is to obscure the alternative causal path, DEF, noted previously. We postpone adjudication between these two causal solutions until we reexamine them in the context of additional results.

Contribution to Development. A developmental institution (DI) emerges, according to the data in table 2.2, as an outcome of the following combinations (frequencies in parentheses):

DI = ABCDEF (3), ABCDE (3), ABCD (1), ABDEF (1), CDEF (1), ADEF (1), BCDEF (1), DF (1) (VI).

The analysis in this instance confronts one anomalous result. This is the Mexican postal service that receives a score of *o* in Institutional Adequacy but is, nevertheless, evaluated as making a significant contribution to development. It is theoretically implausible that a state agency could simultaneously fail to meet the goals for which it was created *and* be capable of furthering the nation's development. This anomaly led us to reexamine the rationale given for these evaluations. The institutional report for SEPOMEX, the Mexican postal service, finds that it is riddled with corruption and is at the verge of extinction. Postal workers even use the term "milking" the mail to refer to the common practice of opening letters in search of checks, money orders, or cash (Luján Ponce 2008).

SEPOMEX was saved from extinction only by the direct intervention of the president of the republic who appointed a new and capable general director and provided the institution with a significant budgetary increase. Still, it is an open question whether this agency can survive. The positive evaluation on contribution to development given to SEPOMEX despite its sorry state is due to its past rather than its present. The author argues that, historically, the post office fulfilled an important integrative function by linking all Mexican regions and representing the only presence of the state in the country's remotest corners (Luján Ponce 2008). While this is a plausible argument, history is no substitute for present performance, as an organization near collapse cannot make any contribution to the nation's progress. SEPOMEX accounts for the last causal expression in equation VI. Its removal allows minimization of the other primitive terms into a parsimonious solution:

DI = D (A+C) (VII).

This solution covers 100 percent of all other primitive terms with a consistency of 1.00. This causal expression highlights the key role of Proactivity (D) in making an institution capable of yielding significant developmental outcomes. In agreement with Evans's (1995) argument, it is not enough for an institution to be meritocratic or immune to corruption if it is inward-oriented. To further economic or social development, it must leave its protected turf and engage with key actors in society, organizing them and creating incentives to achieve various strategic goals. This solution is similar to that reached in our initial study of nine institutions, mentioned previously (Portes and Smith 2008).

An alternative, more complex solution that includes SEPOMEX, despite the problems noted, would yield:

DI = D (ABC + AF + CF) (VIII).

The first term in this equation is similar to the solution just seen, while the second highlights the causal significance of a combination of internal with external predictors. D emerges again as *the* necessary condition for a developmental institution. Hence, inclusion of the anomalous case produces a more unwieldy solution but does not detract from the original conclusion: In every case, Proactivity is the key factor. While not sufficient to create a developmental institution, it consistently does so in combination with other factors, primarily the internal determinants—Meritocracy and Absence of "Islands of Power."

Fuzzy-Set Analysis

Institutional Adequacy. As noted in chapter 2, fuzzy-set methods were introduced to overcome the limitations of exclusively binary evaluations, reflecting more closely the character of complex social phenomena. This is done by giving investigators a more flexible range of options to indicate level of membership in the conceptual set defined by each predictor and each outcome. Table 2.3, above, presents the fuzzy-set codes assigned by investigators to all institutions in the sample. QCA methods allow the identification of necessary and sufficient conditions for each outcome based on these data.

Necessary conditions are always present when the outcome is positive, but they may be present without the outcome materializing. Fuzzy-set algebra translates this condition into the expectation that scores in the predictor will be higher than or equal to those in the outcome. Intuitively, membership in the set defined by the effect is a subset of that defined by membership in the cause (Ragin 2000: chap. 8). Necessary conditions thus create a "ceiling" for the expected effect. Sufficient conditions always lead to the effect, but the latter may also occur in their absence, due to other factors. The logical translation in fuzzy-set algebra is that scores in the set defined by the predictor be equal to or lower than scores in the outcome. In effect, sufficient conditions create a "floor" for the outcome by assuming that membership in that set is a superset of that defined by the outcome. The logic of necessary and sufficient conditions is summarized in table 8.1.

Table 8.2 presents the relevant data for the analysis of necessity and sufficiency for the first outcome of interest, Institutional Adequacy. A perusal of results indicates that no single factor fulfills the requirements for a necessary condition but that two approach them closely. The first is Technological Flexibility (E), which fulfills the rule in 74 percent of the cases. If we add those cases where membership in the predictor is almost the same as in the outcome (separated by no more than half a point), coverage reaches 87 percent. Two of the remaining three cases are the postal service and the health service of Chile. A rereading of the respective institutional reports indicates that in these cases the leadership of the organization was strongly committed to technological innovation but that it was resisted by unionized subordinate personnel apparently fearful for their jobs (Cereceda 2006; Cereceda, Hoffmeister, and Escobar 2008). If these cases are exempted, Technological Flexibility becomes a necessary condition in 96 percent of the cases.

The second factor approaching necessity is D, Proactivity. If cases where membership in D is but a fraction lower than outcome membership are included, sample coverage reaches 78 percent. It would appear that combining D and E could lead to 100 percent coverage. However, this is not the case. By the rules of fuzzy-set algebra, set membership in a complex expression is assigned the score of the *lowest* component. Hence, DE fulfills the requirements for necessity in *fewer* cases than D and E separately. Joining these predictors by the term *or* (+) covers the full sample, allowing for a few fractional differences since, in fuzzy-set algebra, membership in a summated set is the higher of its components. Hence, the solution that comes closest to a necessary condition for Institutional Adequacy is:

$$IA = D + E \text{ (IX)}.$$

TABLE 8.1 Necessary and Sufficient Conditions in Fuzzy-Set Algebra

		Requirement	
		CAUSE ≥ EFFECT[1]	EFFECT ≥ CAUSE[2]
Determinant	NECESSARY	X	0
	SUFFICIENT	0	X

TABLE 8.2 Fuzzy-Set Sufficient and Necessary Conditions for Institutional Adequacy (*N = 23 institutions in 5 countries*)

	Determinants	Necessity Cause ≥ Effect %	Sufficiency Effect ≥ Cause %
Internal	A. Meritocracy	65.2	87.0
	B. Immunity to Corruption	34.8	78.3
	C. No "Islands of Power"	52.2	87.0
External	D. Proactivity	69.6	60.9
	E. Openness to Technological Innovations	73.9	47.8
	F. External Allies	56.5	73.9

No single predictor suffices to bring about this outcome. However, results in table 8.2 show that the three internal determinants approach that standard. In particular, A (Meritocracy) and C (Absence of "Islands of Power") each fulfills the requirement in close to 90 percent of the cases. Complex terms make sense for sufficient conditions since membership in the resulting set is the *lower* of its components. The composite ABC thus becomes a sufficient condition in 96 percent of the cases. The single exception is the Colombian postal service where Institutional Adequacy is minimal, thus preventing fulfillment of the sufficiency criterion. As discussed later, this institution actually ceased to exist in the course of the study. Combining the results of the analysis of necessity and sufficiency in this sample yields the expression:

IA = ABC (D+E) (X).

The first term is identical to that found in the previous Boolean analysis and corresponds as well to that found in the fuzzy-set analysis of our earlier sample of nine institutions (Portes and Smith 2008). The term ABCE, which is a subset of equation X, yields the same solution found in the prior crisp-set analysis when limited to repeated causal combinations (equation V). The major exceptions are

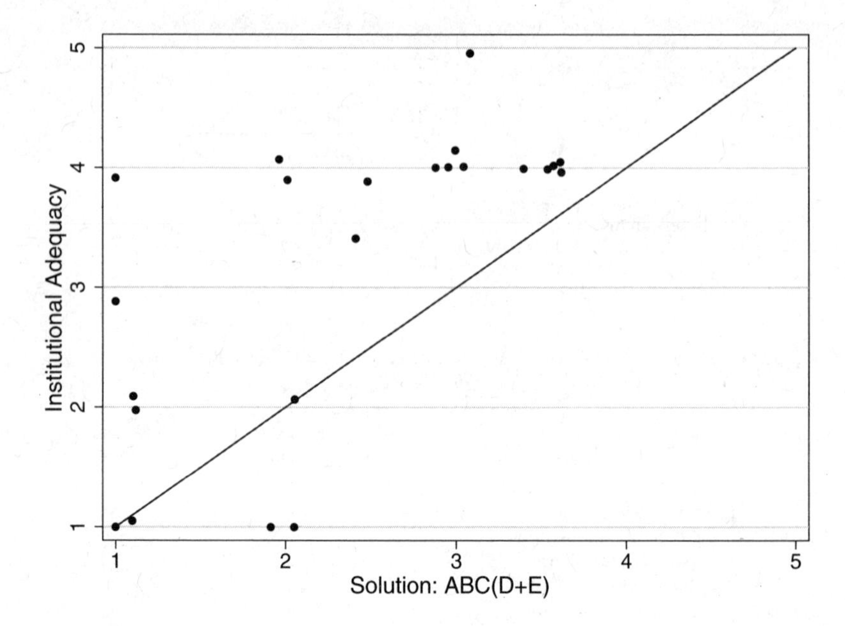

FIGURE 8.1. Membership in the Causal Solution "ABC (D+E)" and Institutional Adequacy

that External Allies (F) disappears from the picture and that the causal expression DEF does not fulfill the criteria for sufficiency.

Figures 8.1 and 8.2 map the position of cases defined by set membership in Institutional Adequacy and its determinants, in equations V and X. Both plots exhibit the expected concentration of cases in the upper-left triangle, with a significant number close to the diagonal. This is an indicator of a satisfactory causal solution. The only exceptions are cases at the bottom where scores in the outcome are minimal and are, hence, exceeded by even very low scores in the predictors. For reasons of parsimony and theoretical plausibility, we select as the final causal solution to Institutional Adequacy:

IA = ABCE

Not only is E a participant in all repeated crisp-set causal combinations in the original truth table 2.2, but it emerges as the strongest necessary condition in the fuzzy-set analysis. It makes conceptual sense that openness to technological innovation should be an integral part of any organization able to fulfill its institutional

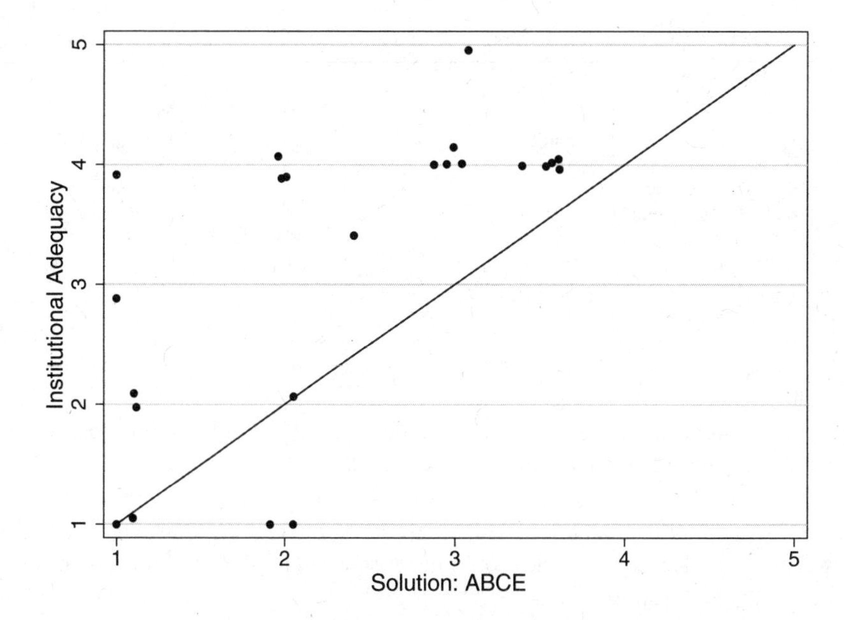

FIGURE 8.2. Membership in the Causal Solution "ABCE" and Institutional Adequacy

mandate. All internal determinants are required for this outcome, but External Allies does not figure in any causal solution.

Contribution to Development. Table 8.3 presents the comparable results, drawn from scores in table 2.3, for an organization's contribution to national development in its own sphere of activity. Again, no individual predictor emerges as a necessary condition but, in a result similar to earlier findings, Proactivity (D) comes closest to fulfilling the criteria. If cases where *D* scores are fractionally inferior (0.5) to scores in the outcome are included, this predictor would cover 91.3 percent of the cases. Second, in the definition of necessity comes Technological Flexibility (E). Joining the two predictors by "or" (+) and disregarding fractional discrepancies, sample coverage would reach 100 percent.

D+E is, of course, the same expression deemed necessary for Institutional Adequacy so that we may conclude that the pattern of causal results for both dependent variables is identical. However, in this case, Proactivity is easily the strongest predictor accounting, by itself, for the bulk of sample coverage. Based on this

TABLE 8.3 Fuzzy-Set Sufficient and Necessary Conditions for Contributions to Development (*N* = 23 *institutions in 5 countries*)

	Determinants	Necessity Cause ≥ Effect %	Sufficiency Effect ≥ Cause %
Internal	A. Meritocracy	65.2	69.6
	B. Immunity to Corruption	52.2	73.9
	C. No "Islands of Power"	56.5	69.6
External	D. Proactivity	82.6	69.6
	E. Openness to Technological Innovations	78.3	34.8
	F. External Allies	60.9	73.9

difference, we conclude that *D* is the "usually necessary" condition for the emergence of a developmental institution (Ragin 2008).

The pattern of results in table 8.3 shows that no individual predictor comes close to the criteria of sufficiency, each registering many exceptions. We are thus forced to consider more complex solutions. A solution produced by the algorithm of the QCA program is:

DI = (AD + BD) (E + F) (XI)

Or, by algebraic manipulation:

DI = D (AEF + BEF) (XII)

While this causal expression again highlights the central role of *D*, it is rather unwieldy, using almost all possible predictors. In addition, solution coverage is only 71.1 percent of the sample. A more parsimonious alternative is:

DI = D (A + C) (XIII)

This solution increases coverage to 83.2 percent with a high level of consistency (92.9 percent). Plotting the two equations, XII and XIII, in figures 8.3 and 8.4, yields quite similar results. In both instances, we see the expected upper-left triangle concentration, with most cases falling on or near the diagonal. Equation XIII is, of course, identical to results produced by the Boolean analysis, once the anomalous case of SEPOMEX was set aside. For this reason, and in the interest of parsimony, we adopt it as the best causal solution.

A final alternative solution is arrived at by inspection of scores of the original fuzzy-set table (2.3) and by taking advantage of the combinatorial rule that equates membership in a complex set with the lowest score of its components. Using this rule, we may join the terms in equation XIII as follows:

DI = ACD (XIV)

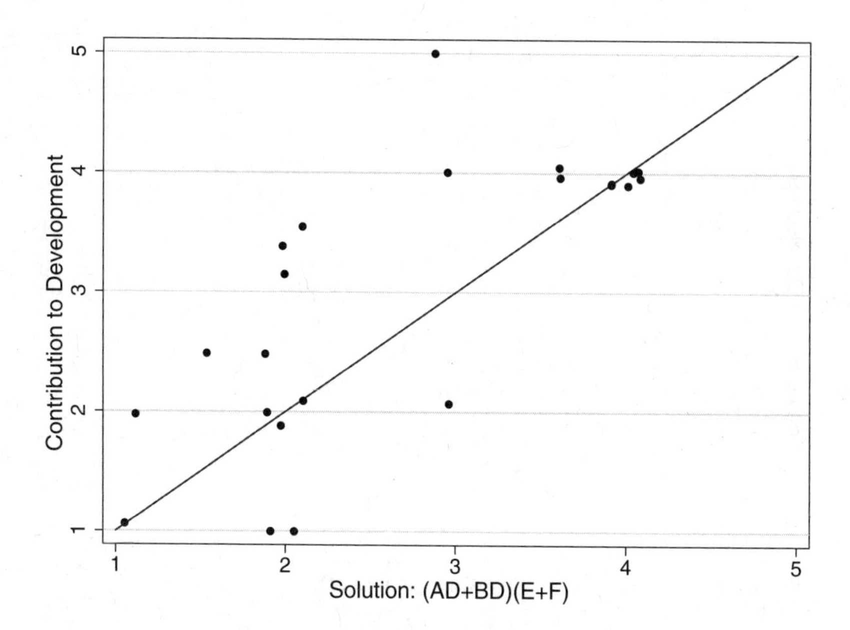

FIGURE 8.3. Membership in the Causal Solution "(AD+BD) (E+F)" and Contribution to Development

This final solution achieves coverage of 91.3 percent, or 21 of 23 cases, without need to adjust for fractional discrepancies. The two exceptions are the Colombian postal service and the Colombian public health service whose developmental contributions were so low as to prevent fulfillment of even a minimum sufficiency criterion.

Whether one chooses equation XIII or XIV as the best solution, the individual components are the same. Theoretically, these causal patterns indicated that Proactivity is necessary but not sufficient for the construction of a developmental institution and that it must be buttressed by one or more dimensions of internal quality. The combination of just one such dimension with Proactivity is usually sufficient to bring about the outcome. This conclusion is quite similar and actually simplifies that arrived at in our earlier analysis limited to nine institutions in three countries (DI = ABCD).

In synthesis, results of crisp- and fuzzy-set analyses of these data do not differ markedly and actually support each other. Adjudicating between alternative causal solutions on the basis of parsimony and prior theoretical expectations leads us to conclude that organizations will fulfill their institutional blueprints if they combine the internal criteria of meritocracy, immunity to corruption, and absence of

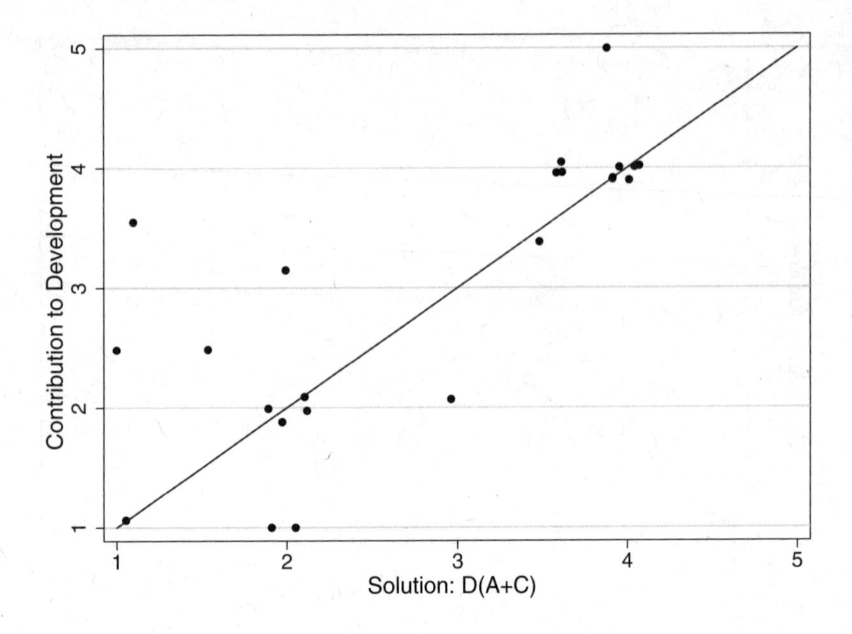

FIGURE 8.4. Membership in the Causal Solution "D(A+C)" and Contribution to Development

entrenched cliques with openness to external innovations, with the latter dimension representing the key necessary condition. By contrast, the contribution that an organization or agency can make to national development depends less on its internal characteristics and more on its capacity to mobilize and energize its external environment. Proactivity toward strategic external actors emerges as the central condition for a developmental institution. In most cases, it just needs to combine with one criterion of internal quality or probity in order to bring about this outcome.

INSTITUTIONAL DIFFERENCES AND SIMILARITIES

Comparative analysis of these data would be incomplete without a more in-depth discussion of what the observed causal patterns mean in terms of similarities and differences between institutions and countries. A perusal of institutional rankings in Tables 2.2 and 2.3 show a marked divide between organizations and agencies whose prime mission is economic and those that focus on services for the general population. Consistently, the stock exchange and the tax authority tend to rank higher; while zeros in the binary scale (table 2.2) and low scores in the continuous one (table 2.3) tend to cluster in the post office, the national health service, and, to a lesser extent, civil aeronautics.

Detailed analysis of individual reports confirms these trends and clarifies their historical origins. Neither stock exchanges nor tax authorities have been historically strong institutions in Latin America. The first were, for the most part, "gentlemen's clubs" that served as much a function of social networking as of rent-seeking and where access was limited to males of the local elite (see chapters 4 and 5). Opportunities for profit in these exchanges were neither universal nor transparent, as they were restricted by particularistic ties. Tax authorities were dormant or corrupt agencies not given high priority by governments that financed themselves primarily from import and export tariffs plus external indebtedness (chapter 7).

The rapid strengthening of both economic institutions across Latin America was directly linked to the Mexican default of 1982, the subsequent regional crisis, and the advent of neoliberal reform inspired by the so-called Washington Consensus (Williamson 1994; Ballassa et al. 1986). Latin American governments were compelled to open up their markets and financial sectors to external actors. For stock exchanges, this meant the entry of powerful foreign players that pushed for greater transparency of transactions and impartial regulation. Not surprisingly, the old elites resisted. As reported in the study of the Chilean stock exchange (Bolsa de Santiago), "The most significant 'island of power' was formed by the traditional brokers who immediately opposed the entry of the banks. . . . A tension emerged between the reproduction of the traditional *ethos* proper of a 'gentlemen's club' and a modern perception that viewed the Exchange as a competitive business" (Wormald and Brieba 2009: 44).

As the same authors continue, to the extent that global financial markets operate under modern norms of universalism and transparency, the interest of brokers in preserving the stock exchange as a traditional agency could not but slow down the integration of the national market into global financial circles. This resistance threatened the institution with obsolescence, a fate that more modern economic actors resisted and that the state could not allow. Gradually, the old elites were pushed back or out, electronic transactions replaced "voice" ones, and new mechanism of regulation and control were put into place to stop the particularistic privileges of the past.

This evolution has led Latin American exchanges to improve significantly their probity and openness to innovation, turning many into organizations capable of fulfilling their institutional blueprints. Stock exchanges in the region ceaselessly copy Wall Street and, to a lesser extent, the Bolsa of Madrid, and monitor each other in search of the latest technological innovations. As the institutional report on the Colombian stock exchange (BVC) concludes, "The entry of the new global actors has been the most transformative force for the BVC and the Colombian financial scene. Dissatisfied with the preferential treatment granted by the Exchange to its stockholders, the new actors forced changes in corporate governance and operational functioning accompanying the Exchange's demutualization" (Rodríguez-Garavito 2009: 20).

Something similar happened to the tax authorities, which had to be urgently revived in the wake of the crisis. Neoliberal reform meant drastic reduction in custom tariffs in order to open previously protected national markets to global trade. This led to significant reductions in the revenues of Latin American governments. They could not substitute them with foreign indebtedness since these flows had also dried up in the wake of the Mexican default and new assistance by global agencies was conditioned precisely on budget balancing, even at the cost of social unrest (Robinson 1996; Roberts and Portes 2006). Governments only had recourse to internal revenues, which, in turn, required extracting fiscal resources from a most reluctant population as well as from economic elites previously untouched by such demands (Roig 2008).

As the report for the Dominican Republic notes, "In 1987, the International Monetary Fund concluded that 'given that the Dominican Republic cannot cut its expenses on a mass scale, a tributary reform to replace the loss of taxes to external trade is the only way to rebuild and maintain social services and investment'" (Guzmán 2008: 11).

In country after country, the tax authority was put directly under the president of the republic, who appointed its director general; the agency received operational and budgetary authority; and fiscal functionaries were placed on a higher pay scale than the rest of the government bureaucracy and rewarded with performance revenues. Two organizational innovations were found to be common throughout the region: first, competent and charismatic directors were appointed, most of whom led the agency for many years thereafter; second, a directorate of large contributors was established in every case. The highly unequal income distribution of Latin American countries translates into a concentration of taxable revenues in a small minority of people and firms. In the Dominican Republic, for example, 80 percent of the total tax take is accounted for by the two dozen largest firms. In Chile, only the top 18 percent of income earners are liable for income tax and just 6 percent of individuals and firms account for 92 percent of tax revenues (Guzmán 2008; Wormald and Cárdenas 2008).

This transformation created the conditions necessary for these agencies to meet their institutional goals and, by the same token, to make a significant contribution to economic development. Personnel started to be recruited on qualifications and merit; bribery and corruption were significantly reduced, if not eliminated; and all agencies went digital and rapidly incorporated new computer-based technology. Proactive steps were taken in most countries—including the Directorate of Large Contributors and educational campaigns aimed at creating a culture of fiscal responsibility among the general population. The best of these organizations, exemplified by the Chilean internal revenue service (SII), introduced technical innovations seldom seen among its peers even in the developed world: "Today, a large number of taxpayers receive their annual tax declaration prepared and sent via Internet by the SII; all they have to do is examine it, sign it, and send it back. This presupposes a level of information by the agency that is ever more encompassing and reliable" (Wormald and Cárdenas 2008: 3).

This level of performance accounts for the high scores received by most of these organizations in both institutional adequacy and contribution to national development. We will discuss the exceptions later on. For the time being, it suffices to point out that these achievements were neither random nor the product of luck but stemmed from a deliberate, concentrated effort by governments, at the highest levels of authority, which assigned top priority to these institutional changes. When the survival of the state was at stake, no effort was spared in producing real institutional reform. No such luck accompanied the evolution of agencies concerned primarily with services to the general population.

For the sake of brevity, we discuss only the two most "socially oriented" of these institutions. As shown in tables 2.2 and 2.3, the lowest scores in the hypothesized determinants of developmental institutions correspond to the public health service and, especially, the postal service. The difficult mission of health services in seeking to extend health care to the entire population is compounded by the limited resources and the absence of resolve by the state to make health delivery a priority, comparable to the tax authority. Throughout Latin America, there is a strong consensus that health care is a human right, not a market good, and this value has molded the organization of the public health system. However, the distance between this worthy goal and its enactment has varied greatly across countries and over time.

Chile, with solid external revenues from high copper prices in the world market and a string of social democratic governments, has been the most successful in turning this aspiration into reality. The Chilean Public Health Service effectively covers the nation. A law enacted in 2004, labeled "Plan AUGE," guarantees free care, in public or private facilities, for the fifty-six most common pathologies affecting the Chilean population. The detailed study of the Barros Luco Hospital in Santiago, which was part of the Chilean public health institutional report, describes a large, well-funded and well-organized facility, highly proactive toward its catchment area (Cereceda, Hoffmeister, and Escobar 2008).

In Mexico, as well, a strong tradition of public service has compelled the state to commit significant resources to the health sector. The Mexican Institute of Social Security runs a complex network of hospitals and clinics covering the country. The Gea González Hospital in Mexico City, elected for intensive study as part of the Mexican institutional report, displays comparable characteristics to its Chilean counterpart: massive size, coverage of almost all medical specialties, technological innovation, and a strong proactive stance. The existence of this system may explain the common tendency, documented by recent studies of Mexican immigrants in the United States, to return home when seriously ill, thus bypassing the costs and obstacles of commercial health care in the United States (Gómez Fonseca and Ruiz 2008; De Juana 2006).

Since the mid-1990s the Dominican Republic has made sustained efforts to imitate these achievements, promulgating a series of presidential decrees to reorganize the health service. Already 98 percent of pregnancies receive prenatal health care and 97 percent of births take place in clinics. However, the levels of maternal and infant mortality are among the highest on the continent, indicating the poor quality of care in public health establishments (Castellanos 2008: 17–18). Most informants for the Dominican institutional study coincide in the big gap that exists between governmental decrees and health realities on the ground. The report reaches the following conclusions:

- *Meritocracy:* Results support the conclusion that hiring and promotion in the Dominican public health service are at the discretion of the authorities and are poorly meritocratic.
- *Probity:* This feature is predominantly absent, and the system is vulnerable to the pressures of outside interests in key decisions.
- *Proactivity:* All agree that most decisions and changes in the public health service are defined by personalistic interests and that the general population has very little say in these decisions (Castellanos 2008: 59–60).

The most catastrophic situation is that of the Colombian health service, which effectively disappeared in the course of the study. The fate of this institution deserves special attention because it illustrates with clarity the consequences of trying to privatize and commercialize a major public service. Heavily influenced by neoliberal ideology, the Colombian government decided to privatize its hospitals and turn them into profitable entities. This was done by the passage of Law 100 in the mid-1990s. The law created a double-payment system whereby state employees and those in private sector firms were covered by private insurance, while the indigent were covered by a state-financed system akin to Medicaid (SISBEN) (Díaz 2008).

This new system excluded the vast population of independent workers, those employed in informal enterprises, and the unemployed. Simultaneously, it decapitalized the old Social Security Institute (ISS), which was left covering the elderly and the very ill. Newly privatized hospitals forced to fend for themselves squeezed down medical salaries and started to refuse attention to the uninsured. This led to a wave of strike actions and other protests by doctors and other medical personnel for most of the 1990s and early 2000s. It also led to the tragic phenomenon dubbed in Colombia the "tour of death," as uninsured but seriously ill patients were turned down, in hospital after hospital, until they died in front of one (Díaz 2008).

By 2008 the ISS and ten large formerly public hospitals had gone bankrupt, with seventy-nine others at the edge of collapse. Today, Colombia is painfully attempting, by fits and starts, to reverse the consequences of a catastrophic policy decision. The situation contrasts sharply with that of other countries in which, despite limited resources, the state never wavered in its commitment to health care as a fundamental human right and the provision of at least basic primary care to the mass of the population.

In all five countries, it became clear that the post office is an organization in crisis, a kind of Cinderella of the governmental apparatus left at the margins by years of neglect and corruption. Although the postal service is expected to meet a key function of social integration by reaching the remotest corners of the country, this function has been perceived by governments as less urgent and less important. In one country at least, it has been common practice to turn the post office into a "consolation prize" to the losing party in national elections (Sánchez Mariñez 2008).

The dominant neoliberal ideology of the 1990s actually favored this turn of events, and in the countries most affected by it, postal services were turned over to private operators. Argentina privatized the post office during the 1990s, while Colombia simply allowed it to expire, an event that happened in the course of the study (Castellani 2009; Díaz 2009). Unfortunately, privatization did not turn out to be the promised panacea. The costs of postal services rose significantly and private companies restricted service to the most lucrative sectors of the market, abandoning small towns and isolated areas of the countryside.

In response to this situation, Argentina brought the post office back into the state apparatus, and in Chile and Mexico last-minute efforts by the respective presidents saved the official service from extinction. In Chile, the post office appears to have surmounted its near-mortal crisis after having been put under direct state control (Cereceda 2006). In Mexico, the fate of SEPOMEX is still in doubt. The state of the agency prior to the recent rescue attempt was described in the corresponding institutional report as follows: "In February 2008, the local press in Ciudad Juárez denounced the theft of more than ten tons of mail coming from the U.S. It was perpetrated by a mailman who, over ten years, opened the mail in search of checks and money orders from Mexican immigrants to their families. This event is only part of a long list of events that, if not so grave, certainly expose the insecurity suffered by users of the Mexican postal service" (Luján Ponce 2008: 22).

This brief review of institutional differences across the continent brings forth two general points. First, the state of the Latin American postal services, national health services, and, to a lesser extent, civil aeronautics show, with clarity, the inefficiencies and limitations that seriously hamper attempts at sustained national development in the region. These results are not abstract disquisitions but concrete empirical evidence that identify the constraints and operational failures of many agencies, preventing them from fulfilling their institutional mission. Second, states are not impotent to overcome this situation, but their efforts so far have concentrated in strengthening those organizations that are directly related to the governments' own economic survival and the interests of business elites rather than those addressing the well-being of the general population. That is why Latin American governments have managed to promote increasingly efficient stock exchanges and to create, in a relatively short period, powerful tax agencies while public health services and postal offices serving the poorest sectors have been allowed to languish or even disappear.

The current absence of a postal service in Colombia and its parlous state in the Dominican Republic and Mexico, the "tour of death" with which the Colombian poor are threatened if they fall ill, and the remarkable insecurity of air traffic in Argentina convey a clear image of why Latin American countries have been unable to implement effective developmental programs and why key social objectives have, so far, eluded them.

COUNTRY DIFFERENCES

A new look at tables 2.2 and 2.3 brings forth a final point, so far unremarked: there are significant differences in the caliber and developmental capacity of institutions among countries. Overall, Chile appears to be in the best situation: all the organizations studied in that country appeared to be institutionally adequate and positively developmental. While this result confirms the common description of Chile as the "success story" in Latin America (Roberts and Portes 2006; Díaz 1996), it could be challenged as a reflection of nationalistic bias on the part of the Chilean team of investigators. This objection does not hold for two reasons: first, there is no a priori basis to assert that members of that research team were more nationalistic than those of other countries; second, a reading of the Chilean institutional reports show them to be carefully nuanced, covering in detail the evolution of each individual agency, as well as its frequent failures.

There does not exist, to our knowledge, a similarly rich and detailed body of information on these organizations. For this reason, we take these reports, for Chile and the other countries included in the study, as reliable sources on the quality and performance of institutions in each. On that basis, it is possible to conclude that while Chilean institutions are comparatively the strongest in the region, Colombian ones are the weakest. Two of them actually ceased to exist in the course of the study, and even those evaluated as the best overall—the stock exchange and the tax authority—were scored lower on average than their peer organizations in other countries. The rather precarious state of Colombian institutions, as shown by these reports, compounds the effects of the civil war afflicting the country for many years. In his synthetic analysis of Colombian results in chapter 5, Rodríguez-Garavito concludes that clientelism is simultaneously the mechanism that keeps the nation's institutions alive and a key source of their weakness, especially in the more peripheral areas of the country. Restoring badly needed public services, especially health to the most deprived sectors of the population, emerges from these results as a top priority.

Although less consistently than Chile, Mexico also approaches the institutionally adequate/developmental pole while the remaining two countries lean in the opposite direction. The generally good quality of Mexican institutions can be attributed to the interplay of two broad forces: first, the opening of the economy, especially after the signing of NAFTA with the United States and Canada, which, as seen previously, forced rapid reforms in its economic institutions; and second, the advent of multiparty democracy that gave greater voice to the citizenry in support of the popular achievements of the Mexican Revolution, in particular a universal and effective public health service (Centeno 1994; Ariza and Ramírez 2005). The attempt to save the post office, after years of neglect, also reflects well on the elected governments' effort to strengthen public agencies serving the general public. The civil aviation authority, although not the best in the region, has also managed to fulfill its institutional mission (Velasco 2008).

Fieldwork for the Mexican institutional studies reached its end just as the country embarked on an all-out war against its powerful drug cartels. The very launching of this war reflected the hope, at the highest level of the Mexican administration, that the country's institutions were up to the task (chapter 7). The uncertain course of the war and the pervasive corruption uncovered during it correspond to the very weaknesses observed by our institutional studies. They point to significant progress but also to major gaps in institutional quality that leave Mexican organizations well below currently acceptable levels of performance in the advanced world.

The quality of Argentina's institutions emerging from this set of studies is also surprisingly poor, although it adjoins Chile and is commonly regarded as the most developed country in Latin America. With the exception of the Argentine internal revenue service (AFIP), which has been thoroughly reorganized and modernized, the state of the other organizations leaves much to be desired, either because of internal organizational weaknesses or a lack of proactivity. The future of Correo Argentino (the post office) is uncertain, having bounced back and forth from private to state management. The civil aviation agency (Comando de Regiones Aéreas), an island of excellence within the state apparatus elsewhere, disappeared in the course of the study. After a series of corruption scandals and near accidents, the agency—run by the Argentine Air Force—was closed by the president of the republic in 2008. As seen in table 2.2, the Comando garnered zeros in all predictors of institutional quality, as well as in the two outcomes. Just prior to its closure, the investigator in charge concluded, "The problems denounced by external actors have been consistently minimized by the Comando which has not shown any capacity to respond, much less to anticipate problems. . . . [T]here are solid indicators of technological obsolescence in civil aviation in Argentina. The lack of training and retraining of the technical personnel reveals a complete absence of flexibility and openness to innovation" (Grimson 2008: 22).

The reorganization of this agency and its transfer to civilian control may lead to a better future, in line with what happened after the end of military control of civil aviation in the Dominican Republic. In general, Argentina's wealth and the level of education achieved by its population stand in stark contrast to the country's persistent institutional weaknesses. It is an open question whether this situation will persist indefinitely into the future or whether Argentina will find a way to follow Chile's path into the ranks of the developed world.

A similar checkered scenario is evident in the Dominican Republic, the smallest of the countries included in the study. Despite the many problems observed in the four institutions studied, which are described in detail in chapter 6, a noteworthy feature is the rapid progress achieved by some of these organizations, starting from very low levels of probity and performance. In particular, major improvements in the civil aviation authority, after being wrestled from control by the military and the rapid development of institutional capacity in the tax agency (DGII), point to a clear upward trajectory in the country's development. Almost alone in the Caribbean region, the Dominican Republic has been following a sustained path toward economic and social progress in recent decades that is well reflected in these studies. Still, major failures, such as the blockage of reform in the public health sector and the parlous state of the postal system linger, reflecting the long road ahead in quest of a mature institutional framework.

CONCLUSION

Past theories of national development evolved from the unilinear version of modernization theory and the dismal predictions of the dependency and world-system perspectives to the analysis of the successful strategies pursued by some "late developers" and the recognition of the role of the nation-state as a key agent in the process of social change (Evans 1995; Portes 1997; Guillén 2001). The advent of the "institutional turn" deepened the analysis of endogenous variables within countries as they interact with the forces of globalization. The intellectual promise of this perspective was limited, however, by the absence of a rigorous definition of the concept "institutions" and the subsequent characterizations of countries as institutionally homogeneous. This comparative study has attempted to overcome both limitations.

Results of the study support and extend sociological theories concerning determinants of institutional adequacy and development capacity. These are captured in the six hypothesized determinants of these outcomes and in the concrete causal solutions that they produce when submitted to systematic comparative analysis. Simultaneously, the findings point to numerous differences among types of organizations and across countries, showing that the institutional landscape of Latin America is neither homogeneous nor simple. Instead, distinct patterns emerge according to various combinations of predictive factors and the variable commitment and effectiveness of national governments and external actors impinging on them. A detailed comparison of institutional reports shows a clear rank order of priority, where economic agencies have been the beneficiaries of vigorous state reform efforts while organizations serving the general public have received less attention, several of them saved at the last minute or placed into receivership.

Similarly, the different trajectories of individual nations show clearly the interplay between the homogenizing forces of globalization and unique factors buried deep in the history and culture of each of these countries. Results of this comparative study demonstrate that it is feasible to bring down the concept of institutions from the heights of theoretical speculation to the level of concrete empirical analysis. It is at this level where it becomes possible to test specific predictions about factors leading to competent developmental organizations. In a field replete with broad generalizations and caveats, knowledge of what these factors are should provide a decisive step ahead. Findings from the five countries buttress the recent sociological contribution to development studies by providing concrete and nuanced evidence of when and where institutions "matter." By the same token, they should give pause to sweeping proclamations about the effects of globalization and policy prescriptions that disregard the institutional complexities of individual nations.

NOTES

1. This solution assumes that logical expressions ABCde, aDEF, bDEF, and cDEF would also lead to a positive result. A perusal of Table 2.2 shows that this solution is plausible since several of these terms exist and actually yield the predicted outcome.

2. The first phase of this study, which included the sample of nine institutions described previously, was limited to the other three countries. This sample produced the causal combination, ABC, as the sole determinant of Institutional Adequacy. Thus, it is the addition of Argentina and the Dominican Republic that brings forth the second alternative causal path.

3. Consistency is defined as the degree to which one set is contained in another:

$$(x_i \leq y_i) = \Sigma \min x_i, y_i / \Sigma (x_i).$$

By counting the portion of x_i values that violate this criterion in the numerator of the formula while counting these values again in the denominator, large penalties are assigned to large inconsistencies but small ones for near misses. See QCA software manual and Ragin 2004.

REFERENCES

Ariza, Marina, and Juan M. Ramírez. 2005. "Urbanización, mercados de trabajo y escenarios sociales en el México finisecular." In *Ciudades latinoamericanas: En el umbral de un nuevo siglo,* edited by A. Portes, B.R. Roberts, and A. Grimson, 299–362. Buenos Aires: Prometeo Editores.

Balassa, Bela, Gerardo M. Bueno, Pedro-Pablo Kuczynski, and Mario H. Simonsen. 1986. *Toward Renewed Economic Growth in Latin America.* Washington, DC: Institute for International Economics.

Castellani, Ana G. 2009. "Instituciones y desarrollo en América Latina: El caso del correo oficial de la República Argentina." Final report to the project *Latin American Institutions and Development: A Comparative Analysis.*

Castellanos, Pedro L. 2008. "La reforma del sistema público de salud en República Dominicana." Final report to the project *Latin American Institutions and Development: A Comparative Analysis.*

Centeno, Miguel A. 1994. *Democracy within Reason: Technocratic Revolution in Mexico.* University Park: Pennsylvania State University Press.

Cereceda, Luz Eugenia. 2006. "Institucionalidad y desarrollo: El caso de Correos de Chile." Final report to the project *Latin American Institutions and Development: A Comparative Analysis.*

Cereceda, Luz Eugenia, Lorena Hoffmeister, and Constancia Escobar. 2008. "Institucionalidad, organización y reforma de la salud en Chile." Final report to the project *Latin American Institutions and Development: A Comparative Analysis.*

De Juana, Cristina. 2006. "Traditional Health Care Practices." In *On the Edge of the Law: Culture, Labor, and Deviance on the South Texas Border,* edited by C. Richardson and R. Resendiz, 17–50. Austin: University of Texas Press.

Díaz, Alvaro. 1996. "Chile: ¿Hacia el pos-neoliberalismo?" Paper presented at the Conference on Responses of Civil Society to Neo-Liberal Adjustment. Department of Sociology, University of Texas at Austin, April.

Díaz, Luz Marina. 2008. "La seguridad social en salud de Colombia." Final report to the project *Latin American Institutions and Development: A Comparative Analysis.*

———. 2009. "Vida, pasión y muerte de la Administración Postal Nacional Colombiana." In *Las instituciones en el desarrollo latinoamericano: Un estudio comparado,* edited by A. Portes, 292–316. Mexico City: Siglo XXI.

Edwards, Jeremy, and Sheilagh Ogilvie. 2008. "Contract Enforcement, Institutions, and Social Capital: The Maghribi Traders Reappraised." *CESifo Working Paper* 2254.

Evans, Peter. 1995. *Embedded Autonomy: States and Industrial Transformation.* Princeton: Princeton University Press.

Gómez Fonseca, Miguel Angel, and María Teresa Ruiz. 2008. "México: Servicios médicos públicos de atención a población abierta." Final report to the project *Latin American Institutions and Development: A Comparative Analysis.*

Grimson, Alejandro. 2008. "La aviación civil en la Argentina." Final report to the project *Latin American Institutions and Development: A Comparative Analysis.*

Guillén, Mauro. 2001. *The Limits of Convergence.* Princeton: Princeton University Press.

Guzmán, Rolando. 2008. "Recaudación y desarrollo: Un análisis institucional de la Administration Tributaria de la República Dominicana." Final report to the project *Latin American Institutions and Development: A Comparative Analysis.*

Luján Ponce, Noemí. 2008. "El tiempo se acabó: El servicio postal mexicano en la encrucijada de su modernización." Final report to the project *Latin American Institutions and Development: A Comparative Analysis.*

Nee, Victor, and Sonja Opper. 2009. "Bureaucracy and Financial Markets." *Kyklos* 62: 293–315.

North, Douglass C. 1990. *Institutions, Institutional Change, and Economic Performance.* Cambridge: Cambridge University Press.

———. 1989. "Final Remarks: Institutional Change and Economic History." *Journal of Institutional and Theoretical Economics* 145: 238–45.

O'Connor, James. 1973. *The Fiscal Crisis of the State.* New York: St. Martin's Press.

O'Donnell, Guillermo. 1994. "The State, Democratization, and Some Conceptual Problems." In *Latin American Political Economy in the Age of Neoliberal Reform,* edited by W. C. Smith, C. H. Acuña, and E. A. Gamarra, 157–79. New Brunswick, NJ: Transaction.

Portes, Alejandro. 1997. "Neoliberalism and the Sociology of Development: Emerging Trends and Unanticipated Facts." *Population and Development Review* 23 (June): 229–59.

Portes, Alejandro, and Bryan R. Roberts. 2005. "The Free Market City: Latin American Urbanization in the Years of the Neoliberal Experiment." *Studies in Comparative and International Development* 40 (Spring): 43–82.

Portes Alejandro, and Lori D. Smith. 2008. "Institutions and Development in Latin America: A Comparative Study." *Studies in Comparative and International Development* 43 (Summer): 101–28.

———. 2010. "Institutions and National Development in Latin America: A Comparative Study." *Socio-Economic Review* 8: 585–621.

Ragin, Charles. 1987. *The Comparative Method, Moving beyond Quantitative and Qualitative Strategies.* Berkeley: University of California Press.

———. 2000. *Fuzzy-Set Social Science.* Chicago: University of Chicago Press.

Roberts, Bryan R., and Alejandro Portes. 2006. "Coping with the Free Market City: Collective Action in Six Latin American Cities at the End of the Twentieth Century." *Latin American Research Review* 41 (June): 57–83.

Robinson, William. 1996. *Promoting Polyarchy: Globalization, U.S. Intervention, and Hegemony.* Cambridge: Cambridge University Press.

Rodríguez-Garavito, César. 2009. "De club de caballeros a mercado electrónico: Un análisis institucional de la Bolsa de Valores de Colombia." In *Las instituciones en el desarrollo latinoamericano: Un estudio comparado,* edited by A. Portes, 238–67. Mexico City: Siglo XXI.

Rodríguez-Garavito, César, and Diana Rodríguez Franco. 2008. "Entre el clientelismo y la modernización: Una etnografía institucional de la administración de impuestos de

Colombia." Final report to the project *Latin American Institutions and Development: A Comparative Analysis.*

Roig, Alexandre. 2008. "La Dirección General Impositiva de la Agencia Federal de Ingresos Publicos (AFIP) de la Argentina." Final report to the project *Latin American Institutions and Development: A Comparative Analysis.*

Sánchez Mariñez, Julio. 2008. "El servicio postal público en la República Dominicana: ¿Un sistema parapléjico y sin dolientes?" Final report to the project *Latin American Institutions and Development: A Comparative Analysis.*

Velasco, José Luis. 2008. "Servicio de Administración Tributaria de México." Final report to the project *Latin American Institutions and Development: A Comparative Analysis.*

Waisman, Carlos H. 1987. *Reversal of Development in Argentina.* Princeton: Princeton University Press.

Williamson, John. 1994. *The Political Economy of Policy Reform.* Washington, DC: Institute for International Economics.

Wormald, Guillermo, and Daniel Brieba. 2009. "La Bolsa de Comercio de Santiago de Chile: Un análisis institucional." In *Las instituciones en el desarrollo latinoamericano: Un estudio comparado,* edited by A. Portes, 155–81. Mexico City: Siglo XXI.

Wormald, Guillermo, and Ana Cárdenas. 2008. "Formación y desarrollo del Servicio de Impuestos Internos (SII) en Chile: Un análisis institucional." Final report to the project *Latin American Institutions and Development: A Comparative Analysis.*

APPENDIX

Investigators
(*1 = Country Leader; 2 = Senior Author; 3 = Junior Author*)

Country Investigator	Affiliation	Institution
Argentina		
Ana Castellani[2]	Institute for Advanced Social Studies (IDAES), General San Martín University and University of Buenos Aires	Postal System
Alejandro Grimson[1,2]	IDAES, General San Martín University	Civil Aviation
Mariana Heredia[2]	IDAES, General San Martín University and University of Buenos Aires	Stock Exchange
Alexander Roig[2]	IDAES, General San Martín University	Tax Authority
Chile		
Daniel Brieba[3]	Catholic University of Chile	Stock Exchange
Ana Cárdenas[3]	Catholic University of Chile	Tax Authority
Luz Cereceda[2]	Catholic University of Chile	Postal System and Public Health System
Constanza Escobar[3]	Catholic University of Chile	Public Health System
Lorena Hoffmeister[3]	Catholic University of Chile	Public Health System
María Angélica Thumala[2]	Catholic University of Chile	Civil Aviation
Guillermo Wormald[1,2]	Catholic University of Chile	Stock Exchange and Tax Authority

continued

Investigators (*continued*)
(*1 = Country Leader; 2 = Senior Author; 3 = Junior Author*)

Country Investigator	Affiliation	Institution
Colombia		
Luz Marina Díaz[2]	National University of Colombia	Postal System and Public Health System
Diana Rodríguez Franco[3]	University of the Andes	Tax Authority
César Rodríguez-Garavito[1,2]	University of the Andes	Stock Exchange and Tax Authority
Iván Hernández[2]	National University of Colombia	Civil Aviation
Mexico		
Miguel Ángel Gómez Fonseca[2]	Autonomous Metropolitan University (Ixtapalapa)	Stock Exchange and Public Health System
Noemí Luján Ponce[2]	Autonomous Metropolitan University	Postal System
María Teresa Ruiz[3]	Autonomous Metropolitan University	Public Health System
José Luis Velasco[1,2]	Institute for Social Research, National Autonomous University	Civil Aviation and Tax Authority
Dominican Republic		
Pedro Castellanos[2]	Institute for Social Development	Public Health System
Rolando Guzmán[2]	Technological Institute of Santo Domingo (INTEC)	Tax Authority
Wilfredo Lozano[1,2]	Ibero-American University	Civil Aviation
Julio Sánchez[2]	Technical Secretariat, Presidency of the Republic	Postal system

CONTRIBUTORS

DANIEL BRIEBA Born in Santiago, Chile, 1977. B.A. in Economics and B.A. in Sociology, both from the Pontifical Catholic University of Chile. MPA in Public and Economic Policy, London School of Economics and Political Science. Currently finishing a Ph.D. in Politics at Nuffield College, University of Oxford. Main areas of interest are the politics of institutions and development, quality of democracy, and state capacity in Latin America.

ANA CASTELLANI Born in Buenos Aires, Argentina, 1969. B.A. and Ph.D. in Sociology, University of Buenos Aires. Associate Professor of Sociology, University of Buenos Aires and San Martín National University. Main areas of interest are sociology of development, entrepreneurship, and political sociology.

ALEJANDRO GRIMSON Born in Buenos Aires, Argentina, 1968. B.A. in Communications, University of Buenos Aires; M.A. in Social Anthropology, University of Misiones, Argentina; Ph.D. in Anthropology, University of Brasilia. Professor and Dean, Institute of Advanced Social Studies, San Martín National University, Buenos Aires. Main areas of interest are culture and development, international migration, political culture.

WILFREDO LOZANO Born in Santo Domingo, Dominican Republic, 1950. B.A. in Sociology from the Autonomous University of Santo Domingo and Ph.D. in Sociology from El Colegio de México. Professor and Director of the Institute for Social Research, Ibero-American University of Santo Domingo. Main areas of interest are sociology of development, international migration, and historical sociology.

ALEJANDRO PORTES Born in Havana, Cuba, 1944. B.A. in Sociology, Creighton University: M.A. and Ph.D. in Sociology, University of Wisconsin-Madison. Professor of Sociology and Director of the Center for Migration and Development at Princeton University. Part-time Research Professor, University of Miami. Main areas of interest are economic sociology, international development, and immigration.

CÉSAR RODRÍGUEZ-GARAVITO Born in Bogotá, Colombia, 1971. J.D. from the University of the Andes, M.A. in Law and Society from New York University, and Ph.D. in Sociology from the University of Wisconsin-Madison. Main areas of interest are political sociology, economic sociology, law and society, and environmental sociology.

ALEXANDRE ROIG Born in Montpellier, France, 1976. B.A. in Political Science, Institute of Political Studies of Toulouse; M.A. in Development Studies, University Institute of Development, Geneva, Switzerland; Ph.D. in Economic Sociology, EHESS, Paris. Associate Professor, Institute of Advanced Social Studies, San Martín National University, Buenos Aires. Main areas of interest are economic sociology and poverty.

LORI D. SMITH Born in Indianapolis, Indiana, 1982. B.A. in Sociology from Indiana University; doctoral candidate in the Department of Sociology at Princeton University. Previously a fellow at the Center for the Study of Social Organization. Main areas of interest are organization theory, economic sociology, sociology of development, and industrial evolution.

JOSÉ LUIS VELASCO Born in Chiapas, Mexico, 1970. B.A. in Sociology from the Autonomous University of Chiapas and Ph.D. in Political Science from Boston University. Researcher at the Institute for Social Research of the National Autonomous University of Mexico. Main areas of interest are political sociology and socioeconomic inequality.

GUILLERMO WORMALD Born in Santiago, Chile, 1948. B.A. in Sociology from the Catholic University of Chile and Ph.D. in Sociology of Development, University of Sussex. Professor of Sociology, Catholic University of Chile. Main areas of interest are economic sociology, sociology of work, and socioeconomic inequality.

INDEX

Page references in italics refer to figures and tables

Acemoglu, Damon, 24, 29, 79
ADIMARK (marketing enterprise, Chile), 82n6
Adpostal (Colombia), 88; center and periphery in, 99; corruption in, 91; culture of waste in, 94; departure from organizational blueprint, 94; effect of geography on, 89; ethnography of, 99, 103; lack of external allies, 93; liquidation of, 98; meritocracy in, 91; modernization attempts in, 89; patronage in, 92; predatory nature of, 96, 98; proactivity of, 94. *See also* postal system, Colombian
Aerocivil (Colombia), 88; compliance with international standards, 89, 93; corruption in, 91, 101, 103; lack of external allies, 93; lack of proactivity, 95; meritocracy in, 91; reactivity of, 92; technological flexibility of, 93
AERODOM (Dominican Airports) consortium, 124–25
Aerolineas Argentinas, 56
Aeroméxico, restructuring of, 12, 145
airlines, Mexican: privatization of, 145, 162n20
Airports and Auxiliary Services (ASA, Mexico), 144
Airport Security Police (Argentina), 57n4
air traffic authority (DGAC, Chile), 61; accident rate of, 73; Build, Operate, and Transfer Agreements of, 72; immunity to corruption, 73; institutional dependency of, 72; islands of power in, 73; military interests in, 72, 73, 76; modernization of, 72; U.S. FAA on, 73
air traffic controllers, Argentine: command of English, 50, 57n3
Alarcón Osorio, Gonzalo, 151, 152; removal from office, 163n30
Argentina: Constitution, 57n1; crisis of 1930, 39; economic policies of, 40–41; educational level of, 39; external dependency of, 40; institutional development in, 26, 39–57; institutional studies on, 57; Law of Co-participation, 44; military dictatorships of, 39, 40, 56; Ministry of Federal Planning, Public Funding and Services (MPFIPS), 43, 50; National Tax Board, 41; natural resources of, 39; neoliberalism in, 39, 56; political instability in, 40; postal laws of, 43; social conflicts in, 40; sovereign debt in, 44; Subdepartment of Systems and Communications, 49, 53. *See also* economy, Argentine; institutions, Argentine

Barros Luco hospital (Santiago, Chile), 61, 181
Bejarano, Ana María, 98
Black Monday (1987), 138
Board for Accident Investigation (Argentina), 58n5

Bolsa de Comercio de Santiago, 61, 73–75; conflicts of interest in, 75; external allies of, 75; immunity to corruption, 75; institutional change in, 74; islands of power in, 75; meritocracy of, 74; modernization of, 73–74, 75; workers' contributions to, 74. *See also* stock exchange, Chilean
Bolsa de Valores de Colombia (BVC), 88–89; circulation of public bonds, 94; correspondence to organizational blueprint, 94; demutualization of, 180; global actors in, 179–80; immunity to corruption in, 91; lack of proactivity, 95; market model of, 89; meritocracy in, 91; and national development, 94; reactivity of, 92; technological flexibility of, 93; Weberian traits of, 99. *See also* stock exchange, Colombian
Bolsa Mexicana de Valores (BMV, Mexico), 131; absence of islands of power, 151–52; automation of transactions, 138; demutualization of, 138; efficiency of, 161; elitism in, 138, 155, 160, 161; external allies of, 155–56; immunity to corruption in, 150; institutional adequacy of, 137–38; meritocracy of, 146, 147; openness to external innovation, 154; proactivity of, 153; securities brokers of, 137, 138; size of, 132; stockholders in, 138, 162n9; transnational capital in, 155–56. *See also* stock exchange, Mexican
Brazil: institutional development in, 39; transition to civilian government, 40
Brieba, Daniel, 74
Buenos Aires: airport shutdown (2007), 50; Postal Treatment Center, 49; relationship with provinces, 39, 51
Buenos Aires Stock Exchange (BCBA), 41; external allies of, 51; institutional values of, 52, 53; integrity of, 46; meritocracy in, 45; organizational structure of, 52; proactivity of, 48; technical flexibility of, 50; traditional/modernizing agents in, 47, 58n6. *See also* stock exchange, Argentine
bureaucracy: of Argentine institutions, 44; of Colombian institutions, 95, 107; of Mexican postal system, 131; role in institutional development, 25, 32; Weberian, 25, 91, 92, 131, 147

Cafaro, Rubén Miguel, 54
Calvinism, effect on social order, 15–16
Campbell, John: *Institutional Change and Globalization*, 14, 17
Cárdenas, Ana, 71
Cardoso, Fernando H., 32
Carey, John M., 104
Carpinteyro, Purificación, 145; dismissal of, 155; on postal staffing, 163n32; Transformation Plan of, 146, 152
Castellanos, Pedro Luis, 122
Catholic University of Chile, Institute of Sociology, 82n6
Centeno, Miguel, x, xiii
Center for Aeronautical Studies (Colombia), 89
Cereceda, Luz, 69
change: cultural, 16, 18; levels and forces of, *17*; multiple dimensions of, 17. *See also* institutional change; social change
Chile: air traffic authority, 61, 72–73, 76; Allende government, 83n13; bankruptcies in, 65; Constitution of 1980, 65, 74, 79; democratic governments of, 64, 65, 66, 77, 78; electoral system of, 65; entrepreneurial freedom in, 63; Higher Education Law (1981), 65, 82n1; import substitution industrialization in, 63; institutional adequacy in, 184; institutional development research in, 26; ISAPRE (private health providers) law, 65; labor laws, 65, 83n14; Lagos government, 69; middle class of, 67; military coup (1973), 60, 64, 77; military governments of, 64–66, 73, 77, 78, 79; Mining Law (1981), 65; OCDE membership, 66, 76, 82n4; Organic Constitutional Law, 82n2; Pension Reform Law, 65; Pinochet regime, 71; post office, 61, 70–71, 82n11, 183; property rights in, 63, 65; Public Corporations Law, 65; public health services, 61, 68–70, 172, 181; right-wing coalition (2010), 67; social redistribution in, 60; state-centered society of, 60; Stock Exchange Law, 65; stock exchange of, 61, 65, 73–75, 179; tax revenue service, 61, 71–72, 76, 180, 181; welfare services in, 66–67. *See also* economy, Chilean; institutions, Chilean; market society, Chilean
Ciudad Juárez (Mexico), postal theft in, 151, 163n33, 183
civil aviation, Argentine, 41, 42; absence of meritocracy in, 50; airport security in, 57n4; Board for Accident Investigation, 58n5; corruption in, 46, 150, 185; crisis in, 50, 52; deterioration of, 54; islands of power in, 47; lack of state support, 51–52; proactivity of, 48–49; scandals in, 57n4; technological

problems in, 50, 186; work culture of, 54. *See also* Regional Air Command (CRA, Argentina)
civil aviation, Colombian, 88, 89. *See also* Aerocivil (Colombia)
civil aviation, Dominican, 113; airport privatization in, 121; contribution to development, 121–22; effect on tourism, 124; external allies of, 127; FAA intervention in, 120, 121, 123, 125, 128n7; institutional adequacy of, 122; islands of power in, 121; laws regulating, 120–21; leadership of, 127; military influence in, 120, 121, 125, 186; pressure from business sector on, 124; security in, 124, 125; state agency in, 123, 124. *See also* Dominican Institute of Civil Aviation
civil aviation, Latin American, x, 27–28, 86; institutional ranking of, 179; role in development, 183–84
civil aviation, Mexican, 131; institutional inadequacy of, 143–45; institutional mission of, 185; market growth in, 144; meritocracy in, 146, 147–48; privatization of, 144–45. *See also* Dirección General de Aeronáutica Civil
class structure: changes to, 16; Chilean, 77; importance for institutions, 95; state, 128n10
class struggle, 17, 63
clientelism, 95; in Dominican Republic, 118, 125; institutional, 95; Mexican, 133
clientelism, Colombian, 185; armed, 101, 107; in electoral institutions, 106; institutional equilibrium under, 103–8; in institutions, 96, 98, 103, 107; in public health services, 101, 106
CNBV (Comisión Nacional Bancaria y de Valores), 146
Colombia: armed clientelism in, 101, 107; Central Intelligence Agency (DAS), 107, 109n13; civil war in, 185; constitutional government in, 86; democratic stability in, 86, 97; double war in, 98; drug trafficking in, 101, 103; elections in, 97; electoral institutions of, 105–6; electoral risk in, 100–101, *102;* elites of, 105; as failed state, 97, 108; Gaviria presidency, 90; geography of, 89, 100, 103; guerrilla expansion in, 100, 103; institutional development research in, 26; judicial system of, 103; Liberal Party, 108n5; mafias of, 100, 101, 106, 107; paramilitary groups of, 92, 100, 101, 103, 109nn12–13; politicians of, 85; postal service of, 88; public health system of, 88, 89–90; state collapse in, 97, 98; technocracy of, 86, 97; territorial controls of, 106; transitional politicians of, 106–7; Uribe presidency, 106; violence levels in, 86, 97. *See also* clientelism, Colombian; economy, Colombian; institutions, Colombian
colonies, European: economic development of, 24
Commons, neoinstitutional analysis of, 3
Compañía Dominicana de Aviación, 121
Convenios Colectivos de Trabajo (CCT, Argentina), 45
Correos de Chile, 61, 82n11. *See also* postal system, Chilean
Costa Rica, development in, 117
crisp-set analysis (QCA): complexity in, 169; of contribution to development, 170–71; of institutional adequacy, 168–70, 173, 174; of institutional blueprints, 168; parsimony in, 168, 169; primitive terms in, 168, 169
culture: cognitive frameworks in, 4; deep factors of, 4; intersocietal diffusion of, 15; language in, 4; sociological view of, 3–5

data, institutional: discursive reports on, 28, 29
Deas, Malcolm, 97
de la Madrid, Miguel: privatization under, 12
democracy, participatory: and institutional monocropping, *11;* thick, 10
De Pablo, Juan Carlos, 40
developing countries: deep structures of, 9; First World institutions in, x, 8–11; power-based institutions of, 9; resistance to change, 10; value-based institutions of, 9. *See also* institutions, developmental
development, national: capitalistic, 1–2, 25; concepts of, 29; determinants of, ix; economics of, 3; institutional dimension of, 80; in modernization theory, 186; role of institutions in, ix, x, 24–36; sociology of, 2, 95, 103, 105, 187. *See also* institutional development; institutions, developmental
Díaz, Luz Marina, 89, 90
diffusion, in institutional change, 14, 15, 17, 63, 81, 122
Dimaggio, Paul, 77
Dirección General de Aeronáutica Civil (DGAC, Mexico), 131; absence of islands of power in, 151, 152; budget of, 157; developmental contributions of, 145; external allies of, 156; formal mission of, 144; immunity to corruption in,

Dirección General de Aeronáutica Civil (DGAC, Mexico) (*continued*)
150; institutional inadequacy of, 143–45; limitations on authority of, 144; meritocracy in, 147–48; openness to innovation, 155; personnel cuts in, 148; proactivity of, 152, 154; safety concerns of, 144; salary levels in, 148; technological flexibility of, 155, 161. *See also* civil aviation, Mexican
Dollar, David, 25
Dominican Institute of Civil Aviation (IDAC), 121; autonomy of, 128n9; meritocracy of, 122; proactivity of, 122. *See also* civil aviation, Dominican
Dominican Medical Association (AMD), 117
Dominican Postal Institute (IMPOSDOM), 118–19. *See also* postal system, Dominican
Dominican Republic: Central Bank, 114; clientelism in, 118; Congress of, 114; expatriate population of, 128n4; institutional development research in, 26; international trade structure of, 114; justice system of, 114; labor markets in, 126; Ministry for Health and Social Assistance (SESPAS), 117; modernization of, 114; mortality rates in, 116; socioeconomic progress in, 186; stock exchange, 127n1; tax evasion in, 119; tourism in, 114, *115*, 116, 120, 127n2. *See also* economy, Dominican; institutional change, Dominican; institutions, Dominican
Durkheim, Emile, 2, 4

Echandía, Camilo, 100
Echebarría, K., 118
economics: of development, 3; neoclassical, 18; neoinstitutionalism in, ix; study of institutions in, 1, 2, 6
economy, Argentine, 40–41; macroeconomy of, 53; provisional sector of, 52
economy, Chilean: bankruptcies in, 65; effect of globalization on, 60, 64, 67, 68, 76; exports in, 63–64; external revenues of, 181; free trade agreements of, 82n3; gross national product, 66, 82n5; market-oriented, 64
economy, Colombian: cocaine in, 100; coffee in, 100; mining in, 100; stability of, 97, 104
economy, Dominican: Central Government income in, *115;* free trade zones in, 114, 116; GDP of, 114; globalization of, 113; growth in, 119; remittances in, 114; service export, 126; state role in, 114; sugar exports, 114; tourism in, 114, *115*, 116, 120, 127n2
economy, Mexican: default of 1982, 11, 179, 180; exports in, 136; federal revenue use in, 142, 162n12; GDP in, 142, 136, 143; growth in, 157; informal, 162n19; manufacturing sector of, 130; *maquiladora* section of, 161n6; market capitalization in, 138, *139;* per capita GDR, *135;* per capita income in, 130; per capita output in, 134; privatization of, 11–14; productive capacity of, 136; securities market, 138, 151; transnational capital in, 155–56; in 2008 recession, 134
elites: in Bolsa Mexicana, 138, 155, 160, 161; in Chilean market society, 66, 67, 77, 78–79, 82n4; Colombian, 105; in Latin American institutions, 179, 184; and Mexican SAT, 156; replacement of, 16
Escobar, Constanza, 69
Europe, northern: governmental institutions of, 25
Evangelical Christianity, effect on American society, 16
Evans, Peter, x, 29, 92; on embedded autonomy, 95; on external determinants, 32; on institutional monocropping, x, 9, 10; institutional typology of, 55, 95–96, *96*, 107; on islands of excellence, 28
exchange, institutional: effect of cultural diffusion on, 81

Faletto, Enzo, 32
Federal Administration of Public Revenue (AFIP, Argentina), 43–44, 47, 185. *See also* tax authorities, Argentine
Foreign Policy magazine, "failed state" indices of, 97
Furtado, Celso, 108n1
fuzzy-set analysis (QCA), 33, 36; of contributions to development, 175–78, *176;* of institutional adequacy, 171–74, *173*, 175; parsimony in, 176, 177; of proactivity, 175, 177

García, Mauricio, 100
Gaviria, César, 90
General Direction of Social Security Resources (DGRSS, Argentina), 43
General Management of Internal Taxes (DGII, Dominican Republic), 119–20; external allies of, 127; immunity to corruption in, 123;

institutional capacity of, 186; islands of excellence in, 120; meritocracy in, 119, 122–23; public image of, 120; role in economic transformation, 124; technological flexibility of, 123. *See also* internal taxation, Dominican
General Tax Department (DGI, Argentina), 43, 49; automation in, 47; corruption in, 46; meritocracy of, 45; openness in, 48; political appointments in, 50; state support for, 51; Subdepartment of Systems and Telecommunication, 47. *See also* tax authorities, Argentine
geography: effect on Colombian institutions, 89, 103; role in institutional development, 25
globalization: effect on Chilean economy, 60, 64, 67, 68, 76; effect on Dominican Republic, 113; effect on institutional development, 167; effect on Latin American institutions, 186; homogenizing forces of, 187
Gramsci, Antonio, 10
Granovetter, Mark, 8, 32, 95
Gurr, Robert Ted: Polity II data of, 24
Gutiérrez, Francisco, 108n5

Hernández, Iván, 89, 94
HGMGG. *See* Manuel Gea González General Hospital
Hirschman, Albert O., 97, 108n1; *A Bias for Hope*, 85–87
Hodgson, Geoffrey, 2, 6
Hoff, Karla, 1; on power distribution, 9
Hoffman, Kelly, 32
Hoffmeister, Lorena, 69

immigrants, Mexican: remittances by, 136; use of Mexican health care, 182
information management: by Argentine tax authorities, 53; role in power, 6
institutional adequacy: causal solutions for, 173–74, *174*, *175*, 187; comparative study of, 167, 168–78; crisp-set analysis of, 168–70, 173, 174; fuzzy-set analysis of, 171–74, *173*, 175; QCA analysis of, 167, 168–78; technological flexibility in, 172; truth tables for, 33, *34*, 121, *160*, 168
institutional adequacy, Mexican, 137–46; crisp-set analysis of, 170; determinants of, 146–57, *159*
institutional arrangements: Chilean, 81; as interorganizational blueprints, 79–80; relationship with institutions, 81; stabilization through, 80
institutional blueprints, 7–8, 62; crisp-set analysis of, 168; organizations' correspondence with, 25, 177; technocrats', 10
institutional change: Chilean, 63–67, 77, 81; descriptions of, 62; determinants of, 14; diffusion in, 14, 15, 17, 63, 81; gradual nature of, 15; indicators of, 62–63; Mexican, 12; at organizational level, 79; path dependence in, 14, 15, 17, 63, 77; problem of, 14–18; radical, 15–16; sociological explanation of, 77; technological, 15
institutional change, Dominican: development actors in, 113, 125–26; diffuse values of, 122; economic transformations in, 114, 116; historical opportunities for, 113; internal framework for, 113; leadership in, 126–27; modernizing ideology of, 126; predictive variables for, 121–23; state role in, 113, 123–25; unsuccessful, 126
institutional development: Chilean, 60–83; comparative analysis of, 24–36, 167–88; data collection and analysis for, 28–29; effect of globalization on, 167; internal conditions promoting, 29, 32, 95; Mexican, 130–61; real versus ideal processes for, 52; research design for, 26–28; role of bureaucracy in, 25, 32; role of geography in, 25; sociological approach to, 25. *See also* development, national; institutions, developmental
institutionalism: historical, 14; rational choice, 14; thin, 3, 18, 79, 80
institutionalism, thick, 3, 8, 18, 87; in Colombian institutions, 85–108; empiricism of, 97; and institutional collapse, 98; sociology of development in, 103
institutional quality: external factors affecting, 41, 96; hypothesized determinants of, xi, 33, *35*, 44, 75, 187; internal factors affecting, 41; measures of, 24–25; meritocracy in, 29, 41; proximate characteristics of, 29
institutional quality, Argentine, 40–41; effect of inconsistency on, 54; external indicators of, 44–45, 52, 55; heterogeneity of, 52; internal indicators of, 44, 52, 55, 56–57; scoring for, 52; separation of powers in, 41; variables determining, 44
institutional quality, Colombian, 86; bias in, 98; international indicators of, 97–98

institutional quality, Latin American: determinants of, 168–78; research design for, 26–28
institutions: clientelist, 95; cultural aspects of, ix–x, 61; definitions of, 2, 62; deliberative, 10; of developed societies, 157; economic theory of, 1, 2, 6; embeddedness in, 8, 32, 95; external determinants of, 32; fast-moving, 9; formal, 161n4; global forms of, 32; hierarchical character of, 3, 8, 32; immunity from corruption, 29, 40; informal, 161n4; innovation in, 41; interdisciplinary study of, 2, 3; inward-looking, 32; islands of excellence in, 28; islands of power in, 32; kinship to norms, ix, 8; latent/manifest realities of, 61; material reality of, 3; measurable definition of, ix; as organizational blueprints, 79; organizational structures of, 52; as organizations, ix; power in, 6, 9; predatory, 55, 95; proactivity in, 32, 41, 95; reactive, 95; rigidity in, 32; role sets in, 5; as rules, 79; slow-moving, 9; social aspects of, ix–x, 2; sociological theory of, 1–3, 60–61, 80; special interests in, 29; subnational diversity among, 25; subversion of, 32; as symbolic instruction sets, 62; technical flexibility of, 32, 41; as values, ix; values of, 52
institutions, Argentine, xi; accumulation of power in, 56; appointment and promotion in, 44; bureaucracy of, 44; crisp-set analysis of, 170; developmental failure in, 39; development studies in, 26, 39–57; discontinuity in, 40, 54, 55–56, 57; External Allies of, 45, 50–52, 55; immunity to corruption in, 46, 55, 56; intermediate, 56; islands of power in, 47, 56; meritocracy in, 44, 45, 55, 56; patronage-oriented, 56; proactivity of, 44, 47–49, 55; regulatory framework for, 44; socioeconomic actors in, 40; state support for, 50, 54; technological flexibility of, 44, 49–50, 55; trajectories of, 41–44; types of, 55–57, *57*; weaknesses of, 185–86
institutions, Chilean: conceptual framework for, 62–63; continuity in, 63; cultural diffusion in, 78; developmentalist, 62, 181; developmental model for, 63–67; development studies in, 26; discontinuity in, 60; empirical analysis of, 61; historical specificities of, 77; institutional blueprints for, 78; isomorphism of, 60, 75–76; lower corruption in, 78; managerial cadres in, 76, 77; meritocracy in, 78; modernization impact on, 61, 62, 63, 68–77; organizational blueprints for, 76; organizational effectiveness of, 62; particularism of, 76–77; path dependence of, 77, 78; performance criteria for, 62; strength of, 184; technological flexibility in, 172; technological innovation in, 63, 78. *See also* market society, Chilean
institutions, Colombian, 103; absence of islands of power, 92; asymmetry of, 99–101, 103–5, 107, 108; case studies of, 87, 88–96; center and periphery in, 98–99, 100, 106; clientelist, 96, 98, 103, 104–7, 107; collapse of, 99; contribution to development, 90, 94–96; correspondence to organizational blueprints, 93–94; development studies in, 26; effect of drug trafficking on, 101, 103; empirical study of, 87, 90, 96; external allies of, 93, 95; external variables affecting, 90, 95; hypotheses concerning, 87; illegal forces affecting, 92; immunity to corruption, 91–92; internal variables affecting, 90, 95; managerial modernization in, 108; meritocracy in, 90–91; paradox of, 85–108; predatory, 96, 98, 99, 103; proactivity of, 86, 92, 95, 107; rational bureaucracy of, 95, 107; reactive, 56, 103, 104; technological flexibility of, 93; technological modernization in, 108; thick institutionalist analysis of, 85–108; typology of, 94, 95–96, *96*, 103; weaknesses of, 107, 184–85; Weberian, 94, 95, 98, 99
institutions, developmental, ix, x; absence of islands of power in, 177–78; causal solutions for, 176–77, *177*, *178*, 187; crisp-set analysis of, 170–71; differences among, 167, 178–86, 187; economic, 178; external actors in, 178; fuzzy-set analysis of, 175–78, *176*; hypothesized factors defining, xi, 181; immunity to corruption in, 177; meritocracy in, 177; power-based, 9; proactivity in, 178; role expectations in, 9; service-oriented, 178; similarities among, 178–84; value-based, 9. *See also* development, national; institutional development
institutions, Dominican, xi, 26; crisp-set analysis of, 170; developmental, 113–27, 182; external allies of, 126; internal identity of, 126; path dependence in, 126, 127; vulnerability to corruption, 119. *See also* institutional change, Dominican
institutions, imported, x, 8–11; resistance to, 9–10
institutions, Latin American: absence of corruption in, 168; absence of islands of power

in, 171, 173, 177–78; Andean, 132; comparative study of, 24–36, *30–31;* contribution to development, 167; data collection for, 28–29; differences among, 167, 178–86; economic, 26, 33, 178, 179, 187; effect of globalization on, 186; elite, 179, 184; external allies of, 170; fieldwork in, x–xi; flexibility of, 170; fuzzy-set analysis of, 171–74, *173;* general trends in, 33, 36; historical origins of, 33, 167; hypotheses concerning, 29, 32–33, 63; immunity to corruption in, 169, 177; meritocracy in, 168, 171, 173, 177; proactivity of, 169, 172, 175; reactive, 56; social, 26, 181, 187; state priorities for, 184; strategic users of, 28; technical, 26; technological flexibility in, 172; technological openness of, 169, 170; thick ethnographies of, 87. *See also* organizations, Latin American

institutions, Mexican: absence of islands of power, 151–52; budgets of, 157, *158;* case studies on, 161n1; consolidation of, 130; constituencies of, 12; continuity in, 132; contribution to development, 185; corruption in, 133, 185; democratization of, 132; determinants of adequacy, 146–57, *159;* developmental, 134, 137–46; development studies in, 26; divestiture of, 11–14, *13;* economic, 161n2; economic reforms of, 132; effect of informal jobs on, 137; external allies of, 155–56, 157, 160; federal, 131; fieldwork for, 185; formal, 133; fragility of, 157; fsQCA software analysis of, 160; immunity to corruption in, 149–51, 159; informal, 133; innovations in, 157; literature on, 132–34; meritocracy in, 146–49; oligopolies in, 133; openness to external innovation, 154–55; political, 161n2; private, 131; privatization of, 11–14, *13,* 33, 133, 145, 162n21; proactivity of, 152–54, 160; public security crisis in, 130; for social development, 132; social equity in, 160; technological flexibility of, 154–55, 159; Weberian, 131, 147–48

institutions, Weberian: of Columbia, 94, 95, 98, 99; Mexican, 131, 147–48

Inter-American Development Bank (IADB), 117

internal taxation, Dominican, 113; evasion of, 119; institutional change in, 123; leadership of, 127; pressure from business sector on, 125–26; state agency in, 124, 125–26. *See also* General Management of Internal Taxes; tax authorities, Dominican

International Country Risk Guide (ICRG), 24

International Labor Organization (ILO), 136

International Monetary Fund (IMF), bailout of Mexico, 11, 12

Islam, fundamentalist, 16

Johnson, Simon, 24, 29

Junta of Civil Aviation (JAC, Dominican Republic), 120, 121, 128nn6,9

Jutting, Johannes, 25

Keefer, Philip, 24

Kirchner, Nestor, 42

Knack, Steve, 24

Kraay, Aart, 25

labor market, Dominican, 126

labor market, Mexican: effect on public health services, 137; effect on tax authorities, 137; under privatization, 14

Latin America: agrarian reform in, 33; civil aviation authorities of, 27–28, 86, 179, 183–84; economic institutions of, 26, 33, 178, 179, 187; institutional development research in, 26–28; neoliberalism in, 183; per capita GDR, *135;* populism in, 105; postal systems of, x, 27, 28, 86; public health services of, 27–28, 86, *141,* 179, 181, 183–84; social institutions of, 26, 181, 187; stock exchanges of, x, 26–27, 28, 33, 86, 178, 179; tax authorities of, 27, 28, 33, 72, 178, 180, 181; unequal income distribution in, 180

Llach, Juan, 40

Lleras Restrepo, Carlos, 108n1

Mail and Telegraph Service (ENCOTEL, Argentina), 43

Malvinas (Falklands) war, 40

Manuel Gea González General Hospital (HGMGG, Mexico), 131, 181–82; absence of islands of power in, 151; autonomy of, 140; budget of, 157; cost of services, 140; coverage area of, 139; external allies of, 156; immunity to corruption of, 150–51; institutional adequacy of, 137, 138–41; Integral System of Hospital Management, 154; islands of excellence in, 141; meritocracy of, 146, 147, 151; patient referral system, 155; patients of, 139; proactivity of, 153; Quality Management Department, 153; research at, 140; specialty services of, 140; strategic objectives of, 140; technical flexibility of, 154–55. *See also* public health services, Mexican

market society, Chilean: authoritarianism in, 64, 65, 66; contradictions in, 67; deepening of model, 78, 80; elites in, 66, 67, 77, 78–79, 82n4; equal opportunities in, 81; institutional change in, 60–83; internalized values of, 77; legislation supporting, 65; legitimization of, 67; neoliberalism in, 66, 68, 77, 82n1; of 1980s, 64–65; political-economic model of, 64; popular support for, 66, 67; private sector of, 64, 66, 73–74; social citizenship in, 81; social transformations in, 62, 63; sociocultural effects of, 67; stability of, 66, 78, 79, 80; working conditions in, 82n6. *See also* economy, Chilean; institutions, Chilean
Marx, Karl, 6, 16
means of production, power in, 6
Mexicana (airline), 11, 145
Mexican Health Foundation (Funsalud), 156
Mexican Institute of Social Security, hospital network of, 181
Mexican Revolution, 185
Mexico: antipoverty programs in, 132; auditing entity of, 143; Central Bank, 157; clientelism in, 133; Congress, 143; Constitution, 145; corporatist structure of, 13, 133; decentralization in, 132, 139, 162n11; drug war in, 185; Federal Electoral Institute, 157; foreign dependency of, 136; foreign direct investment in, 136; Gini coefficient of inequality in, 134, *135*; health workers' union, 147, 151; informal jobs in, 130, 136; institutional adequacy in, 185; institutional change in, 12; institutional development in, 130–61; institutional development research in, 26; institutional divestiture in, 11–14, *13*, 33, 133, 145, 162n21; in international power structure, 136; job creation in, 136, 161n7; labor unions of, 133, 149, 163n27; Law for Social Development, 132; medical drug market of, 150; Ministry of Finance, 150; Ministry of Health, 139; Ministry of the Public Function, 149; Ministry of Social Development, 132; multiparty democracy in, 185; National Decentralizing Accord, 139; neoliberal reforms in, 156, 179; new institutionalism of, 134; parastate firms of, 11–14, *13*; political stability in, 130, 185; poverty levels in, 130, 132, 134, 139; public security in, 130, 133; Salinas government, 138, 155; securities market, 138, 151; social justice in, 137; Supreme Court, 157; telecommunication companies of, 146; Unit for the Divestiture of Parastate Entities, 12–13. *See also* economy, Mexican; institutions, Mexican
Meyer, John, 14, 32
monocropping, institutional, x; alternatives to, 10; failure of, 8–11; participatory democracy and, *11*

National Administration of Civil Aviation (ANAC, Argentina), 42, 54
National Association of Private Clinics (ANDECLIP, Dominican Republic), 117
National Center for Aviation Medicine (CENMA, Mexico), 144
National Commission of Medical Arbitration (Mexico), 152
National Confederation of Enterprises (CONEP, Dominican Republic), 117, 128n5
National Council of Private Business (CNHE, Dominican Republic), 117
National Tax and Customs Agency (DIAN, Colombia), 88; immunity to corruption in, 91; meritocracy in, 91; modernization of, 90; patronage in, 90, 91, 92, 96, 98, 99, 100, 104, 105, 106; proactivity of, 92, 94, 96, 104; technological transformation in, 99. *See also* tax authorities, Colombian
nation-states, as agents of social change, 186
Nee, Victor, 25, 29
neoinstitutionalism, ix, 1–3; in politics, 2–3; potential of, 18
Nigeria, governmental institutions of, 25
norms, societal: kinship with institutions, ix, 8; roles of, 4–5; versus values, 4
North, Douglass: institutional theory of, 2, 9, 24, 80; on norms, 8
North American Free Trade Agreement (NAFTA), 130, 185
Nun, José, 40

O'Donnell, Guillermo, 32, 40
Offe, Claus, 133
Open Electronic Market (MAE, Argentina), 42
Opper, Sonja, 25, 29
Organization for Cooperation and Development (OCDE), Chile in, 66, 76, 82n4
organizations, Latin American: contributions to institutional sphere, 29; institutional blueprints of, 62; institutional goals for, 33. *See also* institutions, Latin American
Ostrom, Elinor, 3, 4

Pareto, Vilfredo, 16
path dependence, institutional, 14, 15, 17, 63; in Chile, 77, 78; in European colonies, 24
patronage. *See* clientelism
Payne, James, 85–87
Pizarro, Eduardo, 97, 98
Plan Auge (Chile), 69, 70, 82n9, 181
Political Risk Services, Inc., 24
populism, institutional equilibrium through, 104–5
Portantiero, Juan Carlos, 40
Portes, Alejandro, 32, 55, 79, 87, 95, 126; on institutional change, 62–63, 77; institutional concept of, 61, 80; on institutional quality, 41
postal system, Argentine, 41, 43; appointment and promotion in, 45; corruption in, 46; deterioration of, 53; discontinuity in, 55; future of, 185; islands of power in, 47; privatization of, 183; proactivity of, 48, 53–54, 55; technical flexibility of, 49–50, 53. *See also* Post Office of the Argentine Republic (CORASA)
postal system, Chilean, 61, 70–71, 82n11; institutional adequacy of, 172; meritocracy in, 71; modernization of, 71, 82n12; social integration role of, 71; state control of, 183
postal system, Colombian: failure of, 184; institutional adequacy of, 173. *See also* Adpostal (Colombia)
postal system, Dominican, 118–19; absence of leadership, 126; corruption in, 118, 123; development actors in, 123; discontinuity in, 118; effect of globalization on, 113; institutional inadequacy of, 122, 124; lack of external allies, 124; meritocracy in, 123; privatization of, 119; state agency in, 124; weaknesses of, 184, 186
postal system, Mexican: bureaucracy of, 131; contribution to development, 170; deficits of, 145; failures of, 159, 184; institutional inadequacy of, 137, 143, 145–46; obsolete technology of, 145; private competitors of, 145; state control of, 183, 185. *See also* SEPOMEX
postal systems, Latin American, x, 27, 86; contribution to development, 181; institutional ranking of, 179; privatization of, 183; role in development, 28, 183–84; social integration function of, 28, 183
Post Office of the Argentine Republic (CORASA): corruption in, 46; deficiencies of, 53–54; institutional values of, 52, 54; islands of power in, 46; organizational structure of, 52; patronage in, 56; prestige of, 43; proactivity of, 48; state support for, 50–51; technological flexibility of, 50. *See also* postal system, Argentine
Powell, Walter W., 77
power: authority-based, 5–6; class struggle over, 17, 63; deep character of, 6; de facto, 79, 80; de jure, 79; hierarchies of, 32; institutional, 6, 9; legitimized, 10; link to information, 53; Marxist, 6; resources enabling, 6; role of information management in, 6; social effect of, 5–6, 79
power relations, state, 128n10
privatization: Argentine, 183; Colombian, 182; Dominican, 119, 121
privatization, Mexican, 11–14, *13*, 133, 145, 162n21; under de la Madrid, 12; effect on labor market, 14; resistance to, 14, 33; under Salinas de Gortari, 12
Programa de Garantías Explícitas de Salud (Chile), 82n8
prophecy, charismatic, 15–16, 17, 63
Protestant Reformation, effect on social order, 15
public health services, Chilean, 61, 65, 82nn8–10; deficiencies in, 69–70; institutional actors in, 70; institutional adequacy of, 172, 181; material resources for, 69; meritocracy in, 69; modernization of, 68, 69–70; socioeconomic status in, 68–69. *See also* Plan Auge
public health services, Colombian, 88, 89–90; clientelism in, 101, 106; failures of, 182–83; Law 109 affecting, 182; patronage in, 92; privatization of, 182; uninsured patients in, 182–83, 184. *See also* Social Security Institute (ISS, Colombia)
public health services, Dominican, 113; clientelist system of, 125; clinical model of, 117; decentralization of, 128n4; development actors in, 123; external allies of, 122; institutional capacity of, 122; interest groups' influence in, 128n8; international development organizations in, 117; islands of power in, 122; legislation governing, 127n3; meritocracy of, 182; private sector in, 117, 126; proactivity of, 182; probity of, 182; reform of, 116–18; resistance to change in, 122; under SESPAS, 117; state agency in, 124, 126
public health services, Latin American, 27, 86; contribution to development, 181; government/private contributions to, *141*;

public health services, Latin American (*continued*)
institutional ranking of, 179; role in development, 183–84; role in social development, 28; state commitment to, 183
public health services, Mexican, 131; contribution to development, 181–82; decentralization of, 139; effect of labor markets on, 137; expenditure on, *140*, 141; health workers' union, 147, 151; institutional adequacy of, 138–41; lack of access to, 150; neoliberal reforms in, 156; for noninsured population, 139, 162n10; per capita total expenditures, *141;* proactivity of, 152–53, 182; use of information technology, 155. *See also* Manuel Gea González General Hospital
Pucciarelli, Alfredo, 40

Qualitative Comparative Analysis (QCA), 29; Boolean analysis in, 33, 36, 168–69, 173; crisp-set analysis, 168–70, 171–74; fuzzy-set analysis in, 33, 36, 171–74; of Latin American institutional adequacy, 167, 168–78

Ragin, Charles, 28, 33, 168
rationality, bounded, 2–3
Regional Air Command (CRA, Argentina), 42; corruption in, 185; external actors in, 186; failures of, 55; islands of power in, 47; lack of state support, 51–52; meritocracy in, 45; proactivity of, 48–49; transition from, 54. *See also* civil aviation, Argentine
religion, effect on value systems, 15–16, 17
Robinson, James A., 24, 29, 79, 104; on Latin American populism, 105, 106
Rodríguez-Garavito, César, 55, 56, 185
Rodrik, Dani, 25, 29
Roland, Gerald, 2, 9
role occupants, relationships among, 14–15
roles (sets of behaviors), 4–5
Rousseau, Jean-Jacques, 133
Rule of Law index, 25

Sachs, Jeffrey, 25
Salinas de Gortari, Carlos: disgrace of, 14; privatization under, 12
Scott, W. Richard, 161n4
Securities and Exchange Commission, Argentine, 42; integrity of, 46
self-interest, and collective good, 3
Sen, Amartya, 10
SEPOMEX (Correos de México), 131; budget of, 157; business clients of, 163n35; corruption in, 151, 160, 170, 183; deficit of, 162n22; external allies of, 156, 160; infringements on, 146; institutional inadequacy of, 145–46; integrative function of, 171; islands of power in, 152; meritocracy in, 148–49; multiservice postal offices of, 153; proactivity of, 153; salary levels at, 149; technological inflexibility of, 154, 155, 159, 160; theft in, 151, 152, 163n33, 183. *See also* postal system, Mexican
Services to Navigation in Mexico's Air Space (SENEAM), 144
Servicio de Administración Tributaria (SAT, Mexico), 131; absence of islands of power in, 151; budget of, 157; business elites and, 156; centralization of, 151; conflicts of interest in, 150; contribution to federal budget, 142; efficiency of, 142, *142*, 161; employee evaluation in, 148; employee turnover in, 148, 162n26; external allies of, 156; illegal resources of, 156; immunity to corruption in, 149–50, 163n28; institutional adequacy of, 137–38, 141–43; Integral Solution Platform of, 154; Large Taxpayers Unit, 153; meritocracy in, 143, 148; norms/practices discrepancy of, 143; openness to external innovation, 154; reporting requirements for, 151, 163n31; revenues administered by, 142; risk management techniques of, 153, 154; secondary collection by, 162n17; tax gaps under, 143; taxpayers' opposition to, 156. *See also* tax authorities, Mexican; taxpayers, Mexican
Servicio de Correos y Telégrafo de Chile, 82n11
Shugart, Mathew S., 104
Sidicaro, Ricardo, 40
skills, enactment of, 5
Slim, Carlos, 161n8
social action: decision making in, 161n5; in technological change, 15
social change, 18; institutionalist understanding of, 3; role of religion in, 15–16, 17; Weber on, 15
social classes, effect of power on, 6, 17, 63
social organizations: state legitimization of, 128n10; status hierarchies in, 7
social psychology, role sets in, 5
Social Security Institute (ISS, Colombia), 88, 182, 183; corruption in, 91, 92; departure from

organizational blueprint, 94; external allies of, 93; liquidation of, 89–90, 98; meritocracy in, 91; patronage in, 92; predatory nature of, 96, 98; proactivity of, 94; technological flexibility of, 93. *See also* public health services, Colombian
social structures, 5–7; deep factors of, 4, 5, 63; power in, 5–6; sociological view of, 3–5
sociology: cultural capital in, 5; of development, 2, 103, 105, 187; historical, 16; Latin American, 87; neoinstitutionalism in, ix; role sets in, 5; study of institutions in, 1–3, 60–61, 80
South, global: organizational blueprints for, 3
status hierarchies: role of power in, 6; in social organizations, 7
Stiglitz, Joseph, 1, 2; on power distribution, 9
stock exchange, Argentine, 41, 42; islands of power in, 47; proactivity of, 48. *See also* Buenos Aires Stock Exchange
stock exchange, Chilean, 61, 65, 73–75, 179; islands of power in, 179. *See also* Bolsa de Comercio de Santiago
stock exchange, Colombian, 88–89. *See also* Bolsa de Valores de Colombia
stock exchange, Dominican, 127n1
stock exchange, Mexican, 131; meritocracy in, 146. *See also* Bolsa Mexicana de Valores
stock exchanges, Latin American, x, 86; historical origins of, 179; innovation in, 179; institutional rankings of, 178; resistance to change in, 179; role in economic development, 26–27, 28; scoring of, 33
Subramanian, Arvind, 29

tax authorities, Argentine, 43–44; communication activities of, 48; corruption in, 46; databases of, 49; export taxation, 57n1; historical origins of, 179; import taxation, 57n1; information management by, 53; institutional adequacy of, 181; institutional values of, 52–53; islands of power in, 47; meritocracy of, 55; organizational structure of, 52; proactivity of, 47–48; state support for, 50, 51; technological flexibility of, 49, 53, 58n8; use of automation, 58n8. *See also* General Tax Department (DGI, Argentina)
tax authorities, Chilean (SII), 61; authoritarianism of, 76; institutional efficacy of, 72; under Pinochet regime, 71; reduction of taxes, 64; tax liability for, 180; technological change by, 72, 181
tax authorities, Colombian, 88; center and periphery in, 99; corruption in, 90, 91, 100, 101; departure from organizational blueprint, 94; islands of power in, 92; lack of external allies, 93. *See also* National Tax and Customs Agency
tax authorities, Dominican, 119–20; corporate revenue of, 180; institutional adequacy of, 122; loss of revenue, 180. *See also* General Management of Internal Taxes; internal taxation, Dominican
tax authorities, Latin American: contribution to development, 180, 181; institutional goals of, 180; institutional rankings of, 178; internal revenues of, 180; modernizing by, 72, 180; neoliberal reform of, 180; proactivity of, 180; reporting structures of, 180; role in economic development, 27, 28; role in social equity, 27; scoring of, 33
tax authorities, Mexican: effect of labor markets on, 137; successes of, 159; unequal taxation under, 131, 143, 161, 162n18. *See also* Servicio de Administración Tributaria
taxpayers, Mexican: auditing of, 142, 153; beliefs concerning citizenship, 162n25; fiscal obligations of, 143, 162n14; inequalities for, 131, 143, 161, 162n18; numbers of, 142, 162n15; opposition to SAT, 156; perception of corruption, 149
technocrats, institutional blueprints of, 10
Thumala, Angelica M., 72, 73
tourism, Dominican: civil aviation and, 124; economic role of, 114, *115*, 116, 120; in GDP, 127n2
Transparency International, Corruption Perception Index, 98
Trebbi, Francesco, 29
truth tables (data analysis), 28–29; for hypothesized predictors, 33, *35*; for institutional adequacy, 33, *34*, 121, *160*, 168

United Nations Programme for Development (UNDP), 117
United States: bailout of Mexico, 11; illegal Mexicans in, 136
United States Federal Aviation Authority: intervention in Chilean aviation, 73; intervention in Dominican aviation, 120, 121, 123, 125, 128n7

Uribe, Álvaro, 106

values: effect of imported institutions on, 10; effect of religion on, 15–16, 17; embodied in norms, 4

Washington Consensus, 179
Weber, Max: on power, 5, 10; theory of social change, 15
welfare services, Chilean, 66–67
Williamson, Oliver, 6
World Bank: effective state model of, 68; Good Governance Index, 25, 97, 98
Wormald, Guillermo, 71, 74
Wright, Erik Olin, 95

Zeitlin, Maurice, 32
Zelizer, Viviana, x